TREASURY OF GRAPHIC TECHNIQUES

FOR ARCHITECTS, GRAPHIC DESIGNERS, & ARTISTS

TOM PORTER AND SUE GOODMAN

Maxwell Macmillan Canada
Toronto

Maxwell Macmillan International
New York · Oxford · Singapore · Sydney

Charles Scribner's Sons · New York

Acknowledgments

The authors would like to dedicate this book to all the past and present students of the Oxford School of Architecture. They would also like to extend their gratitude to the following people for their help and encouragement during the production of this book:

Stuart Adlam, Trevor Avery, Simon Barton, Rahmat Bayudi, Henry Busiakievicz, John Cadell, Tim Carran, David Cripps (Thames Print Room), George Dombek, Jeremy Feltham-King, Jack Forman, Alte Geving, Paul Godfrey, Erika Goldman, John Grimshaw, Ron and Judy Hess, Paul Holden, Andrew Hunt, Peter Ireland, Gary Jemmett, Devinder Kalsi, Gordon Kirtley, Jean A. Koefoed, Steve Lee (Rank Xerox U.K. Ltd.), Mike Leech, Thorbjoern Mann, Kwesi Marles, Andrew Murphie, Ray Semple, Wilson Sng, David Statman, Sue and John Stewart, William Taylor, Humphrey Truswell, and Steve Warburton.

Special thanks are also due to Iradj Parveneh for the photography, to Paul Chemetov for providing prints of his work, to Iain Bramhill, David Downing, and D. Mark Grayson for their help in developing the introduction to computer-generated perspectives, and to Richard A. Abbott (Execuscope, Bournemouth, Dorset, England) for his expert advice and supply of visual material for the section on modelscope photography.

Charles Scribner's Sons
Macmillan Publishing Company
866 Third Avenue, New York, NY 10022

Maxwell Macmillan Canada, Inc.
1200 Eglinton Avenue East, Suite 200
Don Mills, Ontario M3C 3N1

Macmillan Publishing Company is part of the Maxwell Communication Group of Companies.

Library of Congress Cataloging-in-Publication Data

Porter, Tom
   Treasury of graphic techniques: for architects, graphic
   designers, & artists / Tom Porter and Sue Goodman
   p. cm.
   Includes index.
   1. Graphic arts--Technique I. Goodman, Sue II. Title
NC845.P67 1992   741.6--dc20   91-41307
ISBN 0-684-19341-8   CIP

Macmillan Books are available at special discounts for bulk purchases for sales promotions, premiums, fund-raising, or educational use. For details, contact:

Special Sales Director
Macmillan Publishing Company
866 Third Avenue, New York, NY 10022

10 9 8 7 6 5 4 3 2 1

Printed in the United States of America

TABLE OF CONTENTS

Introduction

Treasury of Graphic Techniques is born out of the highly successful four-volume series entitled Manual of Graphic Techniques. Expanded with new material together with some unusual techniques, this book aims to provide the budding designer with a comprehensive and useful aid in the production of visually effective and convincing design graphics.

The now familiar step-by-step frames describing "how to" stages in the achievement of graphic techniques are used throughout. Furthermore, each page or spread presents a self-contained and easy-to-understand package of information--each technique being selected for its ease of application in the design and presentation stage.

Chapter 1 introduces line- and value-making techniques together with their potential in the production of design drawings. By extending graphite and ink techniques into unusual and specialized methods of achieving drawings, Chapter 2 focuses on how architectural graphics can be given a powerful impression of solidarity and depth--in both illusory and physical three-dimensional forms. Next, Chapter 3 explains the geometry of shadow-casting in an easy-to-apply manner and describes the basic methods used for incorporating shade and shadow into orthographics, paraline, and perspective drawings. Chapter 4 introduces a range of graphic tricks and special effects achievable using the diazo and photocopy print processes, while in Chapter 5, the projection drawing theme returns with a fundamental understanding of one-point perspective and its application in the conversion of the plan, section, and elevation into impressive three-dimensional views. This chapter continues with construction methods for two- and three-point perspective drawings together with an introduction to computer-generated perspectives. Chapter 6 presents a review of the various techniques for using photographic prints and slides in the rapid creation of professional-looking images together with a technique for producing more informative modelscope photographs. Then Chapter 7 turns to the function of lettering in design and, particularly, to the construction of freehand lettering, a sans serif alphabet, and the Roman alphabet. Finally, Chapter 8 concludes with hints and tips for improving the presentation of design schemes and includes a survey of some of the more attention-grabbing techniques for communicating design proposals to others.

While concentrating on the achievement of eye-catching graphics, Treasury of Graphic Techniques--like its predecessors--aims to demystify the many image-building processes associated with architectural design and communication. Furthermore, by incorporating some techniques that have been devised by more adventurous students, this book hopes to encourage the beginning designer to experiment with various mediums and techniques and, thereby, broaden his or her visualization skills.

1 LINE AND VALUE TECHNIQUES

Introducing the Pencil

1 The pencil represents the cheapest, most versatile and easily accessible form of drawing instrument. Pencils come in many forms but, generally, can be subdivided into three basic types.

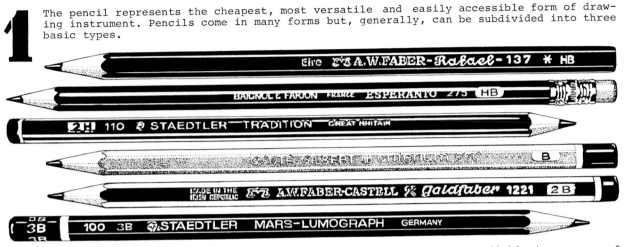

Traditional wood-encased pencils contain a core of graphite that is available in a range of softness and hardness--usually the softer the grade, the thicker the "lead" core.

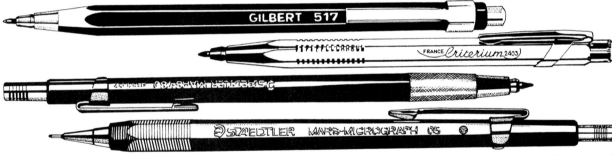

Mechanical, or clutch, pencils employ a push-button action on their plastic and/or metal barrels; this feeds leads made from high polymer or graphite that are available in a full range of hardness, thickness, and color.

The "heavyweight" specialist pencils, such as ebony and carbon pencils and the oval-shaped carpenter's pencil with its oval-shaped lead, contain thick, soft black leads ideal for making large sketches. Their crayonlike boldness relates more to freedom of expression than to precision work.

The versatility of the pencil results from its interaction with the degree of textural grain presented by the drawing surface, the degree of finger-applied pressure during its movement about the paper, and the grade of graphite used. Graphite grades range in descending scales of hardness from 9H to F, and in ascending scales of softness from HB to EE. Generally speaking, pencils represented by the H scale are more suited to technical drafting and will indent softer papers if subjected to extreme pressure. Conversely, pencils represented by the B scale are more conducive to freehand drawing and sketching, with HB and B being ideal for general drawing.

9 H
8 H
7 H
6 H
5 H
4 H
3 H
2 H
H
F
HB
B
2 B
3 B
4 B
5 B
6 B
EB
EE

2

Introducing the Pencil to Paper

1 It is important to experience the effect of the various grades of graphite on a range of different drawing-paper surfaces because such an experience will enhance the ability to match the appropriate pencil to the selected drawing surface. Every type of drawing paper has a surface grain, or tooth, that --in the action of drawing--scrapes the graphite from the pencil and holds it intact. The rougher the tooth, the more graphite will be retained by the surface; the softer the lead, the more graphite will be deposited on the surface. Begin by laying down an even graphite wash on a smooth-surfaced bristol board (cartridge paper) using a 4B grade pencil . . .

. . . and then a 2H grade pencil. Notice the difference in quality between the heavier weight of value offered by the softer graphite and the lighter, almost metallic, silver quality offered by the harder graphite.

2 Next, try a whole range of graphite grades in the production of values on four different drawing-paper surfaces. Explore the differences between the grades of graphite in the creation of even-toned and graduated washes, and in the spontaneity of an unrestricted application of value.

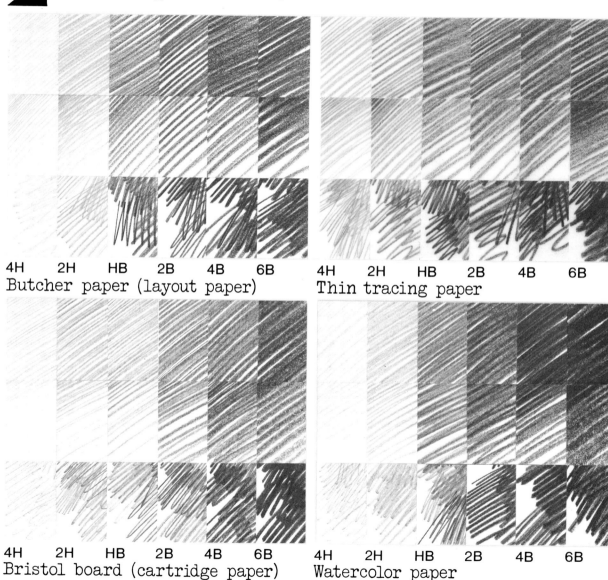

4H 2H HB 2B 4B 6B
Butcher paper (layout paper)

4H 2H HB 2B 4B 6B
Thin tracing paper

4H 2H HB 2B 4B 6B
Bristol board (cartridge paper)

4H 2H HB 2B 4B 6B
Watercolor paper

Some Structured Graphite Shading Techniques

1 Badly rendered shading often leads to the ruination of a pencil drawing. The simple rule is that shading should always bring surface information to forms and give a visual cohesion to the overall drawing. For the beginner, it is a good idea to work graphite shading along the main surface inclination of form, as this reinforces the illusion of three dimensions.

N.B.: Always remember that shading describes surface and value. Therefore, the nature of the drawing will suggest the method best suited to render it.

2 When shading hard-edged areas, avoid "woolly" scribble. Instead, concentrate upon defining a crisp edge for each value region in the tonal structure. This in itself will provide a structured basis for the drawing.

4 When attempting close-grained shading effects, avoid working on the more textured paper surfaces. However, the textured papers can provide a distinctively mottled graphite wash which is used by those who seek a more diffuse and atmospheric effect.

3 Other rapid forms of cohesive shading are the structured "scribble" and variations on the multidirectional cross-hatching technique.

5 When required, the transfer of textured surfaces can be successfully incorporated into shaded artwork. This technique, called "frottage," is the process of making rubbings from variously grained or pitted surfaces. Once the frottage source has been removed, regular linework and shading techniques can be worked over it (see pages 46-47).

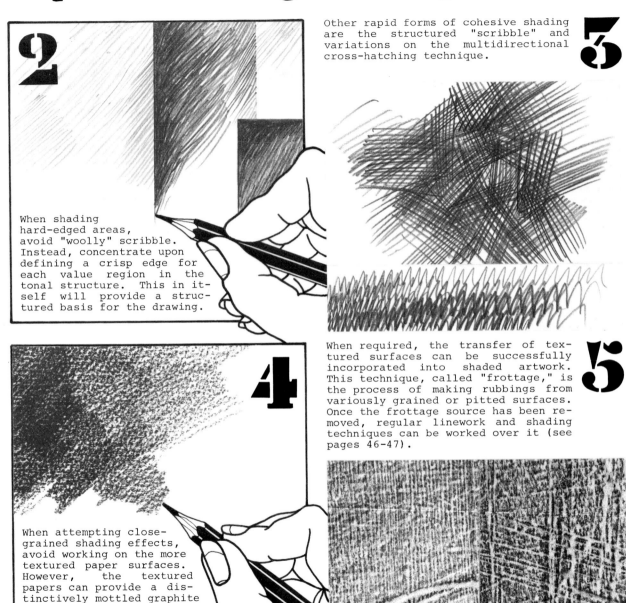

How to Apply a Flat Graphite "Wash"

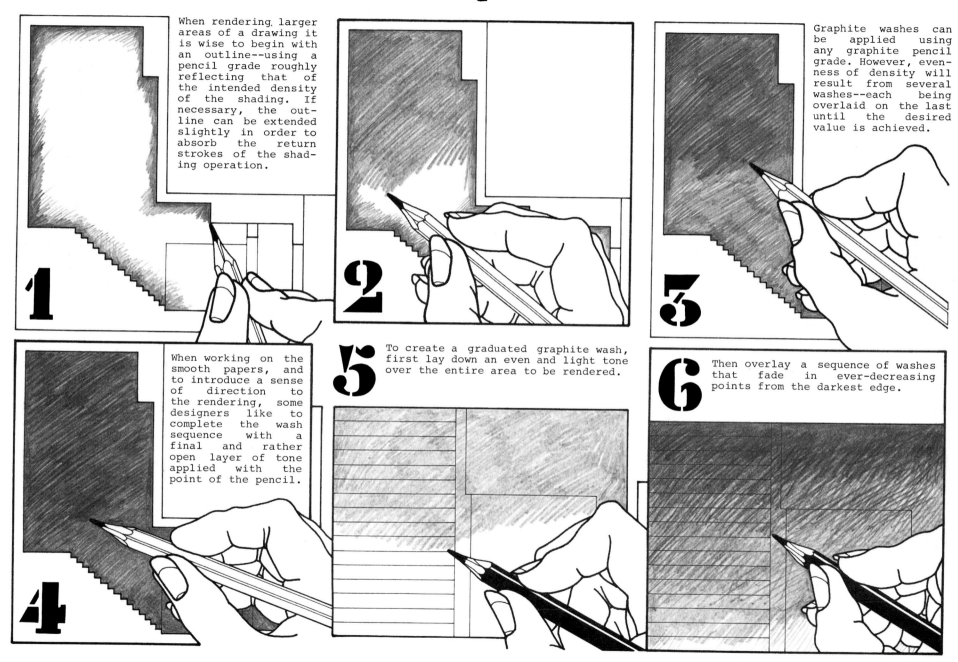

1 When rendering, larger areas of a drawing it is wise to begin with an outline--using a pencil grade roughly reflecting that of the intended density of the shading. If necessary, the outline can be extended slightly in order to absorb the return strokes of the shading operation.

2

3 Graphite washes can be applied using any graphite pencil grade. However, evenness of density will result from several washes--each being overlaid on the last until the desired value is achieved.

4 When working on the smooth papers, and to introduce a sense of direction to the rendering, some designers like to complete the wash sequence with a final and rather open layer of tone applied with the point of the pencil.

5 To create a graduated graphite wash, first lay down an even and light tone over the entire area to be rendered.

6 Then overlay a sequence of washes that fade in ever-decreasing points from the darkest edge.

9

How to Use the Diagonal Shading Technique

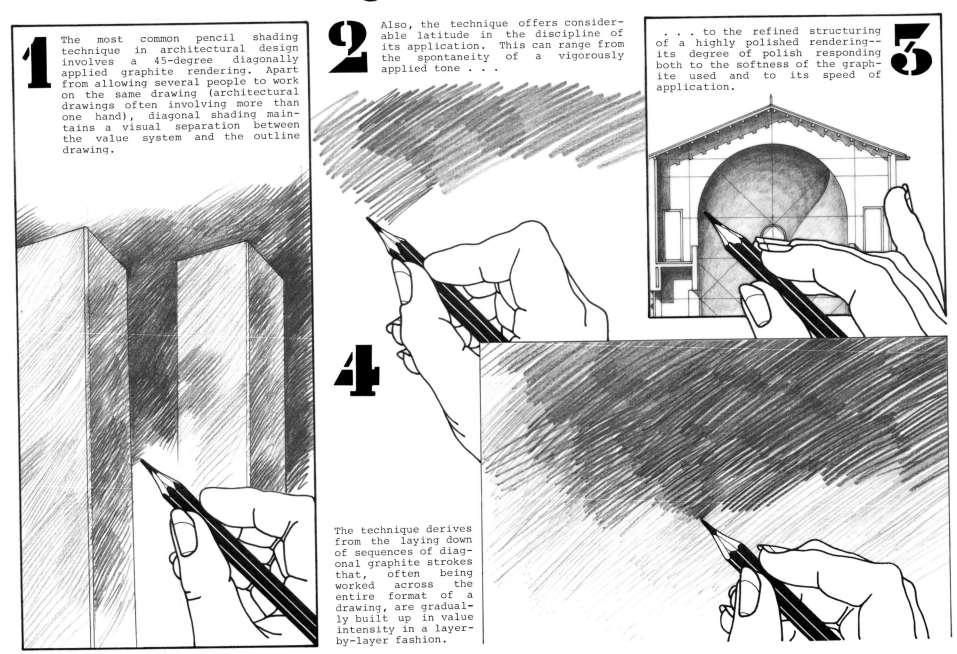

1 The most common pencil shading technique in architectural design involves a 45-degree diagonally applied graphite rendering. Apart from allowing several people to work on the same drawing (architectural drawings often involving more than one hand), diagonal shading maintains a visual separation between the value system and the outline drawing.

2 Also, the technique offers considerable latitude in the discipline of its application. This can range from the spontaneity of a vigorously applied tone . . .

3 . . . to the refined structuring of a highly polished rendering-- its degree of polish responding both to the softness of the graphite used and to its speed of application.

4 The technique derives from the laying down of sequences of diagonal graphite strokes that, often being worked across the entire format of a drawing, are gradually built up in value intensity in a layer-by-layer fashion.

How to Use the Diagonal Shading Technique

5 Obviously, the gradual layering of tonal value should be governed by a clear mental picture of the factors affecting the composition, such as the direction of light.

6 Variations in application of this technique can encompass unpredictable perceptual qualities, such as reflections . . .

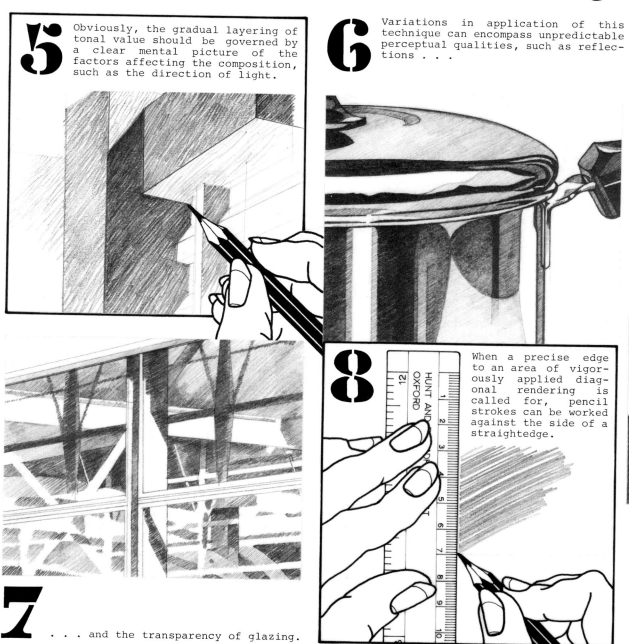

7 . . . and the transparency of glazing.

8 When a precise edge to an area of vigorously applied diagonal rendering is called for, pencil strokes can be worked against the side of a straightedge.

9 The descriptive powers of this system of shading are quite remarkable, and variations in the discipline of diagonal rendering act as signatures of the work of different designers. For example, these three details exemplify the techniques of quite different architects, from the boldness of strokes by Cesar Pelli, the soft accents in the renderings of Guiseppe Zambonini, to the cool, ordered values of George Ranalli.

Introducing the Pen

1 The pen is the oldest drawing instrument, its forerunner possibly being a stick dipped in pigment. Modern pens dispense their ink in two ways: either from a built-in reservoir or via a constant refueling by dipping into an ink source. Nib characteristics and their attendant mark-making abilities vary dramatically both within and across the four basic families of pens.

Fountain pens make an ideal sketching medium--their flexible nibs already being responsive to hand and finger movements. Furthermore, as sketching can be considered an extension of handwriting, their familiarity and portability make them an excellent medium for the beginner.

By contrast, dip pens require some experience in their use. This group of drawing pens includes a vast range of nib types, from the traditional school steel pen and the mapping pen to the traditional reed, cane, or quill pen, together with a host of pens with interchangeable specialist drawing nibs, such as the Gillot and the Hunt ranges.

Technical pens are designed to produce even, continuous lines in a range of thicknesses offered by their interchangeable tubular steel nibs. Technical pens represent the universal drafting instrument but many designers use them also for sketching and handwriting.

Ballpoint pens have enjoyed recent advances in their development. Newly evolved versions, such as the Uni-ball, can simulate the precision of fine-line technical pens, while others, such as Ball Pentel and Pentel Superball, permit a widely expressive line quality never before achievable with this medium.

2 It is important to experiment with the two basically different types of nib. For instance, the range of technical pen styluses is produced in nine internationally recognized line widths or isometric sizes which are specifically designed for the requirements of reduction techniques. Three nibs recommended for beginners are 0.25mm, 0.35mm, and 0.5mm.

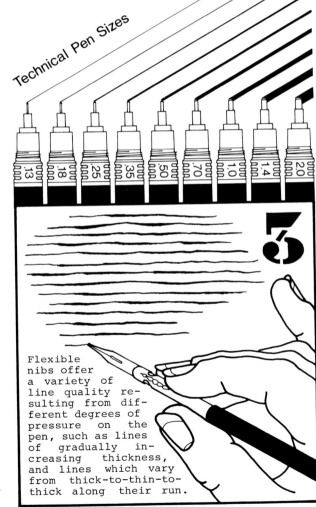

3 Flexible nibs offer a variety of line quality resulting from different degrees of pressure on the pen, such as lines of gradually increasing thickness, and lines which vary from thick-to-thin-to-thick along their run.

Introducing the Technical Pen

1 This is a section through a typical technical pen. The nib is a fine wire held in a tubular sleeve and attached to a plastic weight. The nib and weight move freely in the sleeve at the core of the pen, allowing constant ink flow around its main parts. The ink reservoir is usually a plastic cartridge which squeezes onto the barrel. In some pens a metal band around the cartridge ensures a tight fit and prevents thermal expansion when held in the hand.

Nib--with shouldered tube to prevent smudging when ruling.

Breather holes ensure constant air flow into the ink cartridge which helps keep the ink flow smooth.

Plastic ink cartridge which can be removed and refilled or replaced.

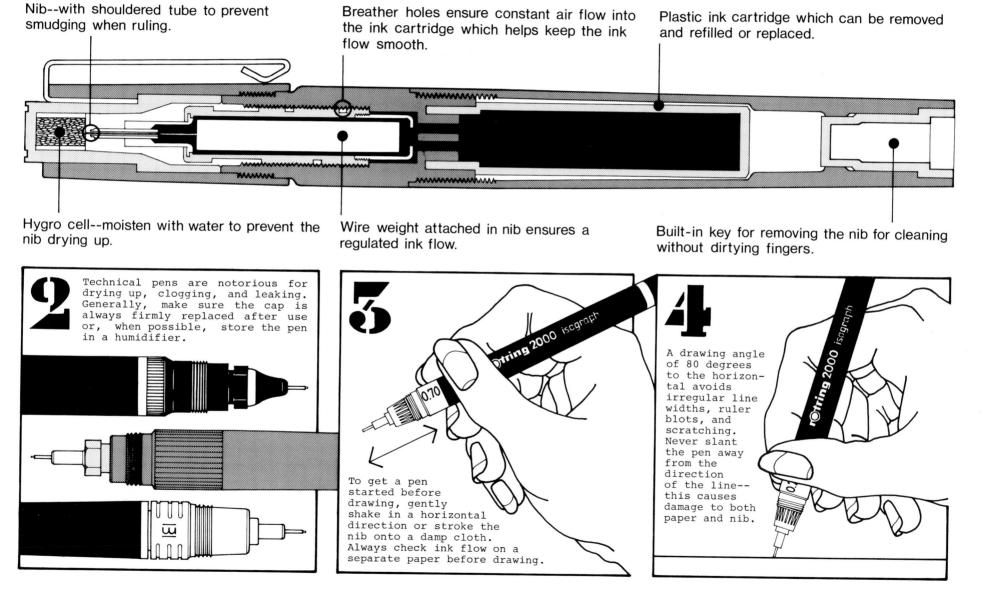

Hygro cell--moisten with water to prevent the nib drying up.

Wire weight attached in nib ensures a regulated ink flow.

Built-in key for removing the nib for cleaning without dirtying fingers.

2 Technical pens are notorious for drying up, clogging, and leaking. Generally, make sure the cap is always firmly replaced after use or, when possible, store the pen in a humidifier.

3 To get a pen started before drawing, gently shake in a horizontal direction or stroke the nib onto a damp cloth. Always check ink flow on a separate paper before drawing.

4 A drawing angle of 80 degrees to the horizontal avoids irregular line widths, ruler blots, and scratching. Never slant the pen away from the direction of the line-- this causes damage to both paper and nib.

An Introduction to Drafting

If we add an adjustable triangle, compass, flexible curve, ruler, and T square to our basic set of drawing instruments, we become equipped for a more mechanical form of drawing. However, when we enter this world of conventional graphics, there is no need--as is often the case with beginners--to abandon an understanding of form, surface, light, and space.

The following exercise is a useful vehicle for helping to familiarize yourself with the drawing equipment, to gain experience in simple drafting techniques, and to gain insight into the creation of convincing three-dimensional illusions in the nonperspective space of a simple projection drawing. Using a large drawing-board format, begin in pencil with the drafting of a spontaneous arrangement of five or more geometric and free-form shapes clustered around the near-center of the paper.

1 N.B.: Keep each shape discrete and separate from its neighbors. Also, with the aid of your drafting equipment, construct each shape clearly and cleanly.

2 Using the triangle and T square, now project the corners and outer edges of each shape in a completely different direction and out to the limits of the format. All projected lines should remain parallel to the chosen direction of each respective shape.

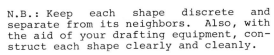

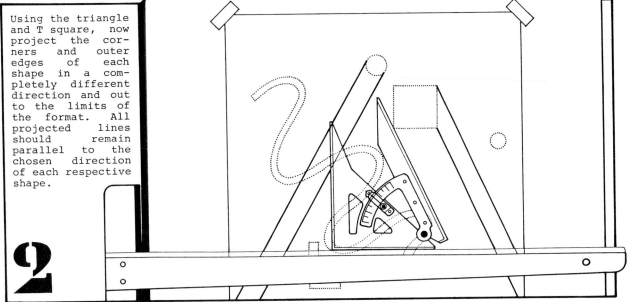

3 During the production stage you should exploit the greatest possible variety of direction. This stage also necessitates decisions concerning near-far relationships of newly projected forms in terms of their sequence of overlap.

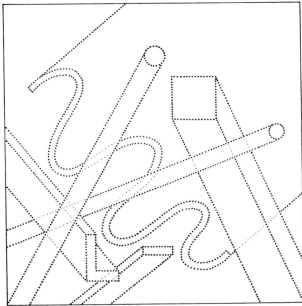

4 Having arrived at this point, we can see that our shapes have transformed into volumes whose forms--without the aid of any other depth cue--occupy a powerful three-dimensional space, an illusion confirmed only by the overlap depth cue. To further reinforce this illusion, we should now turn to rendering each form. However, in order to begin this stage, we first need to assume a direction of light.

An Introduction to Drafting

Begin your technical pen rendering on one of the simpler foreground objects, such as a form with a square section. Use a single-direction line system to reinforce its shaded plane--following either its length or its width.

At the end of the rendering stage, resist the temptation to ink in the outlines of the original shapes. In their new role as profiles of projected forms, they will simply be "painted in" by the perception of the viewer.

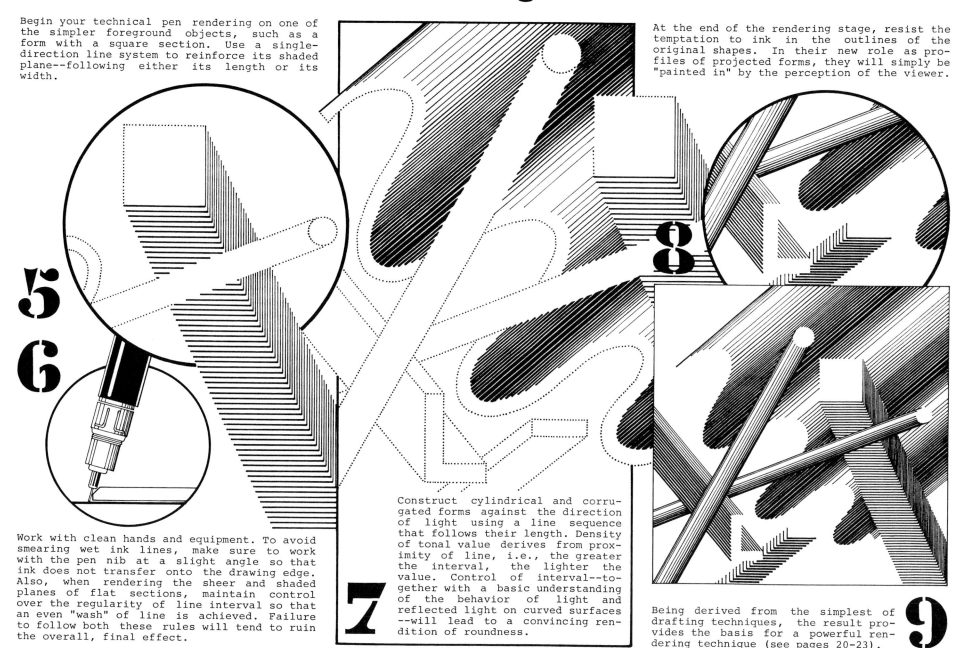

Work with clean hands and equipment. To avoid smearing wet ink lines, make sure to work with the pen nib at a slight angle so that ink does not transfer onto the drawing edge. Also, when rendering the sheer and shaded planes of flat sections, maintain control over the regularity of line interval so that an even "wash" of line is achieved. Failure to follow both these rules will tend to ruin the overall, final effect.

Construct cylindrical and corrugated forms against the direction of light using a line sequence that follows their length. Density of tonal value derives from proximity of line, i.e., the greater the interval, the lighter the value. Control of interval--together with a basic understanding of the behavior of light and reflected light on curved surfaces --will lead to a convincing rendition of roundness.

Being derived from the simplest of drafting techniques, the result provides the basis for a powerful rendering technique (see pages 20-23).

15

An Introduction to Pen Sketching

A deeper experience of ink lines and values will be gained from objective sketching-- either using a technical pen stylus or a flexible nib. Beginners should evolve a sketch via three stages. The first seeks out mass, edge, and shape, which is mapped in line to organize a basic proportional "geometry."

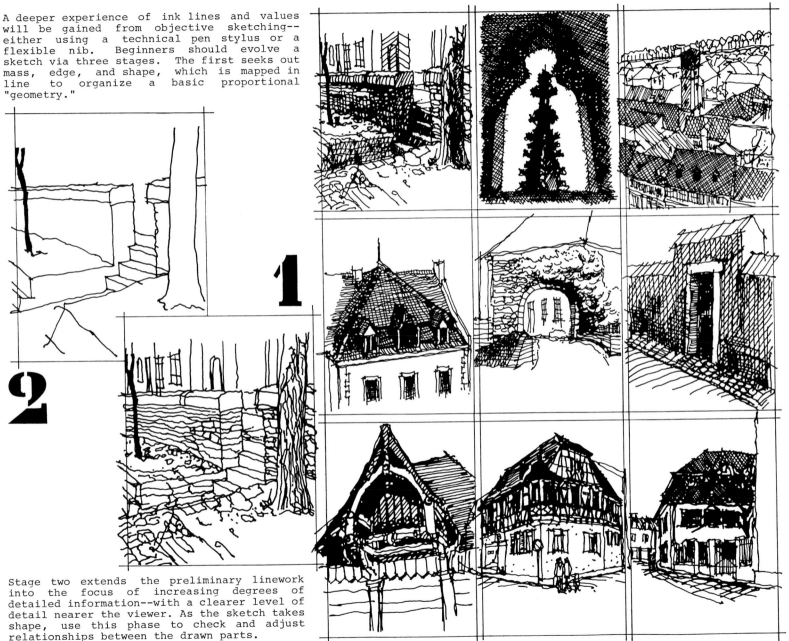

The third stage is extremely important, as it elaborates the under-drawing into values of tone. Their insertion should respond to two observations: the effect of light in creating shade and shadow; the effect of surface and its textural quality. You will discover that these two tonal aspects can be recorded as a single pattern of value--darkest values appearing as nearest the viewer. This third stage also uses the value rendering process to mold the sketch into a unified whole and, simultaneously, increase the illusion of depth.

With some practice, all three stages will gradually blend into one simultaneous sketching technique. This developed experience should also be accompanied by an investigation of different pens so that a sketching vocabulary keeps pace with your developing insight. Initially, you should aim to extract as much as possible from what you observe. However, as this exhaustive seeing process matures and becomes more selective, you should try sketching in line only.

Stage two extends the preliminary linework into the focus of increasing degrees of detailed information--with a clearer level of detail nearer the viewer. As the sketch takes shape, use this phase to check and adjust relationships between the drawn parts.

An Introduction to Pen Sketching

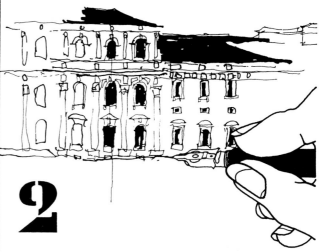

Thor's sketches usually begin with a horizontal or vertical line. In identifying the center of a major mass or the horizon, this guideline immediately challenges the blankness of the paper and establishes the placement of the ensuing delineation.

2

In sketching, the limited mark-making characteristics of the Graphos pen are fully exploited. Its nonflexing nib normally provides a medium stroke; side movements with its edge provide a fine, sinuous line. A broad-stroke effect--useful in simulating shadows and textures--is also achieved by addressing the paper at an acute angle while dragging the side of the nib across the drawing surface.

This series of drawings is from the sketchbooks of Thor Mann, who, using a broad-nibbed Graphos technical pen, produced an illustrated record of his European travels. These drawings--each taking approximately one minute to produce--demonstrate a keen observation in which the descriptive quality of a minimal delineation captures a wealth of information. In striking at the graphic essence of each observation, these drawings also demonstrate the skill of selectivity--a skill that is developed only as a result of a concentrated and continuous experience of the act of sketching.

3

Freehand Rendering Techniques in Design Drawings

1 The potential of freehand pen and pencil techniques to achieve effects of space, surface, and value is limitless. The key to their success in graphics is their structure as controlled systems that rely upon one or a combination of mark-making techniques.

Structured
"scribble"

Dot-and-dash
progression

Dash-to-"scribble"
progression

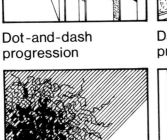

Line and dot

Hatched line
over "scribble"

"Scribbled" dash

"Stitched"
warp and weft

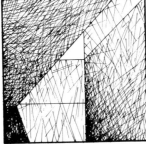

Freehand
cross-hatch

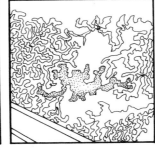

Continuous line
"scribble"

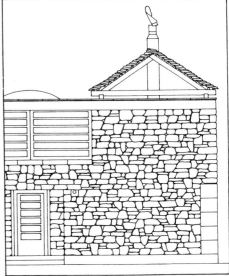

2 When larger scale hatching techniques are developed, a more formal rendering of materials and surface textures becomes possible.

Freehand Rendering Techniques in Design Drawings

3 Many designers who are known for their graphics have evolved highly personal and distinctive value-rendering techniques that are applied in design drawings to emphasize the modulation of light in the space of their designs. The techniques at large are as varied as their personal signatures, but all are flexible enough to depict the subtle graduations of tone at different scales. These details are based on the work of Romaldo Giurgola, Batey and Mack, William Henderson, Site Inc., Franco Purini, and Lebbeus Woods.

4 Apart from sketching, a good way of developing a personal freehand hatching technique is to work directly from photographs. This exercise should aim at the fine-tuning of graduated ink line hatching techniques which will account for the subtle changes in light as it illuminates a variety of surface finishes.

How to Use "Mechanical" Hatching Techniques

1 In complete contrast to freehand value techniques is "mechanical" hatching. This formal approach to rendering value employs sets of parallel lines drawn carefully against a straightedge to create effects of varying tonal density, textural surfaces, and solidity of form.

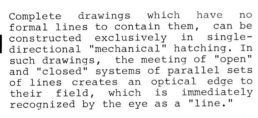

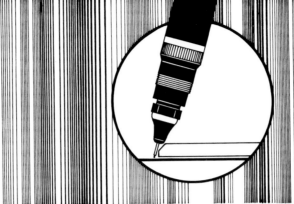

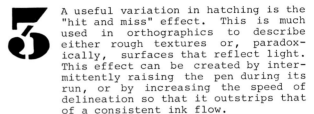

2 As accidental blotches or irregular intervals between lines can cause unwanted visual disruption, great care should be taken when using this technique. For instance, to avoid smearing wet ink lines, make sure to work with the stylus at a slight angle against a beveled straightedge.

3 A useful variation in hatching is the "hit and miss" effect. This is much used in orthographics to describe either rough textures or, paradoxically, surfaces that reflect light. This effect can be created by intermittently raising the pen during its run, or by increasing the speed of delineation so that it outstrips that of a consistent ink flow.

4 Complete drawings which have no formal lines to contain them, can be constructed exclusively in single-directional "mechanical" hatching. In such drawings, the meeting of "open" and "closed" systems of parallel sets of lines creates an optical edge to their field, which is immediately recognized by the eye as a "line."

In this perspective detail, this optical effect is fully exploited in a single-directional hatching to depict a strong illusion of form in space.

How to Use the Bar Shading Technique

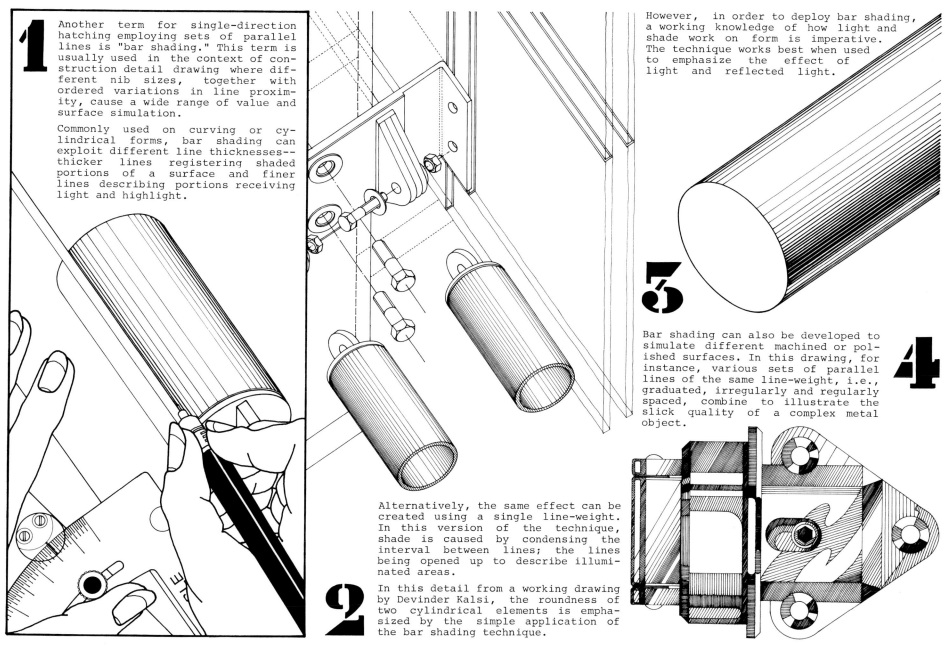

1 Another term for single-direction hatching employing sets of parallel lines is "bar shading." This term is usually used in the context of construction detail drawing where different nib sizes, together with ordered variations in line proximity, cause a wide range of value and surface simulation.

Commonly used on curving or cylindrical forms, bar shading can exploit different line thicknesses--thicker lines registering shaded portions of a surface and finer lines describing portions receiving light and highlight.

However, in order to deploy bar shading, a working knowledge of how light and shade work on form is imperative. The technique works best when used to emphasize the effect of light and reflected light.

3 Bar shading can also be developed to simulate different machined or polished surfaces. In this drawing, for instance, various sets of parallel lines of the same line-weight, i.e., graduated, irregularly and regularly spaced, combine to illustrate the slick quality of a complex metal object.

4

2 Alternatively, the same effect can be created using a single line-weight. In this version of the technique, shade is caused by condensing the interval between lines; the lines being opened up to describe illuminated areas.

In this detail from a working drawing by Devinder Kalsi, the roundness of two cylindrical elements is emphasized by the simple application of the bar shading technique.

How to Use "Mechanical" Cross-Hatching Techniques

1 Cross-hatching occurs when multi-directional sets of parallel lines are superimposed to extend the value range into its darker regions.

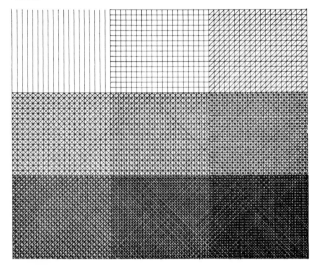

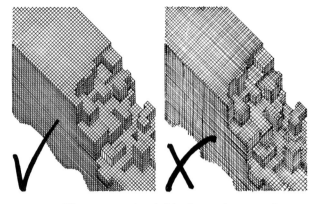

2 When a straightedge is used to achieve a mechanical appearance in hatching and cross-hatching, it is important to retain control over the regularity of line interval and to keep drawing equipment meticulously clean. Failure to do so can cause the rendering of arbitrary lines or smudging that will ruin the overall effect.

3 When required, highlights or softened areas in cross-hatched artwork can be easily "lifted" with an eraser or scraped away with a razor blade.

4 For special effects, a two-directional system of parallel lines can be decomposed (depending on the scale of the cross-hatching) for the depiction of textured surfaces or those receiving fragmented illumination or reflected light.

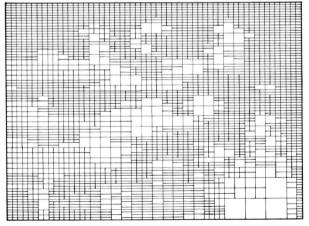

5 Hatching and cross-hatching are extremely effective when harnessed to the receding planes of perspective drawings. Used in this fashion, hatching increases illusions of depth by reinforcing plane inclinations and diminishing texture gradients.

Hatching in Action

Mixed forms of freehand and ruled hatching techniques work well in all forms of drawing but are particularly useful in diazo-printed orthographics. Experience will develop a personal technique after experimentation with the more "closed" effects. These can later be allowed to become more "open" and relaxed during the production of increasingly confident artwork.

Most influential on successive generations of designers are the ruled ink line drawings of Paul Rudolph. His use of superimposed grid lines transcends any mechanical appearance to create a stunning preview of an architecture bathed in a scintillating sunlight.

How to Use the Stippling Technique

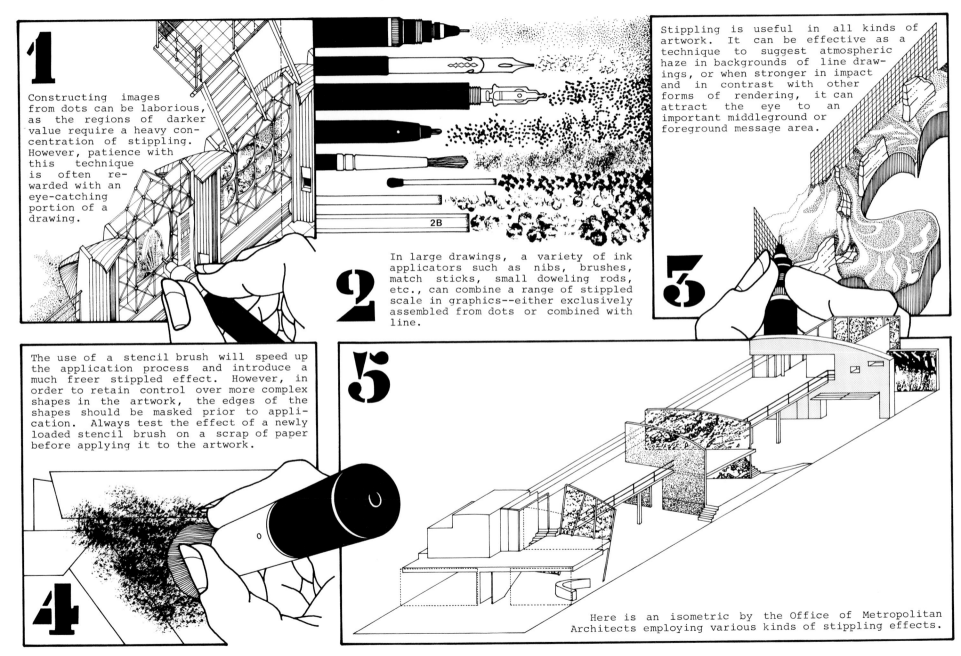

1 Constructing images from dots can be laborious, as the regions of darker value require a heavy concentration of stippling. However, patience with this technique is often rewarded with an eye-catching portion of a drawing.

2 In large drawings, a variety of ink applicators such as nibs, brushes, match sticks, small doweling rods, etc., can combine a range of stippled scale in graphics--either exclusively assembled from dots or combined with line.

3 Stippling is useful in all kinds of artwork. It can be effective as a technique to suggest atmospheric haze in backgrounds of line drawings, or when stronger in impact and in contrast with other forms of rendering, it can attract the eye to an important middleground or foreground message area.

4 The use of a stencil brush will speed up the application process and introduce a much freer stippled effect. However, in order to retain control over more complex shapes in the artwork, the edges of the shapes should be masked prior to application. Always test the effect of a newly loaded stencil brush on a scrap of paper before applying it to the artwork.

5 Here is an isometric by the Office of Metropolitan Architects employing various kinds of stippling effects.

How to Create Coarse-Grain Stipple Effects

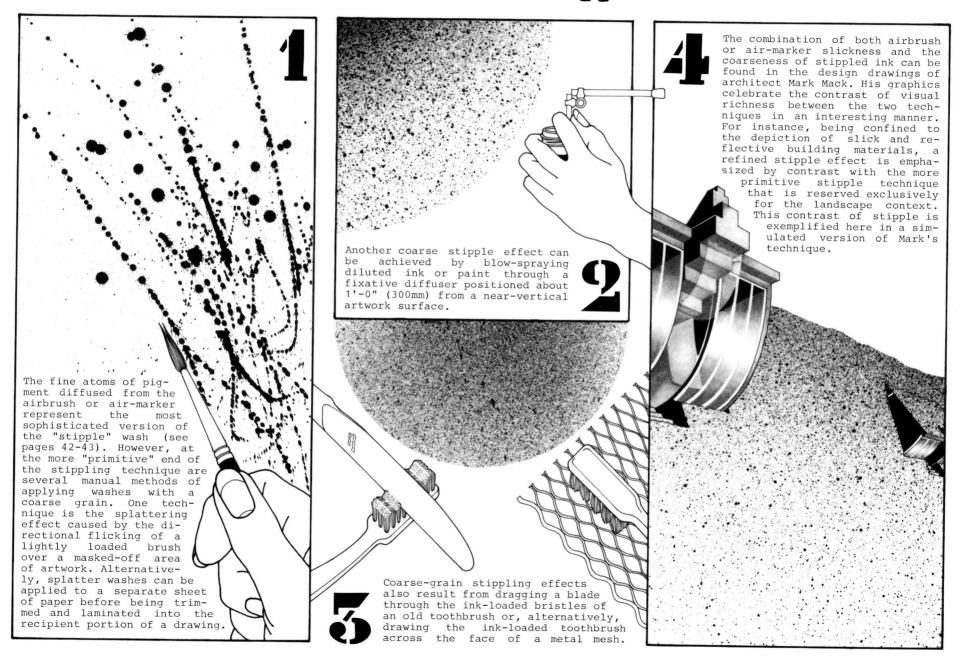

1

The fine atoms of pigment diffused from the airbrush or air-marker represent the most sophisticated version of the "stipple" wash (see pages 42-43). However, at the more "primitive" end of the stippling technique are several manual methods of applying washes with a coarse grain. One technique is the splattering effect caused by the directional flicking of a lightly loaded brush over a masked-off area of artwork. Alternatively, splatter washes can be applied to a separate sheet of paper before being trimmed and laminated into the recipient portion of a drawing.

2

Another coarse stipple effect can be achieved by blow-spraying diluted ink or paint through a fixative diffuser positioned about 1'-0" (300mm) from a near-vertical artwork surface.

3

Coarse-grain stippling effects also result from dragging a blade through the ink-loaded bristles of an old toothbrush or, alternatively, drawing the ink-loaded toothbrush across the face of a metal mesh.

4

The combination of both airbrush or air-marker slickness and the coarseness of stippled ink can be found in the design drawings of architect Mark Mack. His graphics celebrate the contrast of visual richness between the two techniques in an interesting manner. For instance, being confined to the depiction of slick and reflective building materials, a refined stipple effect is emphasized by contrast with the more primitive stipple technique that is reserved exclusively for the landscape context. This contrast of stipple is exemplified here in a simulated version of Mark's technique.

How to Apply a Watercolor Wash

1 Watercolor washes are usually applied to pen or pencil outline drawings on stretched paper (see page 28) or art board. Transparent washes are made from diluted watercolor, ink, tempera, or gouache. A more traditional wash is made from Chinese stick ink gently worked into distilled water to the required intensity. Check the mix on a scrap of paper.

N.B.: When bottled in liquid form, Chinese stick ink is known as "India" ink.

2 Before application, the board should be set at an angle of 45 degrees. Make sure that enough wash is mixed at the outset--then fully load a large sable brush, taking care to avoid any drips.

3 Apply the wash smoothly and evenly --sweeping the horizontal pool of pigment first right and then left across the paper and down the section to be colored. Refill the brush quickly mid-wash to maintain the pool and to avoid tidemarks.

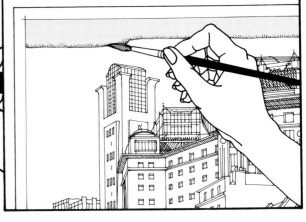

4 Complete the wash in the left- or right-hand corner of the artwork and withdraw the brush. Shake the brush dry before using it to mop up the surplus pool of wash. Successive washes can be applied after the last is dry.

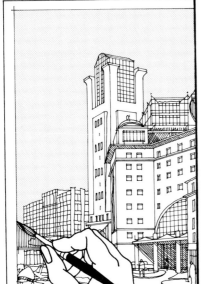

5 Sedimentary washes can be produced by crumbling an asprin into the initial wash mix (a). Textured washes can be achieved by using heavily textured papers (b) or the sprinkling of fruit salts over a freshly applied wash (see facing page).

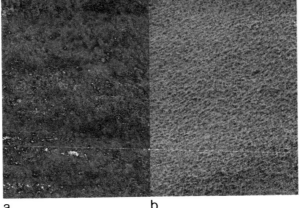

a   b

6 Graduated washes are produced by: (a) progressively diluting a rich initial mix as the wash descends, or (b) by the progressive addition of pigment to the initial dilution.

a   b

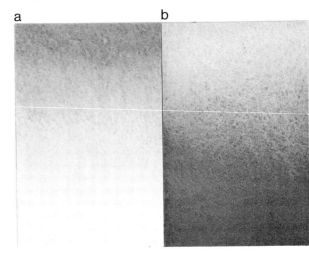

How to Create Textural Wash Effects

Apart from the deliberate or accidental use of dry-brush textures and the delicate back-run effects resulting from the wet-in-wet technique, here are a series of effects that can be selectively incorporated into pen-and-wash drawings using ink or watercolor.

Newly applied washes can be given a directional linear texture using either the point or the side of a pocket or painting knife.

1

Another useful but subtle effect results from a wash composed from a solution of turpentine and fine, soft-grade graphite dust collected from a pointer. The solution is applied vigorously to the paper.

2

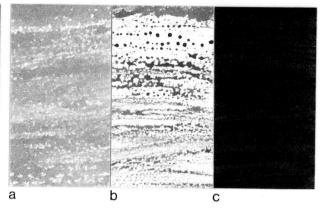

a   b   c

3 Another sequence of turpentine effects is caused when raw turpentine is applied to the paper before a vigorously applied wash (a), turpentine is mixed with a wash prior to application (b), and when a turpentine wash is laid over a dry wash prior to a second coat of watercolor or ink wash (c).

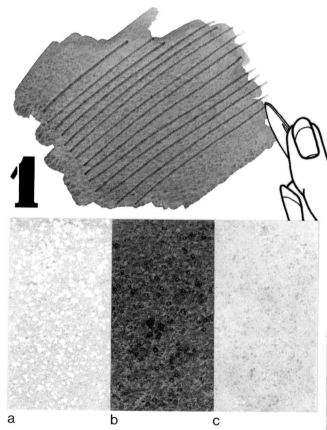

a   b   c

4 Various grades of fine-textured washes result from sprinkling sparingly granules of effervescent fruit salts (a), ordinary table salt (b), and clean builder's sand (c) onto the surface of a wet wash. As the salts dissolve, only the sand needs to be tipped away when the wash is dry.

5 Printed impressions made from various fabrics can be effective but, possibly, the best effect is created by using a moistened sponge dipped into the wash before being pressed onto the drawing surface. Various layers of impression--either from the same or from different types of sponge-- produce textures of great character.

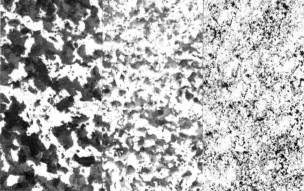

6

Watercolor and water-based ink washes can be drawn into with a household bleach loaded matchstick while the wash still has its sheen. However, this etching effect should be used with care as excessive raw bleach will attack the surface of the paper. Unlike the other techniques mentioned here, bleach will not be confined to the area exposed by a mask of frisk film.

How to Stretch Drawing Paper

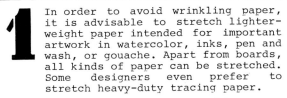

1 In order to avoid wrinkling paper, it is advisable to stretch lighter-weight paper intended for important artwork in watercolor, inks, pen and wash, or gouache. Apart from boards, all kinds of paper can be stretched. Some designers even prefer to stretch heavy-duty tracing paper.

One of two methods of soaking paper is to immerse the sheet in a sink of water for a few minutes. Then carefully remove it, allowing all excess water to drain off before placing it on the drawing board.

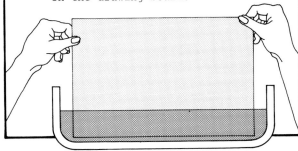

The other method is to carry out the soaking operation on the drawing board, using clean water and a sponge. Both sides should be saturated by first working the sponge around the edges and then in a star-shaped configuration before covering the entire sheet.

N.B.: The presence of a watermark, seen right way round, indicates the correct side of the paper.

2

After making sure that the saturated sheet is as flat as possible, attach it to the board, using a two-inch gum strip and applying half to the edges of the paper, half to the surface of the board. **3**

Make sure that the tape--especially at overlapped corners--is properly stuck down, by burnishing it with a finger. When the paper is dry the artwork can begin.

N.B.: Keep the board flat and away from direct sunlight. Resist the temptation to accelerate the drying process artificially.

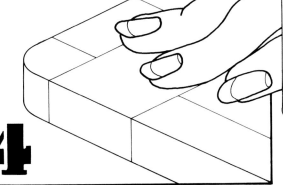

4

5 When the artwork is completed and dry, it should be carefully removed with a sharp scalpel, cutting in one continuous direction along the center of the tape.

When several stretched sheets are required, these can be stretched one on top of another on the same board. After one layer of artwork is finished, it is carefully removed--making sure that only one layer of tape is cut--to expose the next sheet.

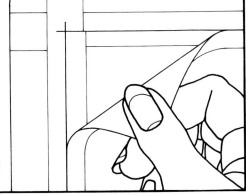

6

How to Use the Pen-and-Wash Technique

Combining pen lines with brush-applied ranges of gray value washes is an effective sketching technique. This usually begins with the basic ink line drawing.

1

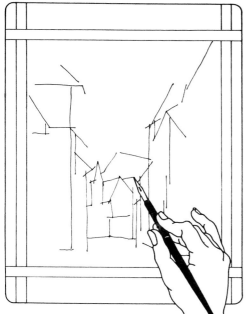

The ink drawing should be made with a pen that you feel comfortable with, using a waterproof ink so that the drawing won't dissolve under ensuing washes.

N.B.: If you feel intimidated by either the blankness of the paper or the permanence of the ink, preplan the drawing in light pencil.

2

3 If a pencil under-drawing has been used, the graphite image can be directly traced in ink or be used as a guide for development into more intricate levels of detail. When penwork is finished and dry, remove the pencil under-drawing with a soft eraser.

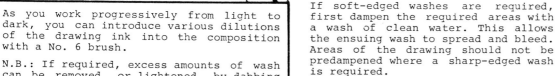

As you work progressively from light to dark, you can introduce various dilutions of the drawing ink into the composition with a No. 6 brush.

N.B.: If required, excess amounts of wash can be removed, or lightened, by dabbing with a blotter.

4

If soft-edged washes are required, first dampen the required areas with a wash of clean water. This allows the ensuing wash to spread and bleed. Areas of the drawing should not be predampened where a sharp-edged wash is required.

5

6

Aim to utilize areas of white paper to simulate the lightest values, and also to extend your value range. When the wash application is finished and dry, final adjustments to the line drawing can be made with the pen.

29

Introducing Felt- and Fiber-Tipped Markers

Since their advent in the 1950s, markers have been considered as inferior to the pencil and the pen, but in the current age of rapid visualization, they have now come of age. Indeed, markers offer a freshness of line, together with an immediate and brilliant spectrum of value and color, and are also capable of producing marks comparable to those achieved by the pen and the brush. Generally, markers dispense two types of ink: permanent spirit-based ink and water-soluble ink. Their extensive range of mark-making abilities falls into three main categories: wide-, medium-, and fine-tipped.

WIDE-
TIPPED

MEDIUM-
TIPPED

FINE-
TIPPED

The range of line potential produced by markers stems from their extensive range of nib types. These include the wide- and soft-tipped felt tips in round, square, oblique, and chisel shapes, through the conical semisoft bullet tips, and on to the fine-line and ultra-fine-line tips of the composition, nylon, and fiber-tipped markers.

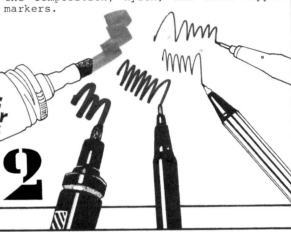

Marker values range from those that are laid down as broad-stroke "washes," through those line-constructed from a loose spontaneity of the intermediate nib thicknesses, and down to the precision and order achievable by fine-line hatching.

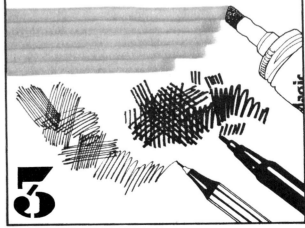

30

How to Apply a Shaped Marker Wash

1 In order to avoid streaking, flat, even marker washes rely upon a constant wet-front. To maintain this, washes have to be applied speedily and with great deftness.

For example, when introducing a wash to a square or rectangular shape, first establish a broadstroke line along the upper horizontal edge of the shape (a) and, after turning the paper anticlockwise, make a second sweep along the newly presented top edge (b).

2 Next, working from the bottom left-hand corner, i.e., the beginning of the first stroke, connect the two boundary strokes using rapid diagonal sweeps. This in-filling stage should be worked quickly in order to maintain a moist leading edge.

3 Now draw a line along the bottom edge of the shape and continue sweeping the wash toward the right-hand side edge, again, keeping the leading edge of the wash wet.

4 Finally, turn the artwork so that the unfinished, left-hand edge is presented horizontally at the top. Finish the wash with a sweep along this boundary line.

5 One technique for achieving a crisp edge on more complicated shaped marker washes begins with a boundary delineation using a colored pencil with a similar hue to the intended wash. This delineation then guides and "frames" the application of the marker.

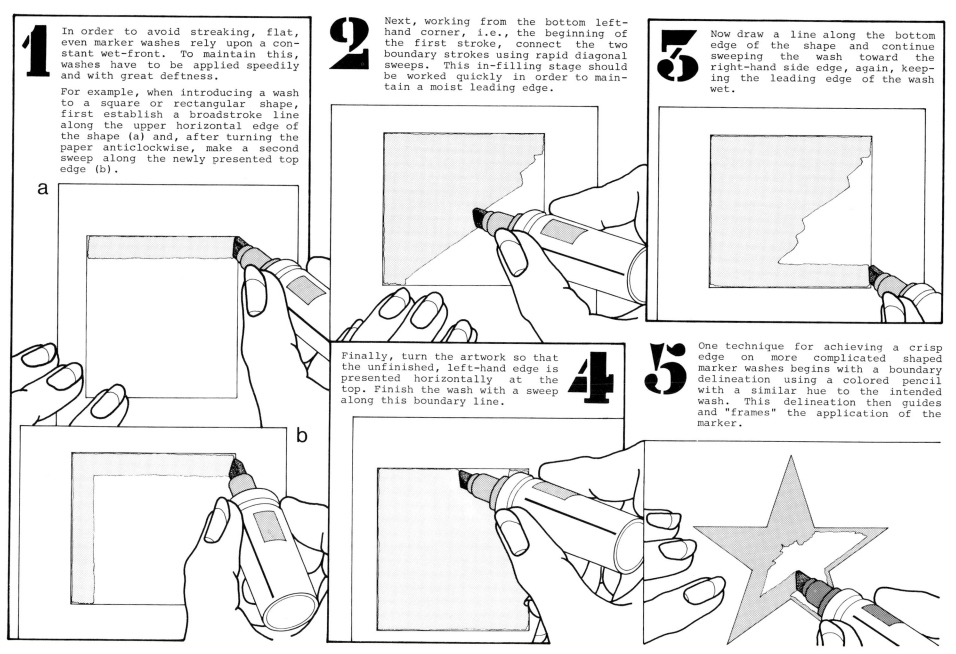

31

How to Develop Marker Techniques

1 Drawing paper has to be selected with care, as the spirit-based markers tend to bleed on soft-surfaced and thin papers. Therefore, you should experiment on a variety of papers, from the thin, absorbent, and bleed-susceptible layout paper, the harder-surfaced Strathmore and the nonbleed wax-backed marker paper to the texture-surfaced watercolor paper. This experiment will identify the effects provided by each surface and how they may work when produced in particular types of drawings.

2 For instance, in a composite image, you might use layout paper for blocking in loose background washes exploiting the bleed to achieve softly blended effects.

3 A bleed-proof paper might then be used for more detailed work that requires crisp edges and accurately defined marks.

The characteristic streaking and bleeding of markers can be used to good effect--especially in more atmospheric drawings. Indeed, some illustrators work a spirit-based marker on the back of thin paper before reversing the sheet to introduce a fine-line drawing into the resultant and diffused effect.

4

As markers are expensive and have a limited existence, there is an economic incentive to extend their working life. Apart from their use in applying faded washes, a run-down marker can be revived by removing its cap and adding a few drops of lighter fluid.

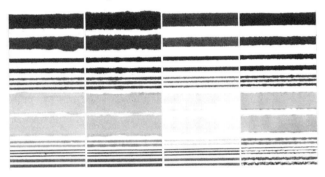

Textural marker effects can be achieved by sprinkling droplets of lighter fuel over a laid down wash. The petroleum-based solvent causes a marble effect that is difficult to render in any other way.

5

6

How to Develop Marker Techniques

There are two approaches to building a line and value drawing with markers. Both involve the use of three markers: a wide-tipped light gray, a wide-tipped medium gray, and a fine-line black. One approach begins by blocking in the main background, middleground, and foreground value shapes with the light gray marker.

1

4

Conversely, a more conventional approach begins with a fine-line black drawing that seeks to establish all the main shapes and details of the composition.

2

The second stage extends the established light gray value pattern with an overlay of middleground and foreground shade and shadow using the medium gray marker.

5

Finally, shape delineation and value and texture details are overworked using the fine-line black marker. This final stage superimposes a network of detail that acts to structure the sketch into an illusion of three dimensions.

This delineation is then elaborated with progressive layers of the two values of gray: light gray to impart an atmospheric distance; dark gray to denote shade and shadows and a feeling of closeness.

In many ways marker is a limited medium. As each marker contains only a single hue or value which dries quickly with a clearly defined edge, designers learn to combine them with other mediums. For instance, marker washes can be modified, refined, and detailed using crayons and, especially, colored pencils (see page 98).

How to Apply Dry-Transfer Materials

1 When using dry-transfer sheets of tone or the self-adhesive sheets of acetate colorfilm, first position the sheet over the artwork and cut the rough shape you require with a scalpel--taking care not to cut through the backing sheet.

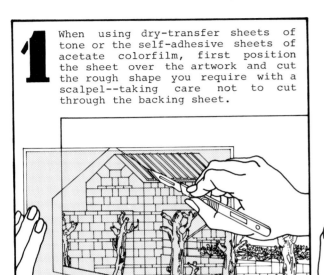

2 Then, remove the film from the backing sheet and lay it on the art surface--the low tack adhesion allows the shape to be repositioned, if necessary.

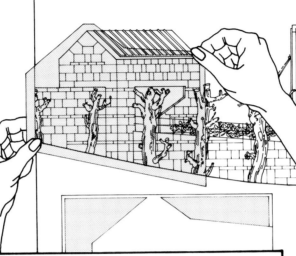

3 Once the film is in position, smooth over lightly with the fingers. Finally, trim around the exact shape before covering the area with paper and burnishing with a burnishing tool.

There are also dry-ink transfer sheets available in a wide variety of black texture screens and a range of about ten colors, both in screens and solid color. The range can be extended by overlaying one color on another.

Remove the backing paper, lay the color sheet over the artwork, and finger-smooth the area to be colored.

4

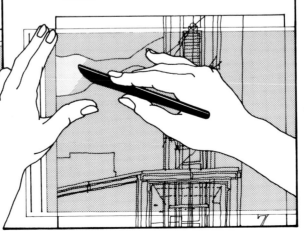

5 Score lightly around the required shape with a stylus (or the point of a brush handle, compass, or scissors) and firmly burnish the area extending to the scored outline.

6 Peel away the sheet toward the center of the colored area. Place the backing sheet over the design and burnish with the finger or a smooth broad-ended burnishing tool.

2 SOME SPECIALIZED TECHNIQUES

An Introduction to Specialized Techniques

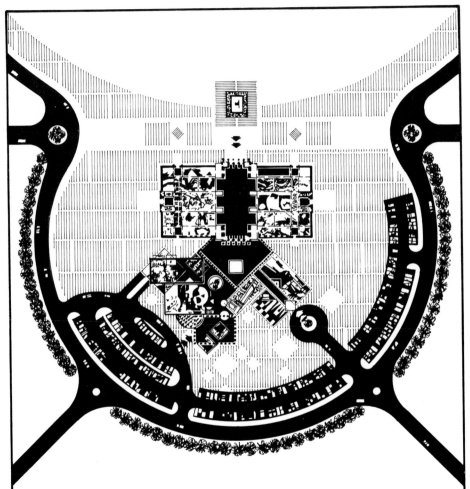

Specialized graphic techniques emanate from the need to create particular graphic effects that are motivated by a design concept, and stem from a more inventive use of unusual mediums or a more adventurous excursion into the application or combination of traditional mediums. For instance, to achieve this abstract and organizational representation of their plan for the St. Louis Art Museum, the office of Hardy, Holzman, and Pfieffer combines a line drawing--embellished with dry-transfer screens and photographic collage--with humble newsprint. The result is a visually powerful architectural footprint symbolized by a rich and variegated pattern of black and white.

However, architectural drawings need not be rendered in their entirety. Often, a line-drawn presentation orthographic can be given an added visual dimension by the selective incorporation of an area of unusual textural effect or a tone. This detail from a drawing by George Ranalli does just that. Here, fragments of photographs are collaged to both highlight the focal point of the drawing and to convey a symbolic message as part of his entry for the Vietnam Memorial competition.

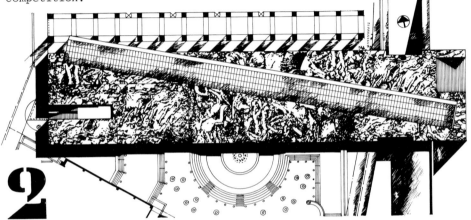

The combination of vigorously applied and tonal renderings with the technical precision of drafted orthographics can provide visually refreshing and attention-catching graphics. Indeed, the juxtaposition of "fixed" and "free" graphic elements is a strategy found in many successful architectural drawings. Generally speaking, having been worked on a separate piece of paper, the specialized effect is introduced into the drawing before being assimilated into a second-stage print via one of the various reproduction processes. The textural effects used can draw from a wide range of both unusual and traditional mediums, such as the colors of shoe polish applied with a wad of tissue paper (see page 91), the effects of ink and bleach and a "printed" watercolor wash (see page 27), and the results of stippling and splattering (see pages 24-25), etc.

An Introduction to Specialized Techniques

4 Specialized techniques can also extend to the invention of drawing aids--especially to shortcut the time consumed by repetitive drawing tasks. One such aid was devised by a student faced with the delineation of a pantile roof in elevation. In order to make a template, she taped a strip of masking tape just below the tips of the teeth of a steel comb.

5 This simple innovation provided an excellent drawing guide for a rapid pen or pencil rendition that simulates the visual appearance of a pantile roof.

Also, an impressive specialized effect was devised by two students who wished to insert a reversed plan, i.e., white-on-black, above a black-on-white elevation drawing. This technique began with the careful masking of the bolder portions of the plan footprint with frisk film before . . .

7 . . . applying a vigorously rendered cloudy sky in charcoal. Once completed, the sky area was thoroughly stabilized using several coats of fixative.

6

8 After peeling away the frisket to reveal that portion of the plan, its footprint was developed directly over the charcoal rendering using the finer lines provided by a pen loaded with white ink.

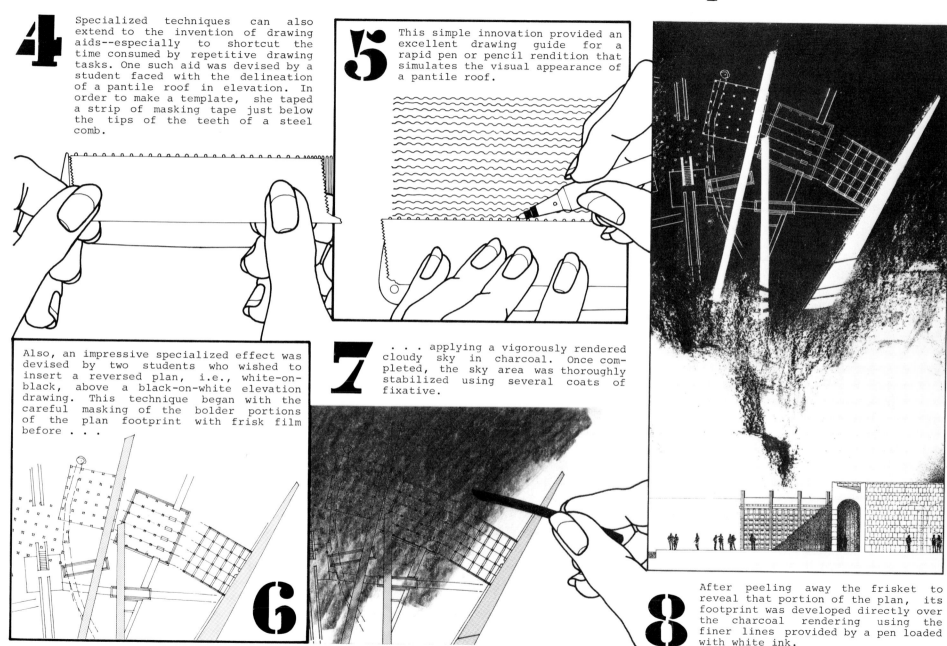

How to Produce Quick Aerosol Spray Effects

1

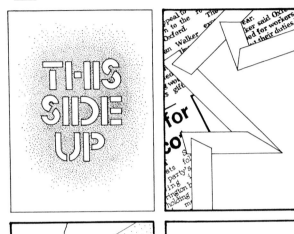

Being quick drying and quick to apply, the aerosol spray method represents a fast medium for rendering color or value on artwork. Color effects can be rapidly built up using a series of oversprayed layers comprising different hues, the edges of areas receiving color being first protected by a mask. Masking methods include the use of cut card templates, masking tape with newsprint, and frisk film. Two paint-on masking methods are liquid frisket and rubber cement, both being finger-rubbed away after the spray application has dried.

2 "Found" stencils can also be introduced as a means of creating patterned or textured spray washes. The "stencil" is placed onto the artwork before spraying or--for effects relying upon interaction among several colors--between spray applications.

3 A variety of objects, such as open-weave fabrics, netting, lace, expanded metal sheeting, string, cut paper strips, confetti, ferns, etc., can function as stencils for simulating a wealth of visual texture in spray-color or monochrome work.

5 The gravel is then tipped away to reveal one of many potential effects using various arrangements and densities of the gravel "stencil."

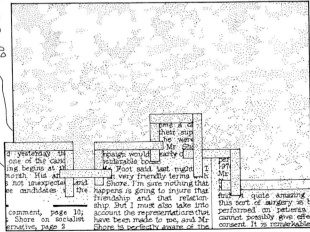

4 For example, a fast way of creating a subtle sky in mixed medium elevations is to first scatter various grades of gravel over a masked-off sky area. Then lightly spray the area with one or two aerosol spray colors.

38

Two Quick Aerosol Spray Sky Techniques

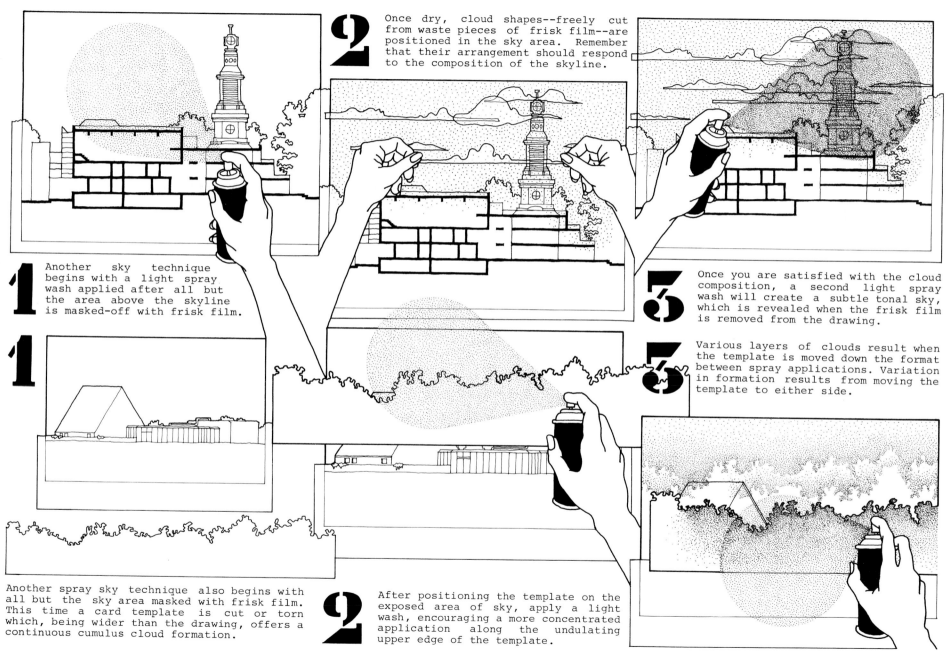

2 Once dry, cloud shapes--freely cut from waste pieces of frisk film--are positioned in the sky area. Remember that their arrangement should respond to the composition of the skyline.

1 Another sky technique begins with a light spray wash applied after all but the area above the skyline is masked-off with frisk film.

3 Once you are satisfied with the cloud composition, a second light spray wash will create a subtle tonal sky, which is revealed when the frisk film is removed from the drawing.

3 Various layers of clouds result when the template is moved down the format between spray applications. Variation in formation results from moving the template to either side.

1 Another spray sky technique also begins with all but the sky area masked with frisk film. This time a card template is cut or torn which, being wider than the drawing, offers a continuous cumulus cloud formation.

2 After positioning the template on the exposed area of sky, apply a light wash, encouraging a more concentrated application along the undulating upper edge of the template.

How to Aerosol-Spray Fast Site Contours

A speedy method of producing tonal progressions for contours in presentation site plans and small-scale site models is the aerosol color-spray technique. As the precision of this graphic technique relies on trace-cutting rather than masking, it short-circuits similar and more time-consuming methods.

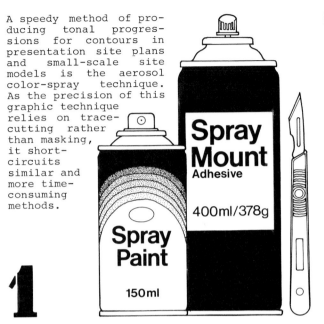

1

Redraw the contours of the plan or model on a separate sheet of paper to same size using pencil or pen. Then cut away any elements such as existing trees and buildings, a proposed building plan, and so on, which may be worked later.

2

3 Lightly color-spray the entire sheet in a hue of your choice, and leave it to dry. This initial wash represents the uppermost level on the site.

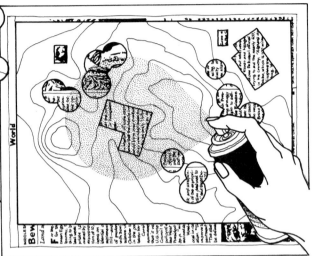

4 Cut away the highest contours with a sharp scalpel or scissors and, using aerosol spray adhesive, mount them into their appropriate locations on the plan or model.

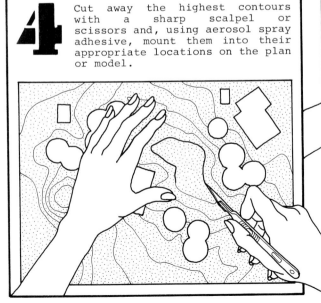

5 Maintaining the same intensity as the initial color wash, respray the remaining area of the sheet and remove the next level for mounting into the site.

6 Simply repeat the process for each subsequent level until all contours are transferred. The act of respraying between each level will establish a descending value scale, with the total number of applications representing the lowest level.

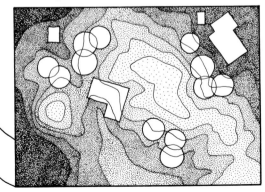

The completed transfer of contours provides a tonal topography on which to draw or laminate further information.

How to Aerosol-Spray Fast Design Plans

1

Many beginners to design presentation find problems when tackling orthographics. Sometimes it is the challenge of the sheet with its sheer size and intimidating blankness, or even the inhibiting effect of a high-quality paper or board. This causes a hiatus in the design process that can often lead to frustrations when working against deadlines.

One valid method around this problem for graphics not destined for diazo reproduction is the composite image: constructing a graphic from separately worked paper components. This is a flexible process allowing experimentation with different color mediums in one graphic and the easy replacement of malfunctioning parts (see also pages 48-49).

2

First, decide upon a structure of tonal value that will establish some organizational control over the total composition.

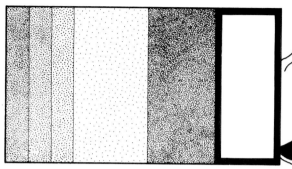

CONTOUR BASETONE EXISTING BUILDING
SCALE   FORMS   PLAN

Within each value range, any color medium may be employed, provided the scale of its mark-making ability fits within the overall textural grain.

Next, carefully outline the elements of the site in ink or graphite on a base sheet. Then, using any wash medium, apply the ground value. Road systems and the like can be established in a slightly lighter version of this value.

3

4

If contours are to be described, these should employ a closely related range of value descending a scale from lighter to darker.

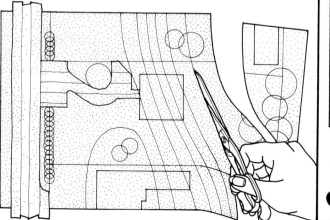

5

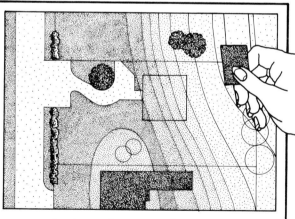

Darker forms such as existing buildings, vegetation, trees, and so on can now be worked in any medium but within their allocated values on separate paper. When dry, cut out and spray mount each element into the support sheet.

6

Drawing the building plan in technical pen on a sheet of white or light-colored paper will maintain a contrast between interior and exterior planning when mounted into position.

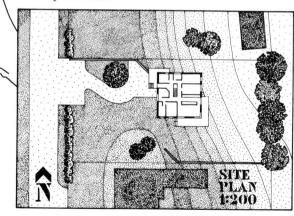

SITE PLAN 1:200

Finally, insert hand-written, stenciled, or dry-transfer labels, plus the north point.

How to Use the Air-Marker

1

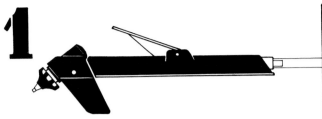

The development of the air-marker represents a medium that bridges the gap between the marker and the airbrush. The Letrajet air-marker is assembled by inserting a fine-line or ultra-fine Pantone marker into a special holder, and attaching the air-hose to a source of compressed air. The resulting jet of air blown across the marker tip works in the same way as a traditional diffuser spray, while achieving pretty good airbrush effects. The resultant ability to create instant airbrush effects without the need to admix colors, together with the ability of switching quickly between marker and spray, makes a welcome addition to the designer's array of mediums.

2

Air-marker assembly begins by attaching the air-hose to a compressor or to an aerosol canister of compressed air and opening the air-supply valve.

3

Next, insert and lock your chosen marker color into the housing.

4

Having assembled the air-marker, simply depress the lever with your finger to blow color from the jet onto the artwork.

Varying the air pressure will alter the texture of spray produced. To achieve greater control over the air flow, steady your forefinger on the knob above the air-nozzle and flex your finger to control the trigger.

5

Various types and densities of wash should first be practiced on scraps of paper. Slight pressure gives a splattered spray (a); full pressure a fine wash (b). To cover large areas with an even splattered wash, the air flow can be controlled by the valve which connects to the canister. As with other spray wash techniques, start the spray away from the drawing to avoid blots, then sweep across the artwork with a steady motion.

Experiment with the effects that can be achieved by masking with paper templates (c,d), by holding the nozzle close to the paper (e), and by directing the flow of spray sideways across the paper surface (f).

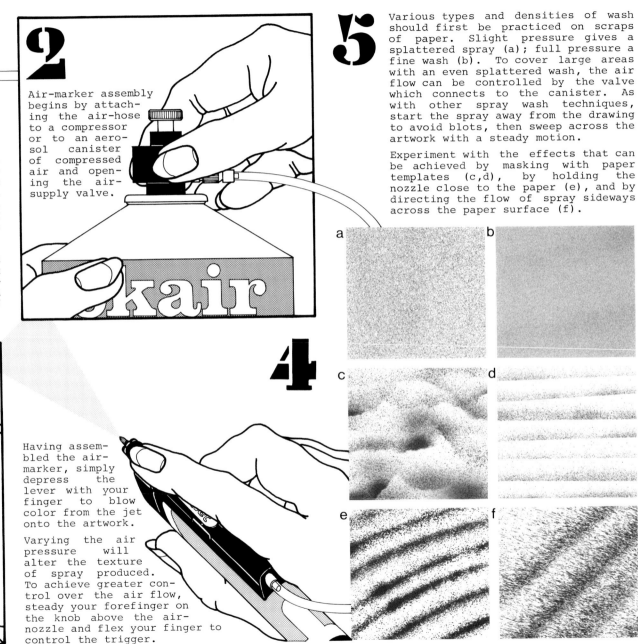

How to Use the Air-Marker

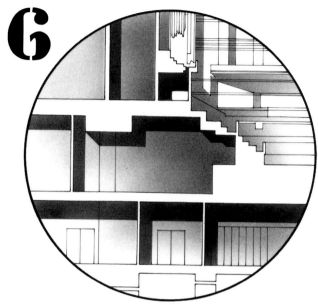

6

Once you have gained confidence with the air-marker you will be able to exploit its most useful potential, i.e., its ability to quickly and cleanly create finely graduated washes.

Used in combination with the frisk film masking technique (see page 44), many subtle and professional-looking effects can be achieved by the relative beginner. The simplest techniques, requiring only one application of frisk film, include graduated sky washes, graduated shadows (see page 81), and the tonal highlighting of sectional cuts (see above).

More advanced techniques, including both flat and graduated washes of various colors, will require several separate applications of masking film. Where different intensities of the same color are required, this is achieved by progressively removing areas of frisk film and building up the overall depth of color. Used with imagination, effects of great luminosity can be achieved with a minimum of colors, such as in the detail on the right based on a silkscreen print by Arata Isozaki.

N.B.: As the overspray tends to obscure the underlying drawing, making it difficult to judge tonal contrast, take care to avoid applying too dark an initial color wash--a common error in all masked spray work.

How to Use the Masking Technique

1 Masking film, such as frisk film, is an essential for precision spray work, but you should always check first that it won't pull away the surface that it is protecting.

To remove the frisk film from its backing sheet, lay the low-tack masking film over the drawing paper--pushing it down smoothly with a ruler while, at the same time, pulling away its backing sheet.

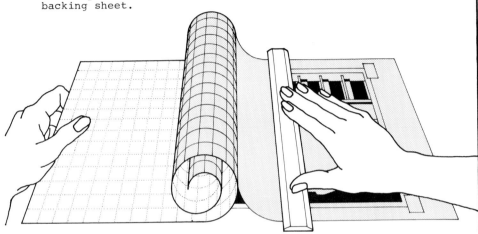

2 Using a very sharp scalpel blade, gently cut out the shapes of the mask-- taking care to cut only through the film, and not the drawing paper underneath.

3 Now carefully peel the masking film away from the shapes to be rendered. Lift at one corner and pull gently-- making sure that the drawing surface is not inadvertently damaged during this process.

4 Having removed the film to reveal the cut-out shapes, you can now briskly and freely apply the selected medium to achieve a perfectly flat wash.

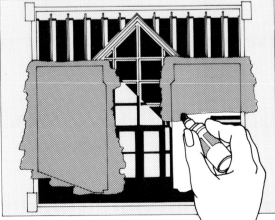

5 Once the application of the medium is completely dry, carefully peel back the film mask to reveal the finished effect.

How to Use the Graphite Dust Technique

The medium for this technique is graphite dust collected from the bottom of a pencil pointer. Graphite dust is useful for introducing subtle and atmospheric values into plans and elevations delineated on opaque or transparent materials (see page 91).

N.B.: Once applied, graphite dust renderings should be thoroughly stabilized with fixative.

2 Large and flat areas of graphite "wash" are simply achieved by masking-off the surrounding area of the drawing with frisk film and applying the graphite using broad, even strokes using a wad of cotton wool or tissue paper.

3 Being a versatile medium, graphite dust can also be employed to create more specific and "three-dimensional" effects. However, before any intensive application, it is important to mask-off surrounding areas of drawing to be left unrendered.

4 Then you are free to apply the graphite dust in a vigorous manner, such as in the rendition of a cloudy sky above an elevation.

5 Once the main areas of value are established, a cotton swab can be used for blending value while highlights in the cloud formation can be "lifted" using the molded point of a kneaded putty eraser. Darker edges and shapes can be intensified using a 6B grade pencil.

6 Used carefully, the same technique can be adapted to render a simulation of different surfaces and materials, such as glazing. However, when large areas of glazing are involved, a reflected version of the sky pattern should be scaled down and formalized into a diagonally stroked application.

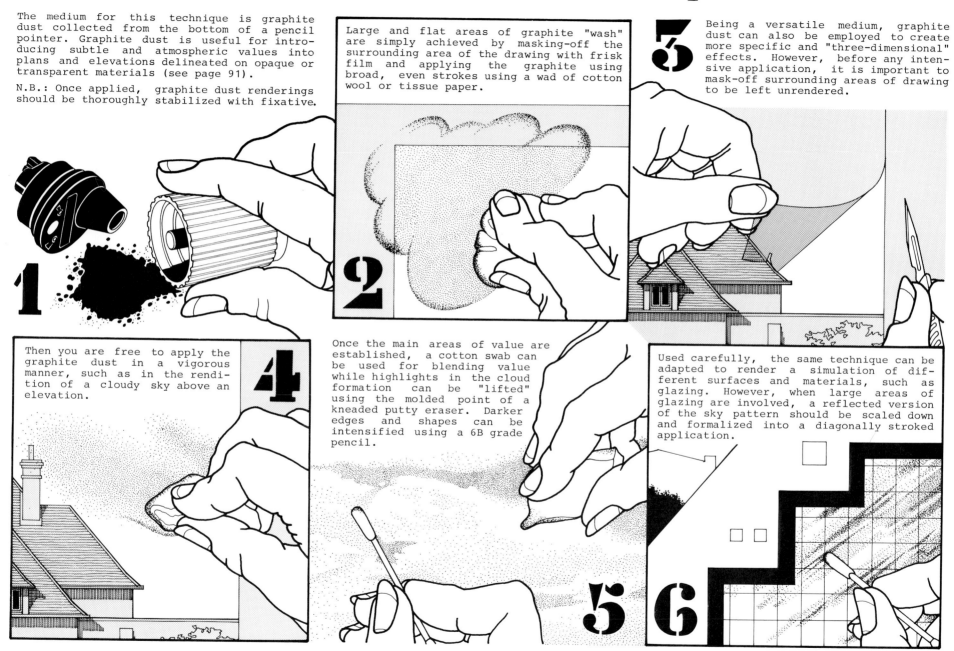

How to Use the Scoring and Frottage Techniques

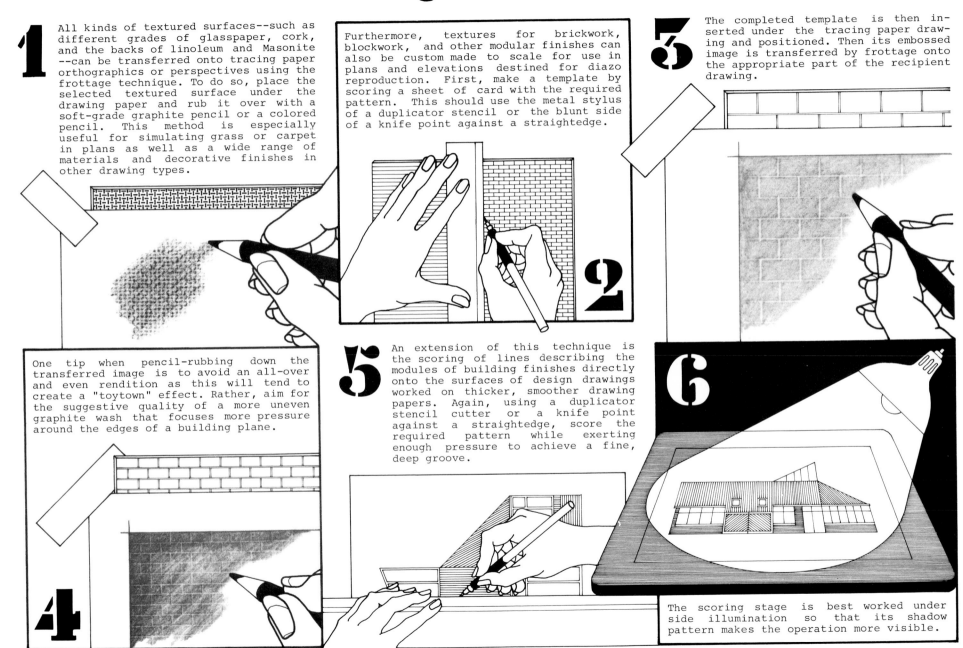

1 All kinds of textured surfaces--such as different grades of glasspaper, cork, and the backs of linoleum and Masonite --can be transferred onto tracing paper orthographics or perspectives using the frottage technique. To do so, place the selected textured surface under the drawing paper and rub it over with a soft-grade graphite pencil or a colored pencil. This method is especially useful for simulating grass or carpet in plans as well as a wide range of materials and decorative finishes in other drawing types.

2 Furthermore, textures for brickwork, blockwork, and other modular finishes can also be custom made to scale for use in plans and elevations destined for diazo reproduction. First, make a template by scoring a sheet of card with the required pattern. This should use the metal stylus of a duplicator stencil or the blunt side of a knife point against a straightedge.

3 The completed template is then inserted under the tracing paper drawing and positioned. Then its embossed image is transferred by frottage onto the appropriate part of the recipient drawing.

4 One tip when pencil-rubbing down the transferred image is to avoid an all-over and even rendition as this will tend to create a "toytown" effect. Rather, aim for the suggestive quality of a more uneven graphite wash that focuses more pressure around the edges of a building plane.

5 An extension of this technique is the scoring of lines describing the modules of building finishes directly onto the surfaces of design drawings worked on thicker, smoother drawing papers. Again, using a duplicator stencil cutter or a knife point against a straightedge, score the required pattern while exerting enough pressure to achieve a fine, deep groove.

6 The scoring stage is best worked under side illumination so that its shadow pattern makes the operation more visible.

How to Use the Scoring and Frottage Techniques

7 The range of patterns achievable by these techniques is only limited by your imagination and your skill in identifying found textures or indenting the paper surface.

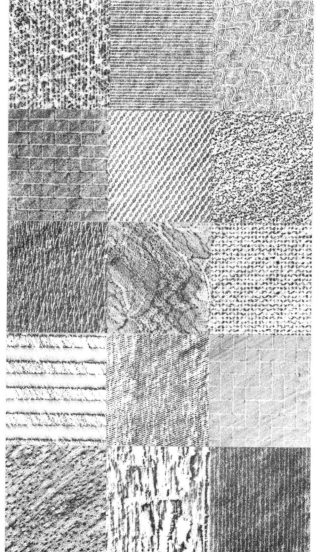

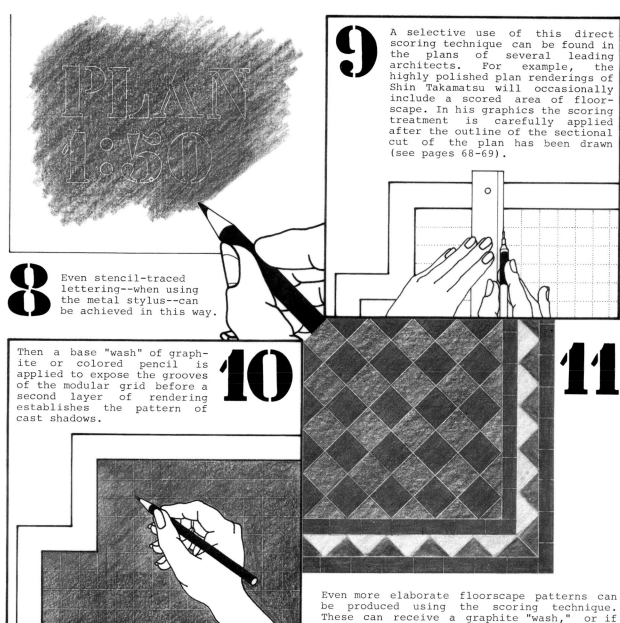

8 Even stencil-traced lettering--when using the metal stylus--can be achieved in this way.

9 A selective use of this direct scoring technique can be found in the plans of several leading architects. For example, the highly polished plan renderings of Shin Takamatsu will occasionally include a scored area of floorscape. In his graphics the scoring treatment is carefully applied after the outline of the sectional cut of the plan has been drawn (see pages 68-69).

10 Then a base "wash" of graphite or colored pencil is applied to expose the grooves of the modular grid before a second layer of rendering establishes the pattern of cast shadows.

11 Even more elaborate floorscape patterns can be produced using the scoring technique. These can receive a graphite "wash," or if color is required, one resulting from a range of colored pencils.

How to Produce Composite Elevations

1

When making composite orthographics, any variation in paper or card thickness will not detract from the ultimate visual effect. On the contrary, precision-cut edges of component parts add a pleasing marquetry effect. When producing elevations using this technique, first set out their outlines in ink or graphite on the drawing board to guide their reception during the image-building phase. If a diazo print of the elevation exists, it can also be used after heat mounting it on a card support.

A separate tracing (or the diazo negative) of the elevation will also be required as a template, because much of the artwork will be produced independently.

After being traced from the template, the design elevation can now be cut from thick paper or card to receive artwork--either directly or indirectly via lamination--in mediums sympathetic to the building's surface finishes.

For example, brickwork, blockwork, cladding, and so on are easily shown in fine-line waterproof inkwork under transparent washes of watercolor, ink, aerosol-spray color, or the subtlety of colored pencils.

An alternative method is the superficial incision of the artwork surface with a scalpel against a straight-edge. The incisions expose the paper fiber which, by attracting more pigment during subsequent color washes, causes them to appear as darker lines.

3

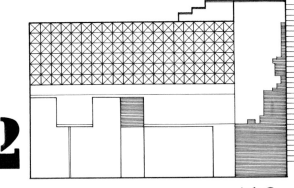

2

5 **6**

4

A further method of representing vertical or horizontal emphasis using either dry mediums such as graphite and colored pencils, or dried ink and watercolor washes, is to score the rendered artwork surface with the back of a cutting blade against a straightedge. This exposes a subtle structure of white lines.

Facade openings present various opportunities. Doors and windows can be drawn directly on the card elevation, laminated as independent graphics, or applied to the artwork after removal from a second diazo print. Alternatively, physical openings can be cut into the elevation to expose windows and doors on a diazo support print, or a pre-mounted artwork, revealed by simulated recesses.

Also, projections such as balconies, canopies, and walls before the main plane of the image can be worked on thin card, cut to shape, and laminated onto the facade as a three-dimensional illusion in relief.

How to Produce Composite Elevations

7

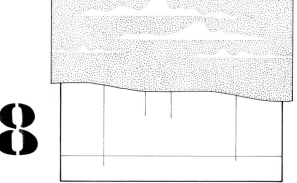

Further modeling of the elevation can be achieved using shadow rendering. This can be introduced as pen hatching or applied in dry-transfer tones.

N.B.: Avoid adding graphite shadows; if badly rendered they will undermine the overall effect.

At this stage, the elevation artwork should be carefully glued into its position on the support sheet. If required, foreground trees, shrubs, and figures can now be added. In-scale dry-transfer figures and silhouette-type foliage are fine for smaller-scale elevations, while drawn or "found" versions cut from magazines can be used to effect in large-scale artwork.

The sky mass will be the first element to be introduced to the support sheet. This can be a transparent watercolor or aerosol spray color wash, worked either directly on the support or on a separate sheet. Otherwise, self-colored paper, magazine photographs, or a proprietary "sky paper" can be shaped and spray mounted into its location.

N.B.: By allowing a margin of overlap into the skyline and elevation outline, time spent in precision-cutting edges will be saved.

8

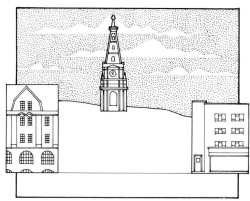

9

Background mass such as existing skyline (i.e., landscape or townscape occurring either side of and behind the elevation area) can now be originated on separate sheets in a medium of your choice. These can then be cut out and mounted on the support, allowing a margin of overlap at the ground line.

10

11

Finally, the ground line section can be added. Being cut from card as thick as that used for the elevation, it will function as a graphic "plinth." For the same reason, this component should be among the darkest values in the completed artwork, utilizing a self-colored surface, or being presprayed with aerosol color.

12

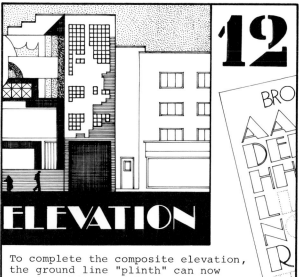

To complete the composite elevation, the ground line "plinth" can now receive white or colored titles using stenciled or dry-transfer lettering.

How to Create After-Dark Elevations

1

The appearance of a building will be transformed completely as it moves from its traditionally rendered daytime experience to that of a nighttime impression. As the source of illumination switches from sunlight to the more localized electric sources occurring immediately outside, on, or inside the building, mass dissolves and surfaces glow, the viewer being drawn to light patterns and given the opportunity of catching glimpses into interiors. Therefore the scope of the nocturnal setting might be considered for elevations, especially when the design exercises a positive after-dark function, or when the fenestration suggests such exploitation. Here is an economical and effective technique for showing nighttime elevations illustrated in a drawing produced in the early 1930s showing neon lighting on a movie theater. It is drawn at a scale of 1/8" = 1' (1:100) and the mediums used are white and black crayon together with red and yellow poster paint and pastels on black paper.

2

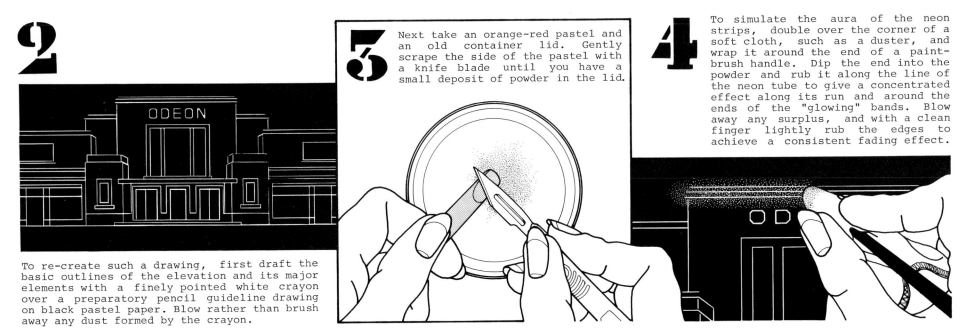

To re-create such a drawing, first draft the basic outlines of the elevation and its major elements with a finely pointed white crayon over a preparatory pencil guideline drawing on black pastel paper. Blow rather than brush away any dust formed by the crayon.

3 Next take an orange-red pastel and an old container lid. Gently scrape the side of the pastel with a knife blade until you have a small deposit of powder in the lid.

4 To simulate the aura of the neon strips, double over the corner of a soft cloth, such as a duster, and wrap it around the end of a paintbrush handle. Dip the end into the powder and rub it along the line of the neon tube to give a concentrated effect along its run and around the ends of the "glowing" bands. Blow away any surplus, and with a clean finger lightly rub the edges to achieve a consistent fading effect.

How to Create After-Dark Elevations

5 If any surplus powder remains on the drawing after blowing, do not attempt to brush it off as this will cause streaking. Instead, lift the drawing off the board and tap its edge onto the board to remove any residue.

Next take a lime-yellow pastel to insert the scattered light effect of fluorescent lamps under the central canopy and behind the first-floor glazing. Prepare some yellow powder, invert the drawing on the board, and mask the top of the drawing with a thin card. Gently finger-rub the powder along this line and blend the edges. The color mixture of the yellow pastel with the black paper will give a greenish tinge that simulates effectively the color of fluorescent lamps.

6 To complete the neon tubes, first dilute some orange-red poster paint with a little water--sufficient to enable it to flow easily in a ruling pen, but not enough to destroy its opacity. Rule a thick line along the position of the neon tube, using a ruler with tapered edges so that the paint will not bleed beneath it. Allow to dry fully.

9 The pastel rendering stage is completed by the indication of reflected light of both neon and fluorescent lights on the sidewalk. This is achieved by mixing the remains of the red and yellow pastel dust and finger-rubbing along the mask placed above the ground line. The resultant orange mix is faded-off as it descends into the pavement zone.

7 Then mix some yellow paint and adjust the ruling pen to give a finer line. Rule lightly over the center of the red line. Do not press too hard as the layer of red paint may flake.

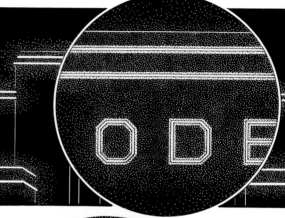

10

Finally add emphasis to the drawing by ruling in shadow lines with a soft black crayon under ledges and window frames. Spray very lightly with a suitable fixative. Allow to dry and apply another coat of fixative. Do not oversaturate the image with fixative as this will loosen the pastel.

How to Create Convincing Design Details

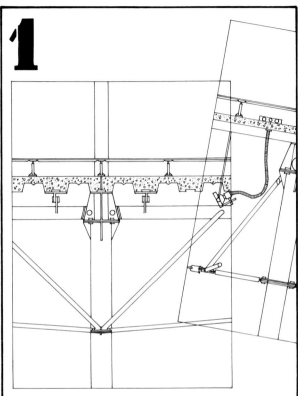

1

Each drawing in the series was then photocopied onto marker bleed-proof paper. Before rendering, a sheet of acetate was placed under the artwork. This functions to slow down the marker ink drying process, thus allowing extra time for the ensuing wet-in-wet marker technique.

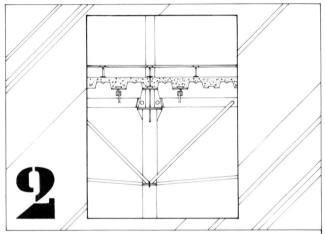

2

For this wet-in-wet bar shading sequence five grades of gray marker were used. Each band steps in 20 percent of grayness from the lightest (10 percent) to the darkest (80 percent), with typist's correction fluid being used to represent isolated highlights.

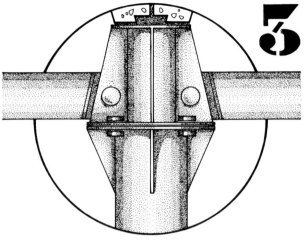

3

The wet-in-wet marker technique was used for rendering all the cylindrical components in the details. The marker ink was applied in bands of gray tone--beginning with the lightest at the center and working outward with bands of increasingly darker grays.

This technique involving markers, colored pencils, and Pantone paper was developed by fifth-year architecture student Trevor Avery to present the working details of his design converting a redundant London church into office units. As the design entailed the insertion of an internal metal deck structure, Trevor wished to focus critical attention on the details of connections and components. Therefore, he devised the following technique to both highlight the metallic quality of the material and create a professional-looking focal point in his subsequent presentation display.

The technique begins with each of his ten representative design details being ink drawn as a simple outline on tracing paper. In this instance the scale used was 1:10.

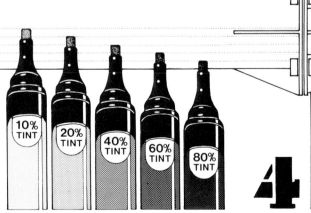

4

10% TINT 20% TINT 40% TINT 60% TINT 80% TINT

5

Immediately after the lightest tone was applied, i.e., along the central axis of the tube, the next tonal step was introduced--allowing the wetness of the first to blend in with that of the ensuing band, and so on until the sequence was completed.

How to Create Convincing Design Details

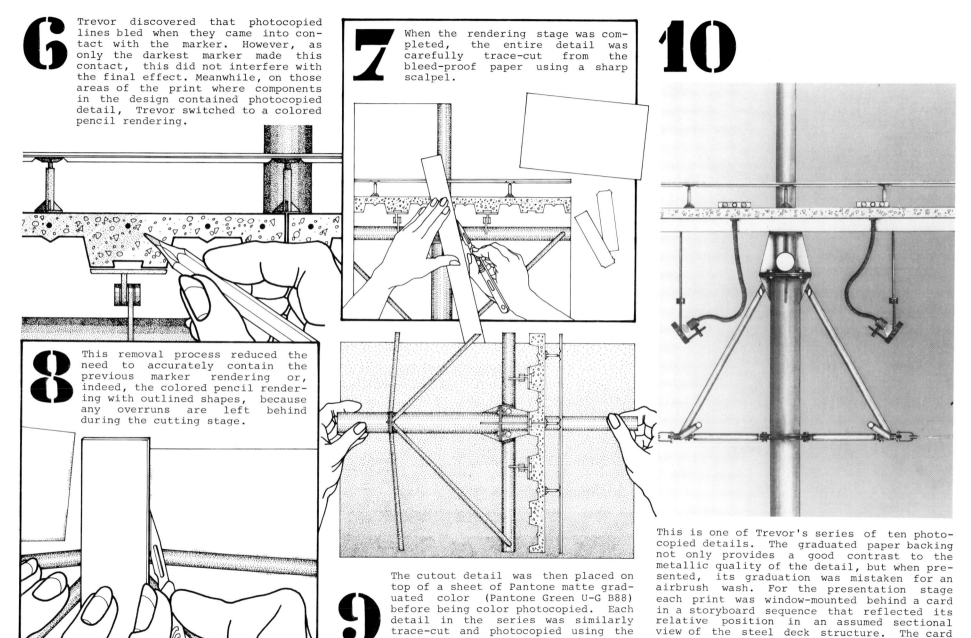

6 Trevor discovered that photocopied lines bled when they came into contact with the marker. However, as only the darkest marker made this contact, this did not interfere with the final effect. Meanwhile, on those areas of the print where components in the design contained photocopied detail, Trevor switched to a colored pencil rendering.

7 When the rendering stage was completed, the entire detail was carefully trace-cut from the bleed-proof paper using a sharp scalpel.

8 This removal process reduced the need to accurately contain the previous marker rendering or, indeed, the colored pencil rendering with outlined shapes, because any overruns are left behind during the cutting stage.

9 The cutout detail was then placed on top of a sheet of Pantone matte graduated color (Pantone Green U-G B88) before being color photocopied. Each detail in the series was similarly trace-cut and photocopied using the same Pantone backing sheet.

10 This is one of Trevor's series of ten photocopied details. The graduated paper backing not only provides a good contrast to the metallic quality of the detail, but when presented, its graduation was mistaken for an airbrush wash. For the presentation stage each print was window-mounted behind a card in a storyboard sequence that reflected its relative position in an assumed sectional view of the steel deck structure. The card mount was then framed behind glass.

53

How to Make "Three-Dimensional" Elevations

1

This technique involves the construction of a relief image from an elevation drawing of a building via a layering process using a series of card-mounted diazo prints. The original drawing should be executed on tracing paper or other transparent drawing material. The technique works well when the original is a line drawing that exploits line weights and is also enhanced when shadows are cast from projecting elements in the design. It is also good for communicating street elevations, especially those including groups of buildings, trees, people, automobiles, and so on.

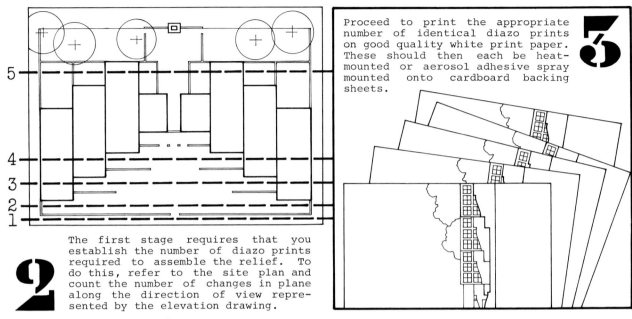

2

The first stage requires that you establish the number of diazo prints required to assemble the relief. To do this, refer to the site plan and count the number of changes in plane along the direction of view represented by the elevation drawing.

3

Proceed to print the appropriate number of identical diazo prints on good quality white print paper. These should then each be heat-mounted or aerosol adhesive spray mounted onto cardboard backing sheets.

4

Next, take one of the mounted diazo prints. This will act as the background sheet or "baseboard" on which the ensuing stages of lamination will be assembled.

5

Now take a second mounted diazo print and, using a sharp Stanley knife, proceed to carefully cut away the sky area by a precision cut along the skyline.

6

This cutaway portion of the elevation should now be aerosol adhesive spray mounted directly over its counterpart on the "baseboard" diazo print.

N.B.: At this stage and between each ensuing lamination it may be necessary to place a weighted board over the newly glued layer in order to ensure a good bond.

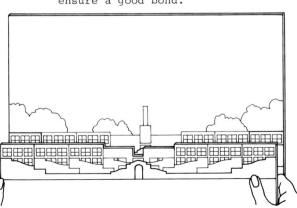

How to Make "Three-Dimensional" Elevations

7 Now take a third card-mounted diazo print and again cut along the skyline in order to remove the sky mass. However, this time all other portions of the elevation that occupy a background plane already represented in the previously laminated diazo print should also be carefully removed.

8 When the cutting stage is completed, glue this laminate into position on the relief.

N.B.: The three-dimensional quality of the relief relies upon the progressive cutting away of background elements as the assembly is built up. The gradual buildup of laminates leaves behind fragments of the elevation that exist at their predetermined plane in the relief--thereby giving a strong sense of depth. Meanwhile, planes that will appear in the final laminate remain intact throughout the entire assembly.

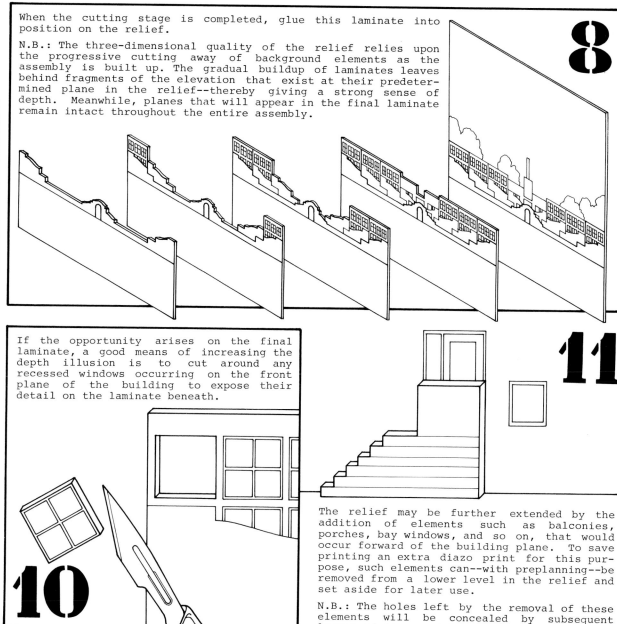

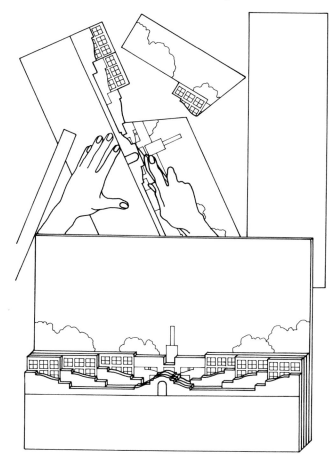

9 Continue this selective cutting and gluing sequence with the remaining card-mounted diazo prints until the final laminate (the plane nearest the viewer) is established on the relief.

10 If the opportunity arises on the final laminate, a good means of increasing the depth illusion is to cut around any recessed windows occurring on the front plane of the building to expose their detail on the laminate beneath.

11 The relief may be further extended by the addition of elements such as balconies, porches, bay windows, and so on, that would occur forward of the building plane. To save printing an extra diazo print for this purpose, such elements can--with preplanning--be removed from a lower level in the relief and set aside for later use.

N.B.: The holes left by the removal of these elements will be concealed by subsequent layers of diazo print.

How to Make Three-Dimensional Orthographics

1 Here is another technique for making elevations appear as three-dimensional presentations. At its simplest the technique works well using elevations with a horizontal bias, such as those of long, low buildings, street elevations, and the like. The depth effect is achieved when the foreground section appears as a cutout and positioned approximately 1/4" (6mm) forward of the main drawing.

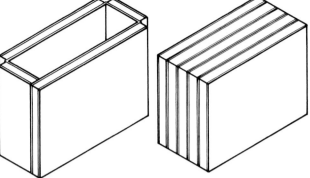

2 This "stage-set" approach to presentation elevations can be produced from two or more card-mounted prints of the same drawing, or from an original drawing worked specifically for the purpose on two or more sheets of paper. The cutout components of the elevation are then glue-assembled using spacer pads made from either folded paper or laminated blocks of card.

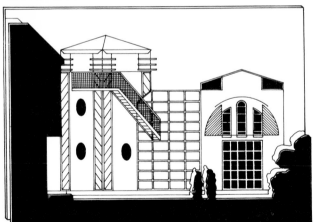

4 A version employing three layers might separate foreground from middleground (the latter containing the building design) with a third layer acting as backdrop and carrying sky and background information.

N.B.: Notice that the technique can be worked successfully with drawings exclusively in line. However, the depth illusion can be further extended by the addition of color or a progressively darkening or lightening value sequence between foreground and background planes.

3 Provided the technique responds to the spatial demands of the elevation, it can be applied in a variety of ways. For instance, another two-layered version might detach foreground buildings to produce a framed view.

How to Make Three-Dimensional Orthographics

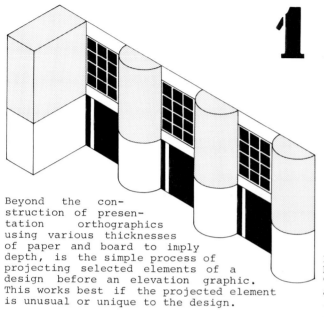

1 **2**

Beyond the construction of presentation orthographics using various thicknesses of paper and board to imply depth, is the simple process of projecting selected elements of a design before an elevation graphic. This works best if the projected element is unusual or unique to the design.

Projections are quickly assembled in paper or board using simple model-making techniques. The form can be cut out and have artwork applied before glue assembly and final gluing into the drawing.

Three-dimensional sections in card can also be quickly assembled in "stage-set" fashion to convey convincing impressions of depth in both interior and exterior spaces. First, cut out the selected sections, apply artwork, and assemble them within an open-ended card box or a balsa-wood space frame.

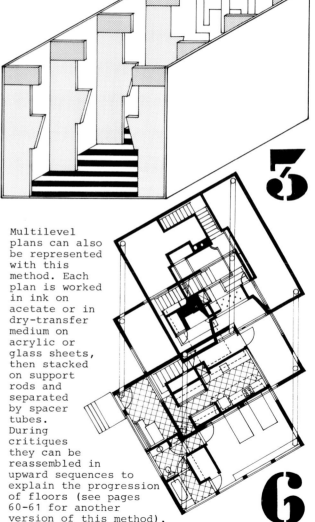

3

4

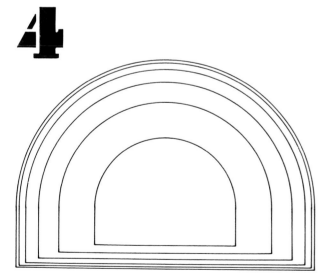

Forms such as domes that are difficult to draw and build are easily constructed using the "stage-set" method.

5

A sophisticated version is the assembly of a series of clear acetate layers which, in carrying ink, dry colors, or collage artwork simulate realistic sections at progressive points through interior or exterior volume. The sections can then be glued into position within an open-ended card box and mounted at eye level for viewing in wall presentations.

Multilevel plans can also be represented with this method. Each plan is worked in ink on acetate or in dry-transfer medium on acrylic or glass sheets, then stacked on support rods and separated by spacer tubes. During critiques they can be reassembled in upward sequences to explain the progression of floors (see pages 60-61 for another version of this method).

6

How to Emboss an Orthographic Drawing

1 The production of an embossed "print" of a plan, section, or elevation begins with a basic line drawing on tracing paper.

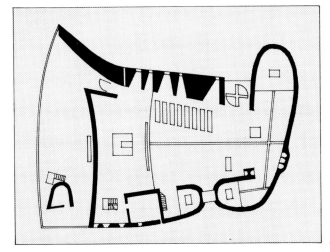

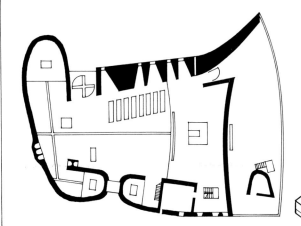

2 The transparency of the tracing paper medium is essential as a photocopy print on plain paper is now made from the back of the original to achieve a handed, or back-to-front image.

3 Next, a laminated paper block that will act as a mold is made by spray-mounting successive layers of thin paper onto a thick cardboard base. The lamination should be one tenth of an inch (2.5mm) thick and cover an area greater than the format of the printed drawing.

4 This stage is completed when the photocopy print--with its handed printed image uppermost--is laminated as the top layer of the paper "sandwich."

5 Now begins the cutting/embossing stage. Two different types of embossing can be used: positive or negative. For instance, in plans and sections the choice is whether to emboss the sectional slice or, alternatively, the areas contained by and surrounding the sectional slice.

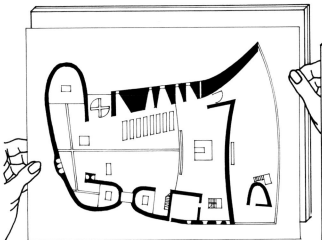

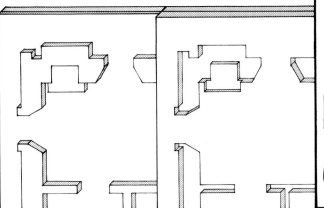

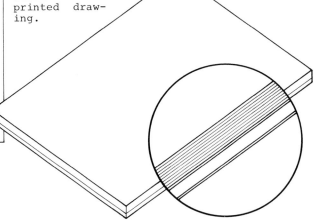

6 The same choice applies to elevations--to which this technique affords the opportunity of raising prominent features in the facade.

How to Emboss an Orthographic Drawing

7

The cutting process involves the use of a sharp scalpel, and using the back-to-front print as a guide, the removal of all the selected negative shapes using a vertical slice into the face of the paper block.

N.B.: Depending upon the desired effect, various depths of incision may be made-- providing that any penetration stops short of the cardboard base layer.

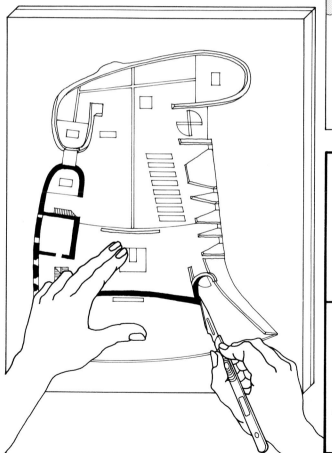

8

Once the cutting process is completed, the surface of the paper mold should be coated thoroughly with a waterproofing agent, such as glue-size or PVC glue, which is allowed to dry completely.

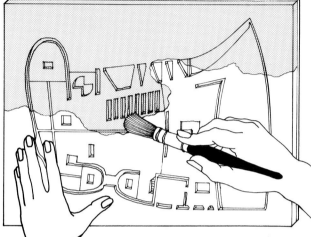

9

Finally, to make the embossed print, take a sheet of heavy-duty watercolor paper and soak it thoroughly in clean water.

10

watercolor paper

PRESS

foam rubber
foam rubber

mold

PRESS

After removing any excess moisture with a clean sponge, position the watercolor paper over the mold and cover this with several layers of felt or foam rubber before placing the complete assembly into a heavy-duty book press. After applying extreme pressure, the paper is left in the press to dry completely into its new shape.

11

Once removed from the press, the embossed image can be rendered with watercolor or airbrush washes--both being applied to exploit the intaglio nature of the surface. For example, prior to airbrushing, the embossed and selectively masked surface can receive an angled wash that exploits the raised nature of the "print."

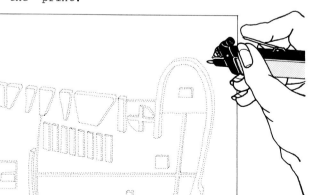

How to Make a "Glass Axonometric"

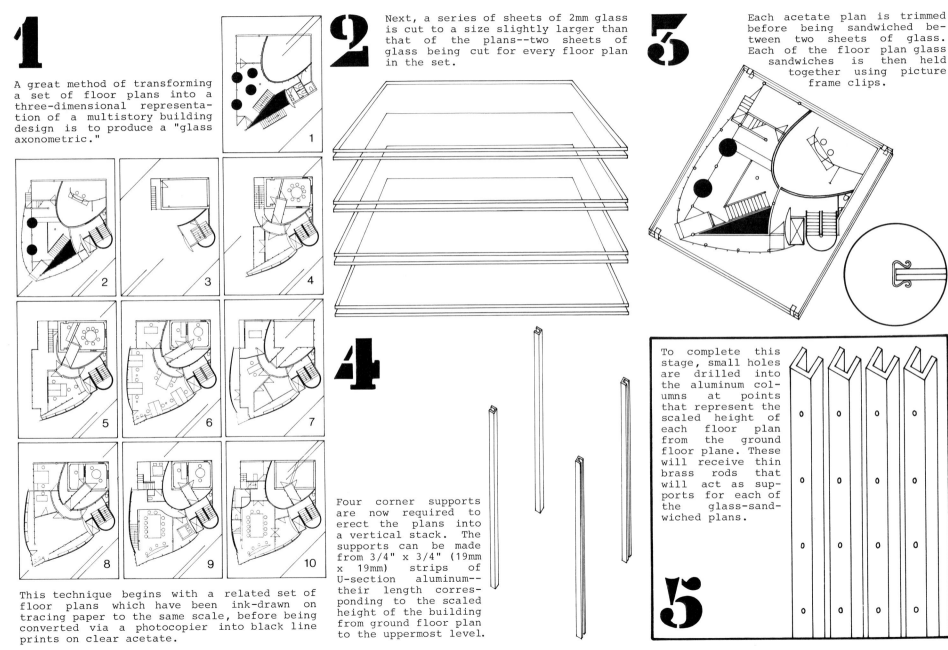

1

A great method of transforming a set of floor plans into a three-dimensional representation of a multistory building design is to produce a "glass axonometric."

This technique begins with a related set of floor plans which have been ink-drawn on tracing paper to the same scale, before being converted via a photocopier into black line prints on clear acetate.

2

Next, a series of sheets of 2mm glass is cut to a size slightly larger than that of the plans--two sheets of glass being cut for every floor plan in the set.

3

Each acetate plan is trimmed before being sandwiched between two sheets of glass. Each of the floor plan glass sandwiches is then held together using picture frame clips.

4

Four corner supports are now required to erect the plans into a vertical stack. The supports can be made from 3/4" x 3/4" (19mm x 19mm) strips of U-section aluminum--their length corresponding to the scaled height of the building from ground floor plan to the uppermost level.

5

To complete this stage, small holes are drilled into the aluminum columns at points that represent the scaled height of each floor plan from the ground floor plane. These will receive thin brass rods that will act as supports for each of the glass-sandwiched plans.

How to Make a "Glass Axonometric"

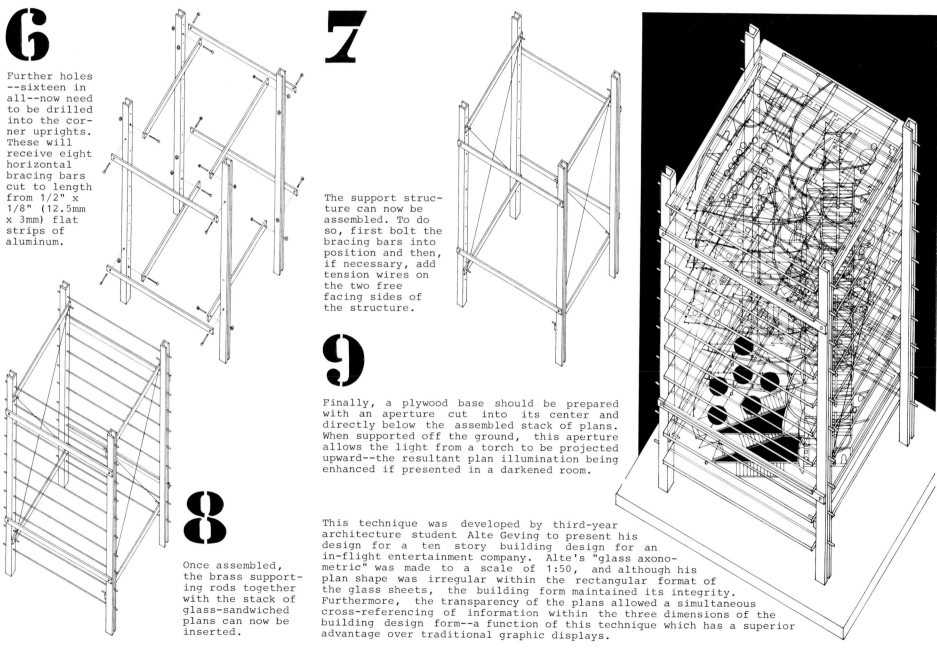

6 Further holes --sixteen in all--now need to be drilled into the corner uprights. These will receive eight horizontal bracing bars cut to length from 1/2" x 1/8" (12.5mm x 3mm) flat strips of aluminum.

7 The support structure can now be assembled. To do so, first bolt the bracing bars into position and then, if necessary, add tension wires on the two free facing sides of the structure.

9 Finally, a plywood base should be prepared with an aperture cut into its center and directly below the assembled stack of plans. When supported off the ground, this aperture allows the light from a torch to be projected upward--the resultant plan illumination being enhanced if presented in a darkened room.

8 Once assembled, the brass supporting rods together with the stack of glass-sandwiched plans can now be inserted.

This technique was developed by third-year architecture student Alte Geving to present his design for a ten story building design for an in-flight entertainment company. Alte's "glass axonometric" was made to a scale of 1:50, and although his plan shape was irregular within the rectangular format of the glass sheets, the building form maintained its integrity. Furthermore, the transparency of the plans allowed a simultaneous cross-referencing of information within the three dimensions of the building design form--a function of this technique which has a superior advantage over traditional graphic displays.

How to Draw for Reduction

1

As we turn to reprographic techniques in Chapter 4, we conclude this section on specialized techniques with some pointers concerning drawings that are destined for reduction.

When artwork is reduced, such as on the photocopier, its format area becomes smaller while its width and height dimensions, though diminished, remain proportionally the same. However, when designers speak of producing originals "half-up" and "twice-up," they refer to linear rather than area scaling. For example, a twice-up or 2:1 ratio gives a reduced format area of one-quarter that of the original. Similarly, a 3:1 reduction is one-ninth of the original area, and so on.

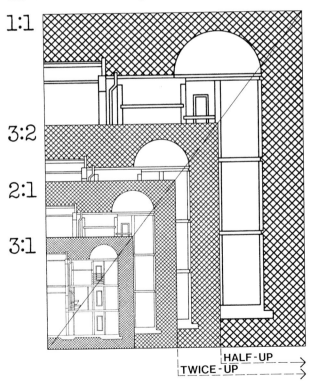

1:1

3:2

2:1

3:1

HALF-UP →

TWICE-UP →

2

As contrast and clarity are salient ingredients in all forms of reprography, it is vital to structure images from a discernible hierarchy of line weights. A basic hierarchy may comprise three or four line thicknesses, from fine to heavy.

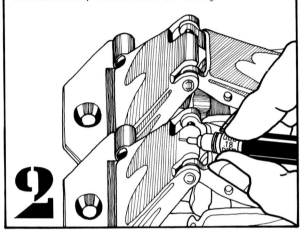

A further factor in reduction is the allowance made for intervals between lines. A common error, for example, is to draw a series of lines or hatching in proximity which, when reduced, will tend to fill in. The basic rule is therefore: the larger the reduction, the wider the spacing --and never draw lines with less than their own thickness as the interval between them.

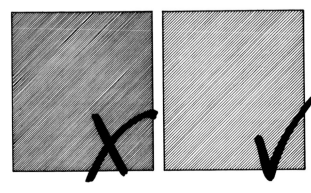

Being more susceptible to erosion by reduction, pencil lines and the thinner lines of ink drawings are the most critical. For this reason their weight should be determined at the outset, and on the basis of their intended reduction ratio.

A fine line weight can be established by calculating backward from its intended thickness when printed. For instance, if a fine line is to exist in printed form at 0.1mm, then the line, prior to a 2:1 reduction, should be drawn to a thickness of 0.2mm. The same reduced line thickness should be drawn at 0.3mm prior to a 3:1 reduction. From this fine line, the other line weights can be determined. The accompanying table is offered as a basic guide. However, if in doubt, always tend toward a line thickness of a bolder size.

3

REDUCTION	FINE LINE	INTERMEDIATE LINE	HEAVY LINE
3:2	0.15mm	0.3mm	0.6mm
2:1	0.2mm	0.4mm	0.8mm
3:1	0.3mm	0.6mm	1.2mm

4 **5**

FULL SIZE

2:1

3:1

As a 2:1 reduction of a dry-transfer screen gives twice the number of lines to the inch in its printed version as a same-size print, and a 3:1 reduction gives three times the number of lines, it is a good idea to predict the effects of dry-transfer tones when applied to drawings destined for reduction. For this reason it is worth avoiding the darker end of ranges of dot and line screens, for instance 70 and 80 percent, as they tend to fill in as a solid black when reduced.

3 SHADOW PROJECTION

An Introduction to Shadow Projection

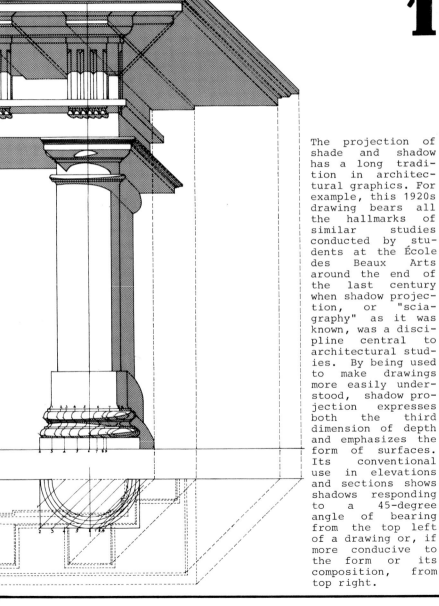

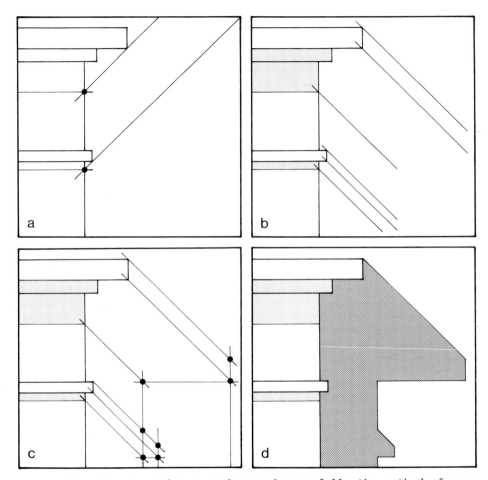

1 The projection of shade and shadow has a long tradition in architectural graphics. For example, this 1920s drawing bears all the hallmarks of similar studies conducted by students at the École des Beaux Arts around the end of the last century when shadow projection, or "sciagraphy" as it was known, was a discipline central to architectural studies. By being used to make drawings more easily understood, shadow projection expresses both the third dimension of depth and emphasizes the form of surfaces. Its conventional use in elevations and sections shows shadows responding to a 45-degree angle of bearing from the top left of a drawing or, if more conducive to the form or its composition, from top right.

2 However, in order to understand more fully the method of construction, we should first examine some of the basic principles. For instance, the rays of light entering the drawing are considered as parallel (a). Therefore, when it falls on a plane surface, the shadow of any straight line can be located by finding the shadows of the ends of the line and connecting them with a straight-line shadow (b). This gives shadow widths which, when a figure is parallel to the line of sight and parallel to the plane receiving the shadow, are equal to its vertical and horizontal projections. In simple terms, therefore, a shadow projection is a 45-degree projection of the form that casts the shadow (c). Also, when light does not strike it, any line within shade or a shadow cannot cast a shadow. In other words, only those lines, or those parts of lines, receiving direct light will cast shadows (d).

An Introduction to Shadow Projection

3
Shadow projection, therefore, is very similar to orthographic projection. The major difference is that whereas in orthographic projection points are projected at right angles to the horizontal and vertical planes respectively, shadow points are projected at 45 degrees upon horizontal and vertical planes. Thus, to find the shadow projection of any point it is necessary to define its position, both on plan and elevation, or on section and elevation.

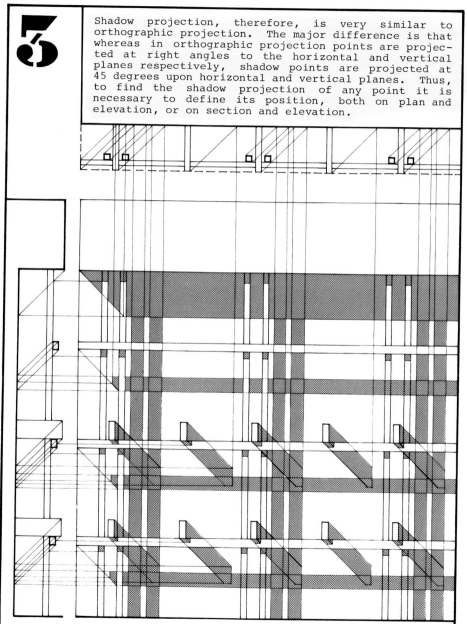

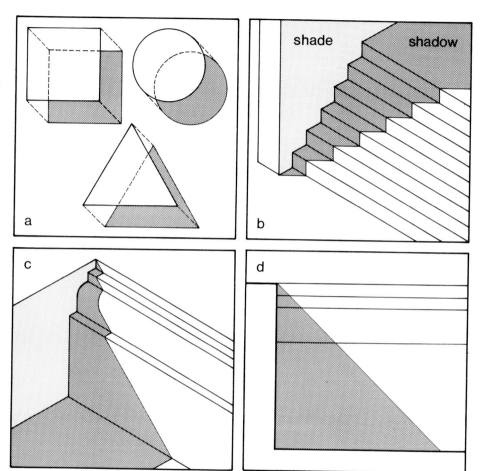

a

b   shade   shadow

c

d

4
Here are some further basic principles of shadow casting. The shadow of any plane figure on a parallel plane is identical in shape, size, and direction with the figure (a). Most important is to be able to identify the difference between shade and shadow. For example, shadows are projected onto another surface from an object that intercepts light, whereas shade represents the unlit areas of the surface of an illuminated object (b). Finally, when the observer looks at the end of a straight line so that it is seen as a point, then the shadow cast by that line appears as a straight line, regardless of the form of the surface receiving the shadow (c,d).

How to Plot Shadows in Site Plans

1

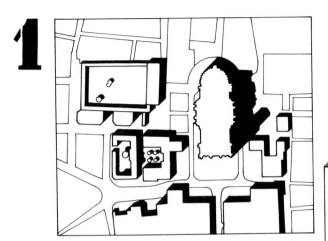

When the degree of detail allows, the projection of shadows provides an invaluable spatial clue to that dimension inherently absent from building and site plans, i.e., verticality. For instance, shadows emphasize the existence of both the shape of the plan and the height of its implied mass above ground level.

2

Shadows also describe the physical nature of the terrain and, at larger scales and when using open systems of rendering, can hint at its surface texture.

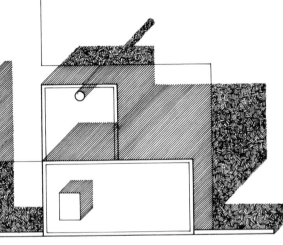

3

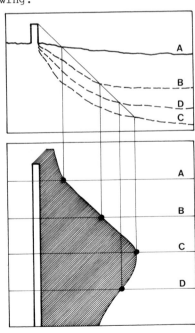

Conventionally, shadows in plan are simply a 45-degree projection of the form along an angle of bearing from the bottom left of the drawing. However, shadows can be cast in any convenient projection, i.e., at any angle that does not impede vital information conveyed in the drawing.

4

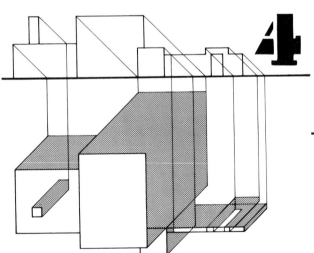

Shadows cast from more complicated forms are plotted with reference to an auxiliary elevation. Therefore, their construction necessitates a degree of familiarity with the building design.

Increasingly more complicated forms require the plotting aid of both side and front elevations.

5

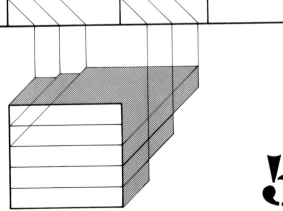

6

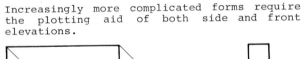

As the shape of shadows will also help to describe the nature of irregular terrain, a basic knowledge of the site topology will bring a more pictorial dimension to their inclusion in site plans.

How to Plot Shadows in Floor Plans

1

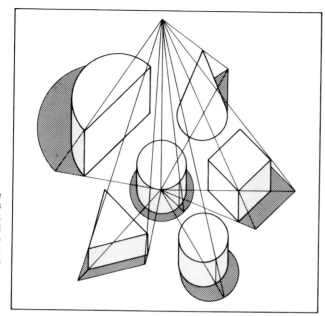

By contrast to the convention that sees the rays of sunlight as parallel and following a single bearing line, the rays of light from electric sources are seen as radiating around their point, or points, of source.

Therefore, in plan, electric light rays are plotted to cut all the casting edges of objects, such as furniture, that lie in their path. From this simple principle, floor plan shadows can be quickly constructed to represent the effect of overhead lighting patterns.

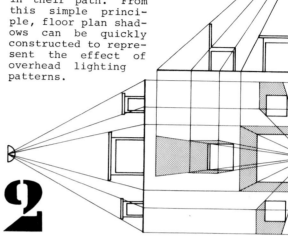

2

3

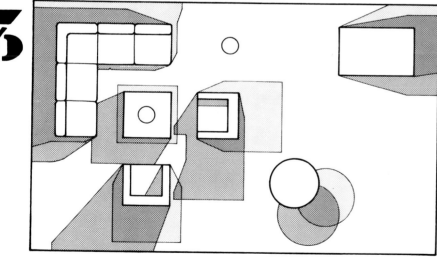

By shading in pencil, ink, wash, or dry-transfer materials, shadows can be invested with different values to simulate strength of light. Also, a value emphasis of any areas of "overlap" will clarify the components of a multishadow cluster.

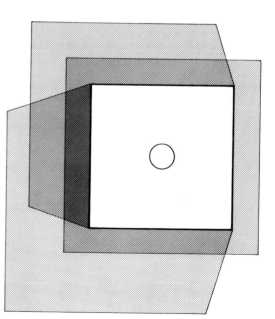

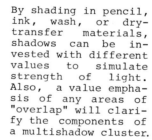

Also, in larger scale interior plans, a multishadowed effect caused by more than one point of source can be represented. Furthermore, light sources of unequal strength or at unequal proximity to the objects in question can be clearly indicated by their corresponding shadows.

4

How to Render Convincing Shadows in Floor Plans

1

The following technique is popular with students who wish to create a highly realistic rendering depicting the impact of sunlight on floor plans. Adapted from the work of Shin Takamatsu, this technique involves the use of a technical pen, a colored pencil, and a graphite pencil.

The technique begins with a fine-line ink drawing of the plan which simply delineates the outline and extent of its cutting plane. To accommodate the next stage in the sequence, the plan outline is drawn on good-quality cartridge paper.

2

Now follows the selective application of a scoring treatment to insert the incidence of floorscape modules. This is applied carefully using the blunt side of a thin blade or a duplicator stencil against a straightedge (see pages 46-47).

N.B.: An alternative to scoring is the delineation of floorscape patterns using a very fine ink line. Another option is the combination of both scored and ink-lined modules introduced to different spaces within the plan.

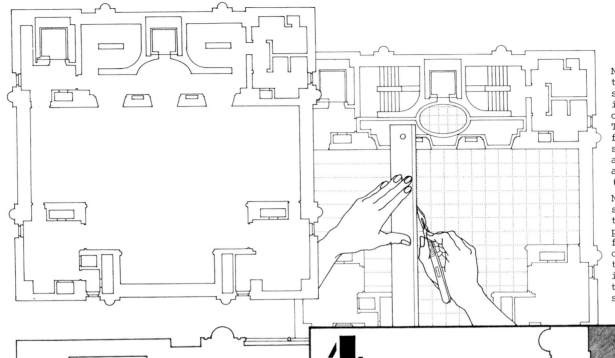

3

The next step involves the application of an overall 45-degree "wash" of colored pencil or graphite to the floor area as defined by the plan. If colored pencil is chosen, this should be applied as a muted or neutral hue so as not to cause a distraction. However, whichever is used, it is important that the rendering is applied in a structured manner, i.e., a tight layering of fine lines deposited to produce an even tone.

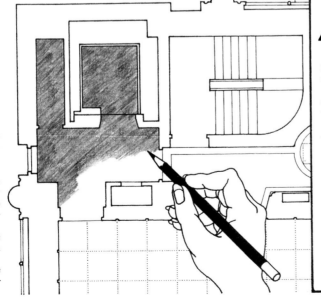

4

During the application of this flat, 45-degree "wash" of tone (or color), the gridded effect of the scored floorscape pattern will reveal itself as a negative, or ghosted impression. Also, two points should be considered during this rendering stage: first, make sure that the "wash" of tone or color is maintained across the entire area contained by the plan--making sure that a crisp edge is achieved around the inside of the walls; second, as the "wash" represents a value step between the white of the sectional slice and the darkness of the ensuing shadow treatment, it is important to achieve a mid-tone.

5

Now begins the introduction of the shadow pattern to the plan. This can enlist an HB grade pencil and be worked in the same 45-degree angle as that of the initial background "wash." First, draw in all the edges of cast shadows from the corners of walls and apertures, such as doors and windows, at 45 degrees and to a length corresponding to the height of the sectional cut.

N.B.: Make sure to avoid a common error, i.e., project the shadow's edge from the outer corner of wall openings rather than the inner corner.

6

The three-dimensional illusion associated with this technique results from a darker shadow tone emphasizing the casting plane of the wall and fading as it approaches its extremity. Therefore, begin by establishing the darkest portion of the shadow and then, using controlled strokes, render its 45-degree directional progression from dark-to-light.

N.B.: An added dimension of visual information is gained from the subtle recognition of tonal changes in floorscape materials.

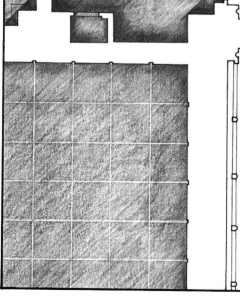

7

Here are some points which help to increase the illusion of depth. Most important is the insertion of a narrow "aura" of tone along all the wall planes receiving light. It is this tonal emphasis that causes the sectional slice to appear perceptually detached and to occupy a plane forward of the ground plane. Also, irrespective of their relationship to direct sources of light, make sure that all internal wall planes cast shadows. It is this comprehensive insertion of shadow that imbues this rendering technique with its powerful sense of depth.

The result is a convincing rendition of light entering a building plan-- the final drawing inviting the viewer to look "into" rather than "at" an architectural space from above.

69

How to Plot Shadows in Elevations

As with the projection of shadows in plan, shadows cast across the face of elevations follow a convention that assumes the sun to be in a fixed position, i.e., emanating parallel rays of light from top left along a bearing angle of 45 degrees.

To plot the shadow of a square column standing forward of an elevation plane, reference is made to an auxiliary plan. First project 45-degree lines from the corners of its elevation together with similar projections from the plan.

1

ELEVATION

PLAN

2 Where the lines projected on plan make contact with the vertical plane (in plan), perpendicular lines are projected upward to intersect the 45-degree projections on the elevation.

3 The resulting intersections will find the outline of the shadow in elevation. Once plotted they are ready for rendering.

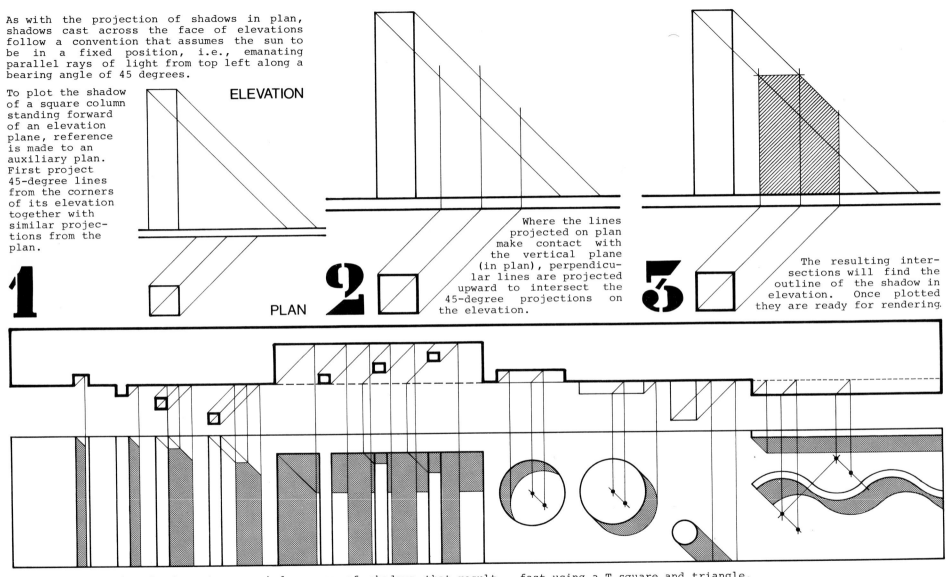

4 Using this basic setup, a whole range of shadows that result from recesses, projections, and objects forward of the elevation can be quickly plotted. The effect of the 45-degree shadow convention appears convincing as it corresponds to average daylight conditions. Also, as the dimensions of shadows are generally the same as the objects from which they are cast, construction is fast using a T square and triangle.

N.B.: Notice that the shadows cast from the cylinder and cylindrical recess are found by slipping the circle along the appropriate direction of the 45-degree angle to a length equal to their depth.

70

How to Plot Shadows in Elevations

1

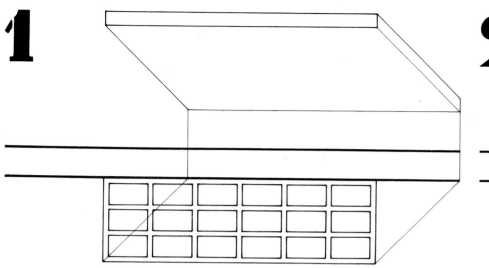

This construction sequence in the plotting of a shadow cast from a perforated canopy demonstrates how both an auxiliary plan and a section can function to determine a more complex shadow. First, the main outline of the canopy is quickly plotted from the plan.

2

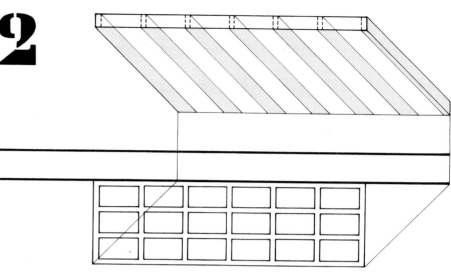

Then, the edges of the shadows formed by the lines of the structure that appear perpendicular to the eye are found from a skeletal view of the canopy in elevation.

3

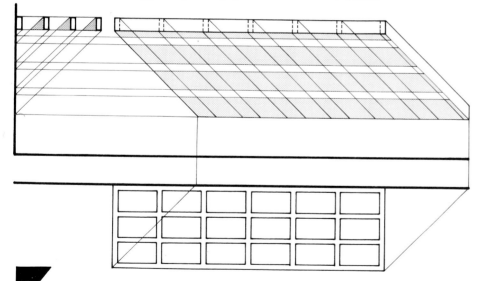

However, to find the lateral edges of shadows describing the perforations, we need to enlist the aid of an auxiliary section.

4

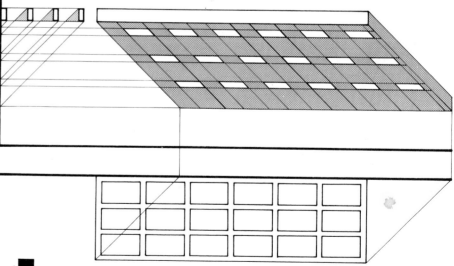

Once established, the shadow pattern is ready to be rendered in a medium or technique of your choice.

How to Plot Shadows on Interrupted Planes

The shadow cast by a semioctagonal canopy onto a flat plane is perfectly straightforward to construct using an auxiliary plan.

1

N.B.: When using an auxiliary plan, section, or side elevation to plot a shadow, it is important that it is carefully aligned to the drawing receiving the shadow. Then a 45-degree line from any given point in one view will locate the same point in the other view. This method of transferring points equidistantly from one graphic view to another is the one used throughout this chapter.

However, the points of the same shadow cast onto an interrupted plane are constructed in a step-by-step manner as it breaks over the various planes of the surface receiving shadow. For example, the effect on the shadow of the two forward planes is determined by 45-degree projectors struck from their front corners which intersect at points A, B, C, and D on the plan. These are then projected up to the underside of the canopy to find their equivalent points in elevation and down at 45 degrees to intersect with the vertical planes. Connection of these points of intersection traces the shadow line on the raised portions of the plane.

2

As the remainder of the shadow from the canopy falls onto the flat portion of the wall, this can be constructed as shown in Frame 1. The construction stage is completed when the shadows from the vertical elements are inserted with reference to the plan.

N.B.: Notice how the thickness of the canopy is projected into the shape of the shadow.

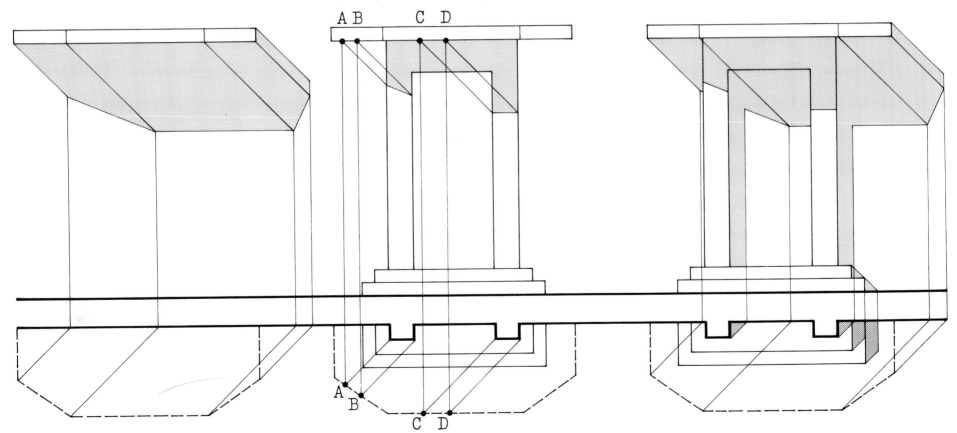

How to Plot Shadows on Interrupted Planes

1

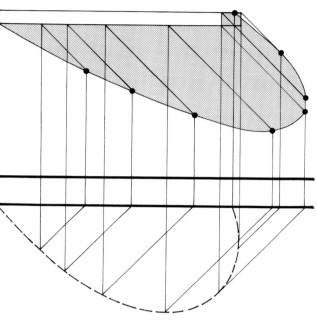

The same principle of point transfer is applied for tracing the shadow line of this irregularly curved canopy. However, in order to trace the smoothness of the curve of the shadow, a whole series of shadow points--taken at key points--should be transferred.

2

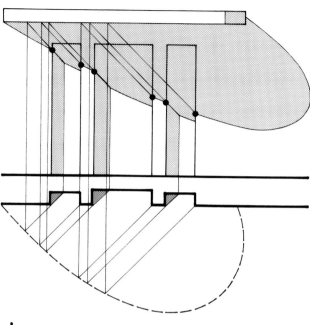

If the same shadow falls onto an interrupted plane, then the principle described on the facing page comes into play, i.e., critical points in plan being projected at 45 degrees before being transferred vertically to the elevation and reprojected at 45 degrees to find their equivalent points in the vertical plane.

3

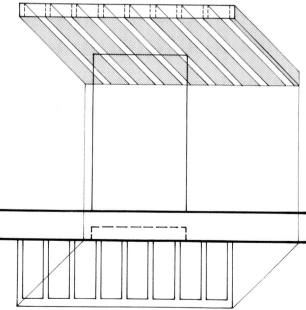

To find the shadow cast from this slatted overhang onto a plane with a recessed doorway, reference is made to both plan and side elevation. When connected with 45-degree projectors made from the corner of the overhang, the same projectors from the plan find the extent of the shadow on the wall plane.

4

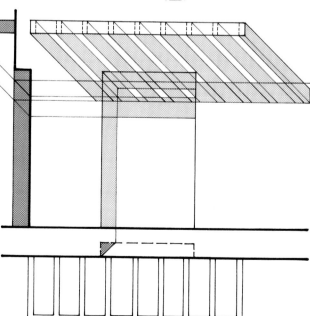

Meanwhile, 45-degree projectors from the overhang in side elevation confirm both the thickness of the horizontal shadow on the wall plane as well as its interrupted location in the recess. Notice the silhouette of the shadow at its extreme lower-right corner. Here, its outline configuration simply describes the form of the overhang as it would appear in an axonometric drawing.

How to Plot Shadows on Inclined Planes

1 The plotting method for shadows cast from a chimney onto a pitched roof follows the principles already established. An auxiliary section or side elevation is necessary in order to find the point at which the shadow from the top of the stack strikes the inclined plane.

2 To plot the shadow from a dormer window, first project points A, B, C, and D on an auxiliary side elevation back at 45 degrees onto the inclined plane. The points of intersection are then transferred horizontally to the front elevation.

3 The equivalent points A, B, C, and D on the front elevation are now projected along the 45-degree bearing of the shape of the shadow on the pitched roof. Notice that only when a shadow is cast from one parallel plane to another is the edge of the shadow at the same angle as the casting edge.

4 This architectural form together with its shadow projection is one of the most recurrent in building design presentation.

5 To plot the shadow of the form forward of the main elevation, first project points A, B, and C along the 45-degree bearing of the sun on an auxiliary side elevation. If the line projected from A intersects the roof, extend the line of the slope to cut the line projected from B. This will establish the secondary angle of the shadow on the roof plane. Next transfer all points of intersection horizontally to the front elevation.

6 Now, from the equivalent points A, B, and C on the front elevation, project the 45-degree shadow casting lines. Their intersection with the appropriate horizontal projection will form the shape of the shadow cast on roof and wall planes.

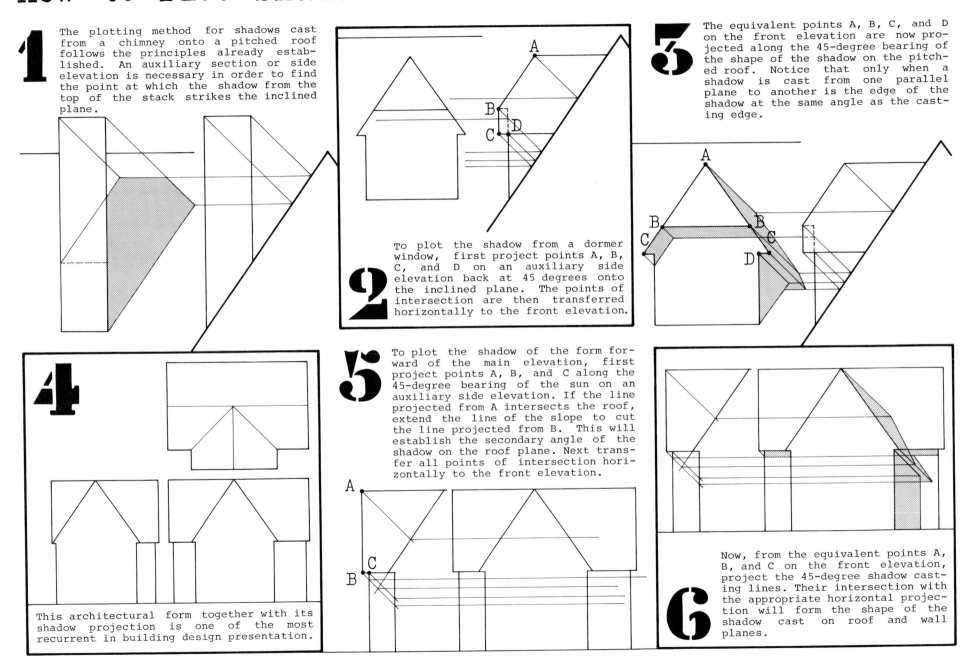

How to Plot Shadows from Circular Planes

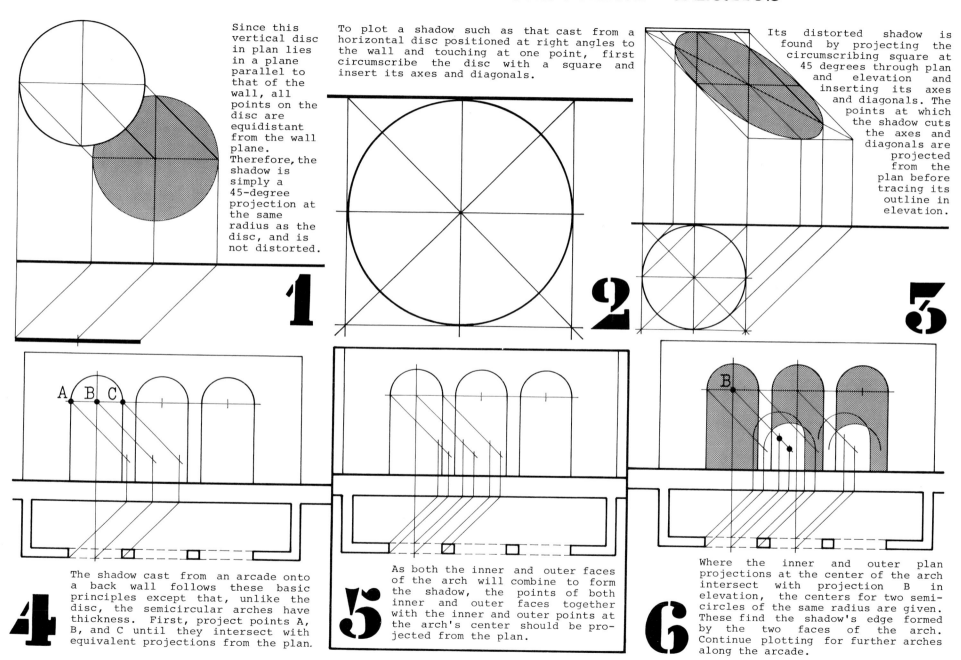

Since this vertical disc in plan lies in a plane parallel to that of the wall, all points on the disc are equidistant from the wall plane. Therefore, the shadow is simply a 45-degree projection at the same radius as the disc, and is not distorted.

1

To plot a shadow such as that cast from a horizontal disc positioned at right angles to the wall and touching at one point, first circumscribe the disc with a square and insert its axes and diagonals.

2

Its distorted shadow is found by projecting the circumscribing square at 45 degrees through plan and elevation and inserting its axes and diagonals. The points at which the shadow cuts the axes and diagonals are projected from the plan before tracing its outline in elevation.

3

The shadow cast from an arcade onto a back wall follows these basic principles except that, unlike the disc, the semicircular arches have thickness. First, project points A, B, and C until they intersect with equivalent projections from the plan.

4

As both the inner and outer faces of the arch will combine to form the shadow, the points of both inner and outer faces together with the inner and outer points at the arch's center should be projected from the plan.

5

Where the inner and outer plan projections at the center of the arch intersect with projection B in elevation, the centers for two semicircles of the same radius are given. These find the shadow's edge formed by the two faces of the arch. Continue plotting for further arches along the arcade.

6

How to Plot Shade on Spherical Planes

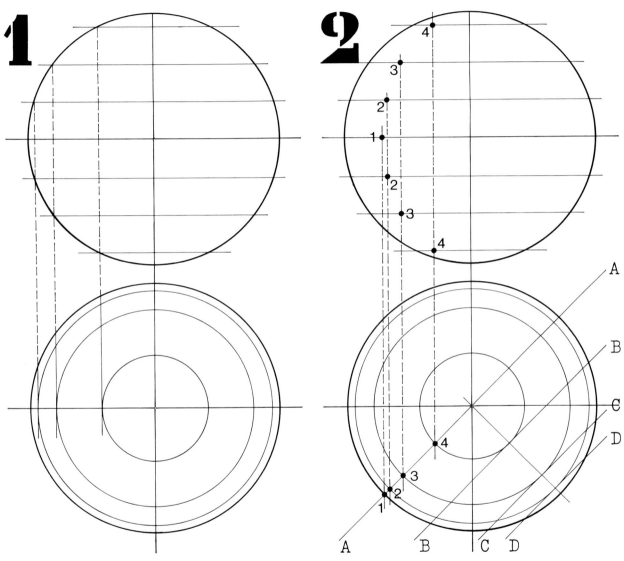

1

To find the line of shade on a sphere in elevation, first draw a series of equally spaced horizontal lines above and below its diameter. Then project down their points of intersection with its circumference to find their equivalent contours along the diameter in plan.

2

As the convention of light in plans travels at 45 degrees, draw a series of lines (AA, BB, CC, DD) angled at 45 degrees to strike the established contours tangentially. Next project the points 1, 2, 3, and 4 upward to find their corresponding points (4,3,2,1,2,3, 4) in the elevation.

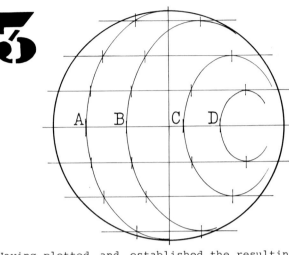

3

Having plotted and established the resulting contour with a continuous line, repeat the transfer process by projecting up the equivalent points along the remaining section lines BB, CC, DD, on plan to find their corresponding contours on the elevation.

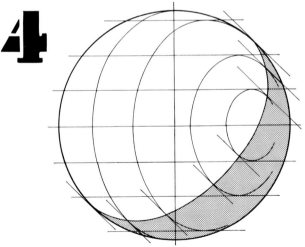

4

To plot the line of shade on the elevation of the sphere, finally strike tangential lines at 45 degrees that represent the parallel rays of light to touch each of the contours. A continuous line drawn through these points will establish the line of shade in elevation.

76

How to Plot Shadows from Spherical Planes

As the sphere is the only form whose elevation appears the same from every direction, and as any plane that cuts the sphere is circular in section, its shadow can also be plotted by finding the shadows of a number of circular sections. Making sure that the sections are parallel to the surface receiving their shadow, transfer their centers in elevation to the 45-degree bearing line in plan before inscribing circles, each with a diameter corresponding to their length in section.

The insertion of two additional circles, each corresponding diametrically to those already established at each end of the construction, provides a framework from which the elliptical shadow of the sphere can be traced.

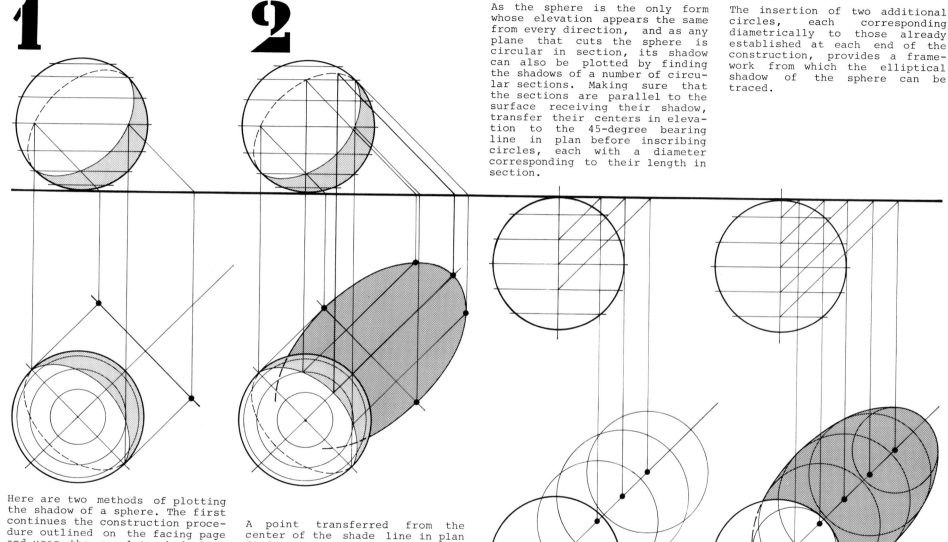

Here are two methods of plotting the shadow of a sphere. The first continues the construction procedure outlined on the facing page and uses the complete shade line in elevation and plan to plot the shadow. For instance, when transferred at 45 degrees via the elevation, projectors from the extremities of the shade in plan find the minor axis of the elliptically shaped shadow.

A point transferred from the center of the shade line in plan finds its equivalent point at the farther extremity of the major axis of the shadow. Using the point-transfer method, additional points transferred from along the shade line continue and complete a trace of the shape of the shadow.

Plotting Shade and Shadows on Cylindrical Planes

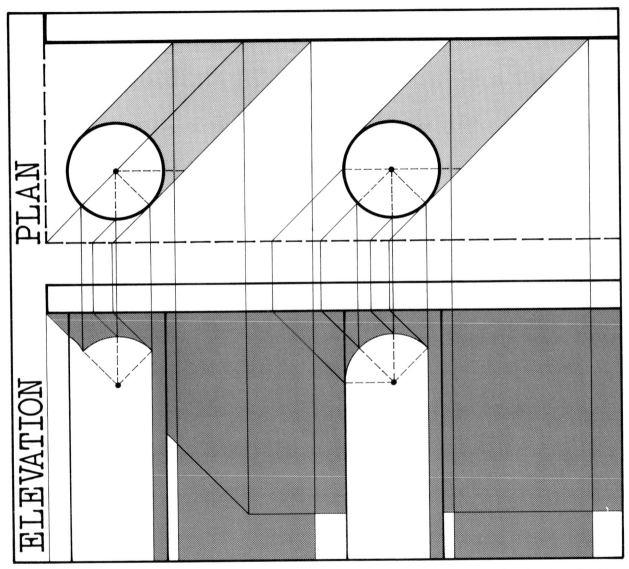

PLAN

ELEVATION

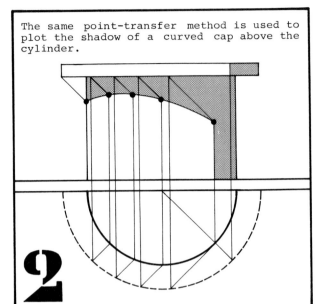

The same point-transfer method is used to plot the shadow of a curved cap above the cylinder.

2

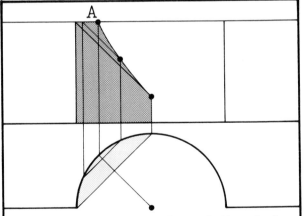

3 The curved portion of the shadow of an uncapped hollow cylinder begins at point A and ends on a 45-degree projection from the top casting corner of the recess. The shadow's curve is then plotted using the point-transfer method.

1 The construction of the shadow from a square block above a cylinder begins by plotting the 45-degree shadow line from the corner of the block. The curved line of shadow is determined by transferring 45-degree projectors along key points between the cylinder and the casting edge of the block in plan. The elevation of the shadow's curve is then drawn by connecting the transferred points until it meets the vertical line of shade. Notice the two different effects of the block's shadow on the two columns.

How to Plot Shadows on a Niche

To determine the shadow on a niche, first draw contours A, B, C, D through the spherical head of the niche in elevation before reproducing these contours in plan.

Then draw the lines EE, FF, and GG at 45 degrees on plan and, with reference to the points where they cut the contours, trace these sections on the elevation.

Next, a 45-degree line drawn from point H on the section AA finds the extent of the vertical portion of the shadow at J. Similar projections from the points at which the remaining sections cut the face of the niche find their equivalent points along the curvature of the shadow line through the spherical head of the niche.

Finally, a tangent through the top of the head of the niche determines the point where this shadow line meets the face of the niche and completes the area of shadow which is now ready for rendering.

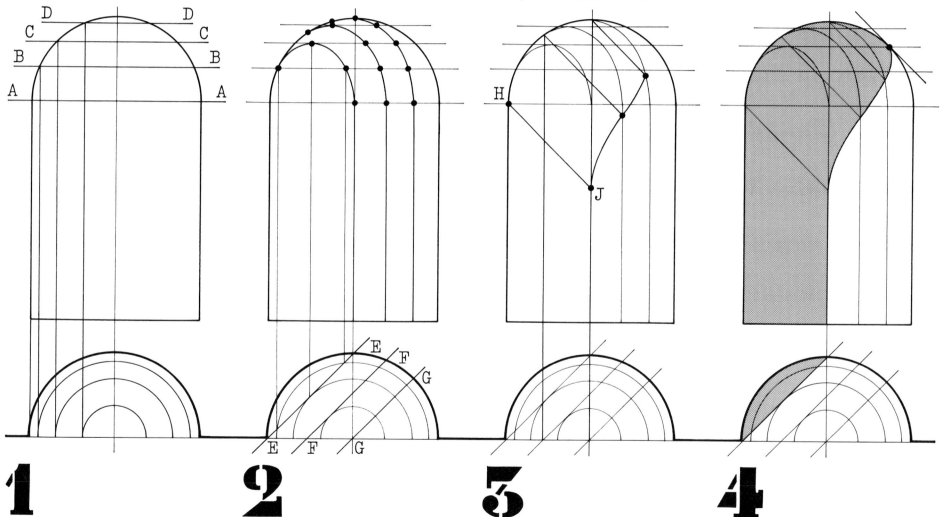

1   **2**   **3**   **4**

How to Plot Shadows on Stepped Planes

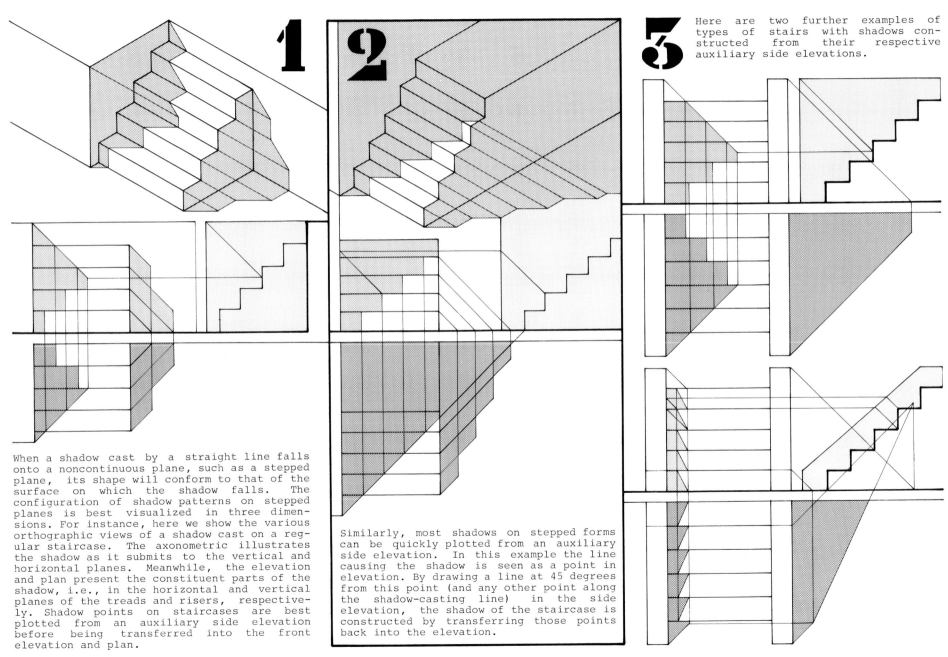

1

2

3

Here are two further examples of types of stairs with shadows constructed from their respective auxiliary side elevations.

When a shadow cast by a straight line falls onto a noncontinuous plane, such as a stepped plane, its shape will conform to that of the surface on which the shadow falls. The configuration of shadow patterns on stepped planes is best visualized in three dimensions. For instance, here we show the various orthographic views of a shadow cast on a regular staircase. The axonometric illustrates the shadow as it submits to the vertical and horizontal planes. Meanwhile, the elevation and plan present the constituent parts of the shadow, i.e., in the horizontal and vertical planes of the treads and risers, respectively. Shadow points on staircases are best plotted from an auxiliary side elevation before being transferred into the front elevation and plan.

Similarly, most shadows on stepped forms can be quickly plotted from an auxiliary side elevation. In this example the line causing the shadow is seen as a point in elevation. By drawing a line at 45 degrees from this point (and any other point along the shadow-casting line) in the side elevation, the shadow of the staircase is constructed by transferring those points back into the elevation.

How to Plot Shadows in Sections

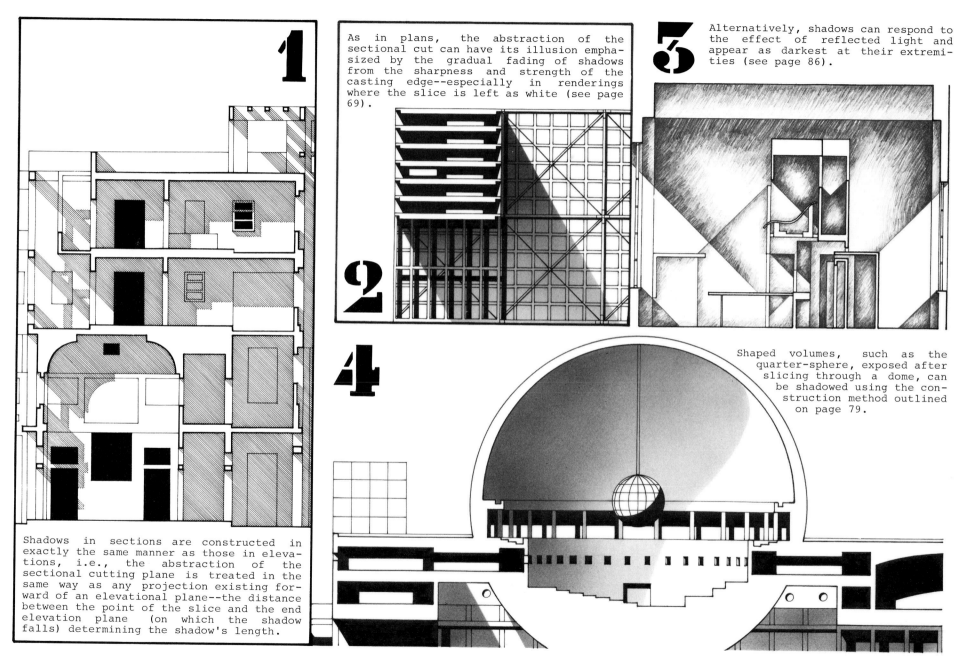

1

2 As in plans, the abstraction of the sectional cut can have its illusion emphasized by the gradual fading of shadows from the sharpness and strength of the casting edge--especially in renderings where the slice is left as white (see page 69).

3 Alternatively, shadows can respond to the effect of reflected light and appear as darkest at their extremities (see page 86).

4 Shaped volumes, such as the quarter-sphere, exposed after slicing through a dome, can be shadowed using the construction method outlined on page 79.

Shadows in sections are constructed in exactly the same manner as those in elevations, i.e., the abstraction of the sectional cutting plane is treated in the same way as any projection existing forward of an elevational plane--the distance between the point of the slice and the end elevation plane (on which the shadow falls) determining the shadow's length.

How to Plot Shadows in Axonometrics

1

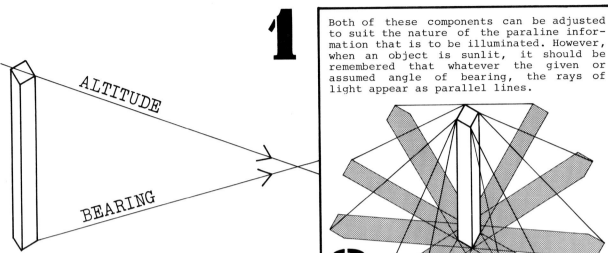

The length of a shadow cast from an object is found at the intersection of the two components: the plan direction of the light, and the angle, or altitude, of the sun's rays.

Both of these components can be adjusted to suit the nature of the paraline information that is to be illuminated. However, when an object is sunlit, it should be remembered that whatever the given or assumed angle of bearing, the rays of light appear as parallel lines.

2

3

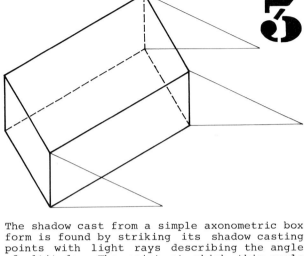

The shadow cast from a simple axonometric box form is found by striking its shadow casting points with light rays describing the angle of altitude. The point at which this angle meets the bearing line--in this instance describing a horizontal ground plane--finds the shadow point.

In architectural drawing a distinction is frequently made between the rendering of shade and shadow. This convention renders shade as less dark than shadow so that shaded planes can receive fenestration and other detail.

4

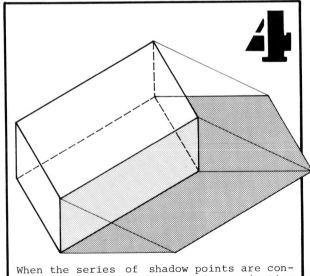

When the series of shadow points are connected, the shape of the shadow projection is completed and ready for rendering.

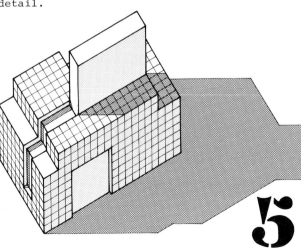

5

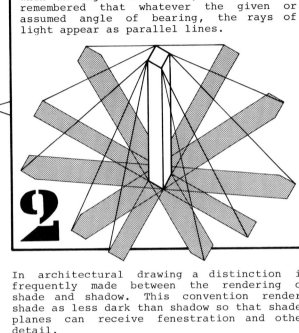

6

When casting shadows from slightly more complex forms, simply project each element of that form separately. For example, with an axonometric of a basic gabled house form, first project the shadow of the "box" element.

How to Plot Shadows in Axonometrics

7

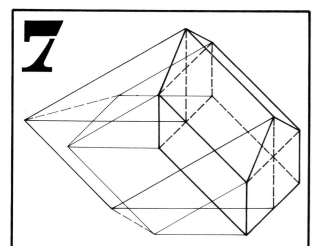

Then project the shadow of the gabled section of the form as an extension of the shadow already established before completing its shape by connecting all the shadow points.

8

Notice that the shadow points corresponding to each end of the ridge are found by bearing lines projected from points perpendicularly below them--the length of the shadow being found at their intersection with the corresponding angle of altitude.

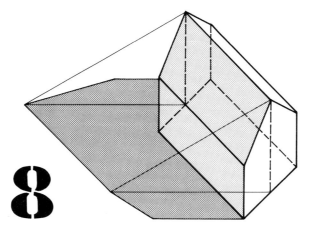

9

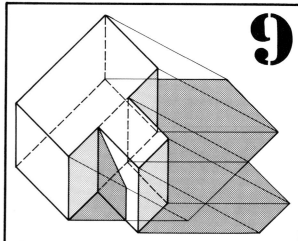

The same technique of separate shadow projection is used when one form projects from another, i.e., the shadow of each is projected independently to form the whole shape.

10

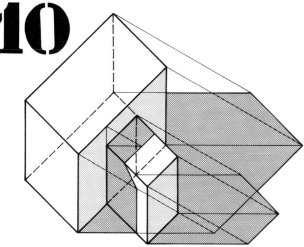

However, when a projecting form occurs below the casting edge of a larger object situated between it and the light source, the shadow of the latter will fall partly across it.

11

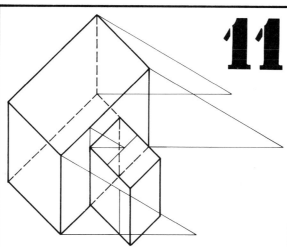

To find this shadow length, take any point along the casting edge of the larger form and triangulate the angle of light with that of the bearing line.

12

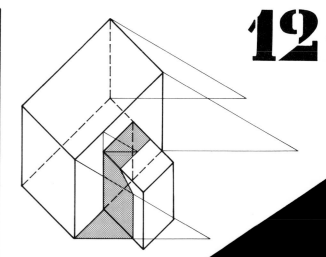

The resulting intersecti̶ of the shadow line a̶ lower form to connec̶ the nearside plan̶

How to Use the Lockard Shadow-Construction Method

1
The casting of shadows in both axonometric and perspective drawings is made more accessible to beginners by a highly useful technique devised by W. K. Lockard. Known as the "flagpole assumption" method, this technique enlists an analogy that clearly focuses the mind of the user on the shadow-casting principles already established; namely, that at any given moment in the sun's cycle all similar verticals will cast shadows that describe the same ratio of casting line to shadow length (a). Also, that as the sun's rays are parallel, all shadows of a casting line parallel to the surface on which the shadow is cast will be parallel to, and of the same length as, the line that casts them (b).

2
Lockard's "flagpole assumption" method begins with a sun/shade analysis of the drawn form in which all the shaded and sunlit planes are identified . . .

3
. . . and a determination of the casting edges, i.e., those lines in the drawing that describe all the vertical and horizontal edges of the form that will cast the shadow.

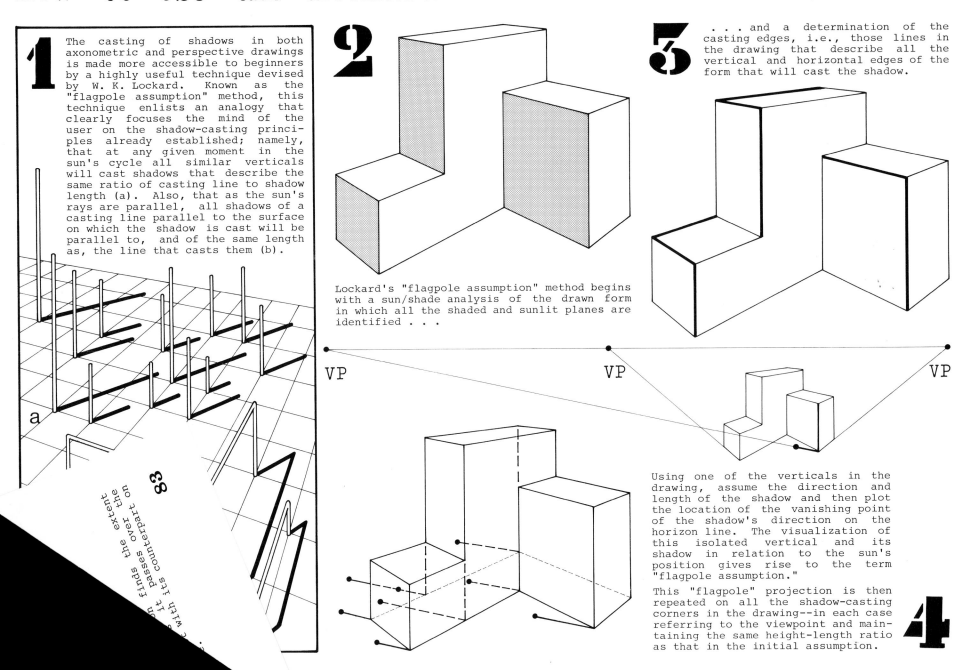

VP   VP   VP

4
Using one of the verticals in the drawing, assume the direction and length of the shadow and then plot the location of the vanishing point of the shadow's direction on the horizon line. The visualization of this isolated vertical and its shadow in relation to the sun's position gives rise to the term "flagpole assumption."

This "flagpole" projection is then repeated on all the shadow-casting corners in the drawing--in each case referring to the viewpoint and maintaining the same height-length ratio as that in the initial assumption.

How to Use the Lockard Shadow-Construction Method

5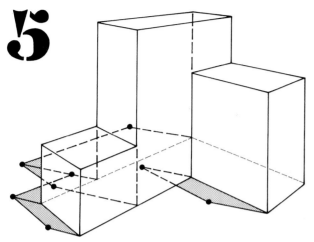

Now connect all the "flagpole" shadows from the vertical lines with lines describing the edge of the shadow in the horizontal plane.

N.B.: Notice that these shadow lines are parallel, i.e., in perspective, to the horizontal edges which cast them.

6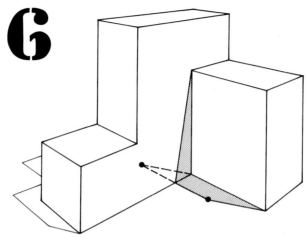

When a connecting shadow intersects a vertical plane the casting relationship alters. In this situation the shadow's edge continues along that plane at an angle necessary to rejoin its casting line or adjacent connecting shadow.

9

However, it is important to remember that assumptions during the initial sun/shade analysis should aim for the most flattering pattern of shadow. As the impact of sunlight on an object will vary dramatically throughout the day cycle, it is wise to make an exploratory analysis so that the best possible configuration of light, shade, and shadow is achieved.

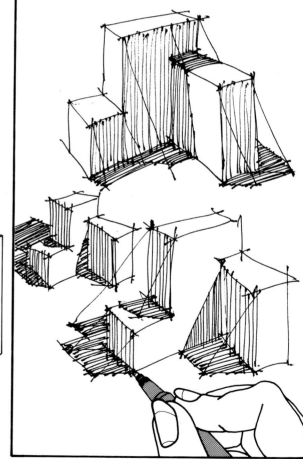

7

On partially shadowed horizontal planes other than the base plane, an additional "flagpole assumption" and connecting shadow construction will trace the shadow's edge.

8

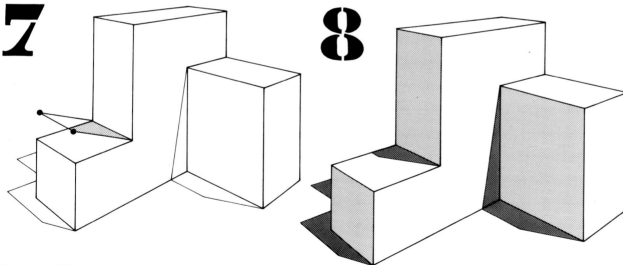

Once the shadow pattern is plotted, the drawing is ready for rendering.

Some More Shadow-Rendering Techniques

Shadows are generally rendered in a value light enough to maintain the visibility of lines that occur within them. This need for transparency is reflected in the various mediums and techniques that are commonly used in their depiction, such as graphite dust (a), pencil shading (b), watercolor wash (c), dry-transfer screens (d), stippling (e), and hatching (f).

1

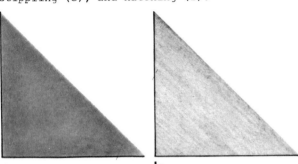
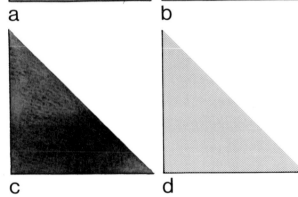
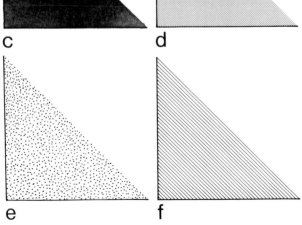

a

b

c

d

e

f

2

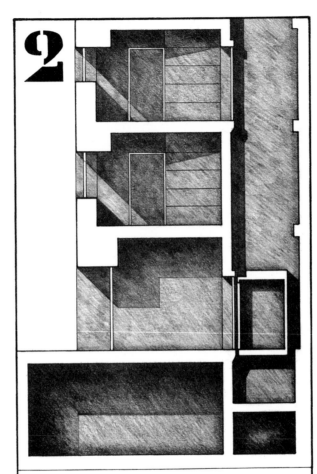

However, on larger drawings a graduating shadow rendition following a light-to-dark projection from the edge of the casting plane responds to the principle of reflected light. This principle recognizes the incidence of light as being scattered back from surrounding planes in the vicinity in the opposite direction of the main light source. Consequently, this deflected light is often shown as appearing in the vertical planes of sections and, in turn, being redeflected into the body of shadows occupying the horizontal plane of plans (see pages 68-69).

3

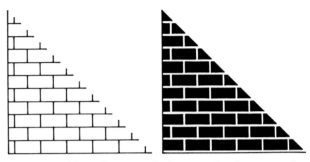

Occasionally, denser shadow renderings can be found in elevations and plans. This technique renders the shadows by delineating mortar joints--either positively or negatively--exclusively within the area occupied by the shadow.

4 Another version of this technique is useful when indicating shaded curving or cylindrical forms. Here, a fragmented hatching, or the use of two line weights (the bolder line being reserved for the shade) to describe modular materials, will simultaneously convey the shade and describe the form.

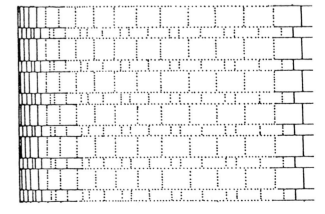

4 PRINTING TECHNIQUES

An Introduction to Diazo Printing

1

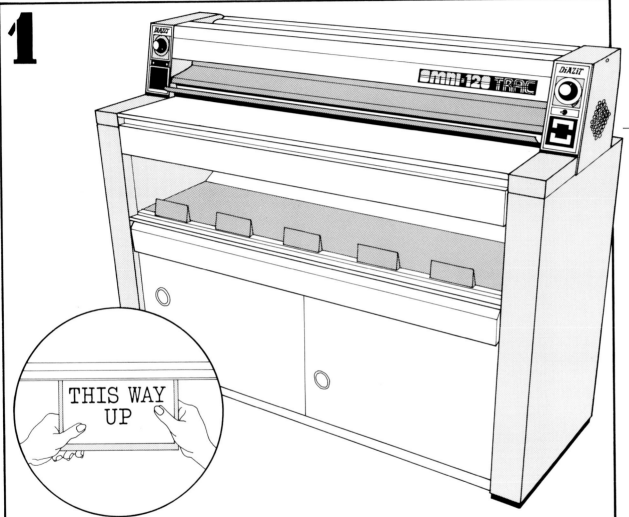

THIS WAY UP

2

The second operation depends upon which diazo process is used. In the ammonia process--after automatic or manual separation from the original-- the exposed print is developed in ammonia vapors; in the semidry process, the print passes through rollers carrying a developing solution.

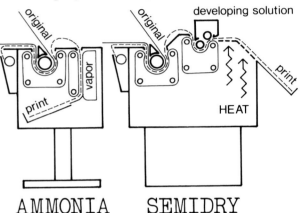

original · original · developing solution · print · print · vapor · HEAT

AMMONIA   SEMIDRY

The ammonia process reproduces superior-quality prints--potential for color being inherent in the print paper, i.e., black-, blue-, sepia-, or red-line. The semidry process developers offer black, blue, red, and yellow color images--the print paper finish being more receptive to subsequent color washes. In the latter process, exposed glossy prints may be retrieved from the machine and various developers applied by hand to create multicolored images.

3

Diazo (dyeline or whiteprinting) is a fast process of same-size printing from large original drawings worked in opaque mediums on translucent papers and film. The chemically treated print papers offer a basic range of image colors on finishes such as textured, matte, and glossy on various weights of paper.

Originals are placed faceup over the side of the print paper with the light-sensitive coating, and fed into the machine for the first printing phase. This involves the exposure of the print paper as it rotates around a glass cylinder emitting a high-intensity ultra-violet light.

An Introduction to Diazo Printing

Levels of contrast between printed image and background are regulated by the exposure setting on the machine. The faster the setting, the less time the coating is exposed to the light, and, therefore, less coating will be burned off--producing a darker print. Experimental prints should be made with originals carrying tonal variations.

6 In order to discover the potential range of diazo effects, it is worth compiling an annotated reference "dictionary" of line weights, tonal values, and textures. Various inks, graphites, and methods of application on tracing paper and film should be explored (top). Colored pencils, water-based markers, and aerosols used on diazo negatives are also potentials for creating tonal values and textures on the ultimate print (bottom). Experiment with colored lines, tonal gradations, and solids and, after printing, mark and code the more useful pencils and pens for future diazo use.

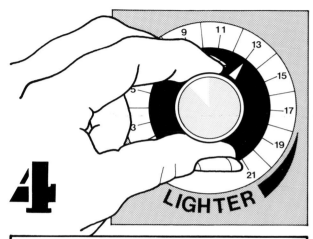

4 LIGHTER

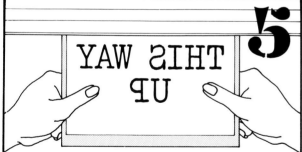

5 THIS WAY UP

The original drawing is referred to as a "negative." For making extended print runs, amended drawings, and copies of negatives for the addition of different types of information, the negative can be transposed onto coated tracing paper, sepia paper, or polyester film--the latter being more durable. This print is known as an "intermediate" or "copy negative." To make an intermediate, place the negative facedown onto the coated surface of the recipient material and feed into the machine.

BLUE   PURPLE   RED   YELLOW   GREEN

Some Hints for Diazo Prints

In diazo printing, different graphite grades print as different values. Hard grades become lighter than softer grades, the latter requiring stabilizing with fixative before printing. Combinations of graphite grades, together with the range of technical pen point sizes, offer a variety of mark-making abilities, emphasis occurring when differences in line weight and quality are exploited. At a basic level, contrast between the clarity of an ink line used for written notes and indicating important zones in pencil drawings aids communication in tracing paper drawings.

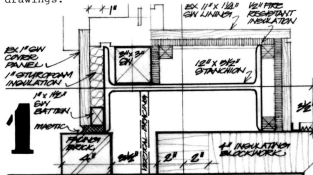

1

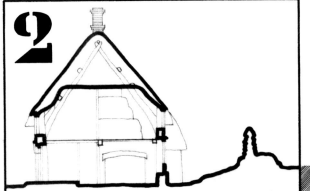

2

Similarly, areas of emphasis (such as the fixed structural points in pencil-drawn plans and sections) will benefit from a change in medium. These could be added as a ruled or freehand fiber-tip-pen line. Its thicker, softer quality brings an added dimension to the drawing. Red is a good choice for this purpose, for in diazo it prints as a dark gray.

5

The convention of the heavy ground line functions as a visual ledge on which to view sections and elevations. This can be simply elaborated for added visual interest using any one of a series of pen or pencil hatching techniques.

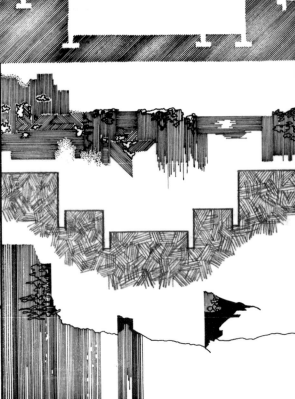

The visually refreshing quality of free-hand drawing can be used to modify the often sterile appearance of exclusively ruled orthographics. The process of converting them is easy. First, draft the complete image in ruled pencil work. This is then ghosted in freehand using a technical pen, exploiting line weights.

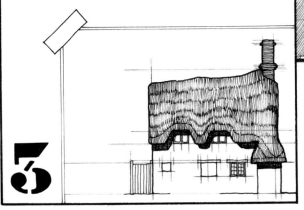

3

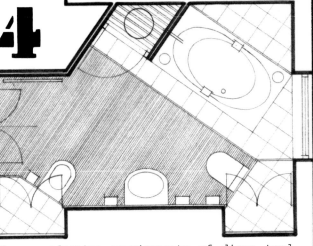

4

The reproduction requirements of diazo tend to encourage a graphic simplicity. However, in all forms of line-drawn orthographics, the addition of even a solitary area of value will become a center of interest or at least impart a little drama.

N.B.: Make sure that the textural grain of ground line elaborations does not overpower the main body of the drawing.

Some Hints for Diazo Prints

The main reason for adding value to drawings destined for diazo is to emphasize an element or an area of importance in the drawing.

1 When areas of lighter value are required in tracing-paper drawings, the quickest method is to trace the required shapes on a second, same-size tracing paper sheet. Next, remove the shape with a scalpel, place it as a "stencil" over the original drawing, locate it with "invisible tape," and print.

As more light penetrates the single layer in the diazo machine, a lighter value is printed.

2 Conversely, when isolated areas of a darker value are required, precision-cut shapes of tracing paper fixed in position over the drawing with "invisible tape" will print as a deep contrasting value.

N.B.: Proprietary "invisible tape" is a nonprint tape for use in diazo printmaking. As dust prints, extreme care should be taken to keep it clean.

3 Graphite dust makes an excellent medium for achieving large areas of even values on tracing paper. Simply collect it from a pointer and, using tissue paper, apply evenly to the premasked shape on the back of the drawing. Stabilize with spray fixative before printing.

N.B.: It is recommended that this and the following techniques be applied to the backs of drawings, to allow an unimpeded drawing surface.

4 The extensive range of values and patterns offered by self-adhesive dry-transfer tones is ideal for small areas of value in drawings for diazo. After removing it from its backing sheet, apply the selected film to the shape and trim away surplus with a sharp scalpel, making sure not to damage the tracing paper.

N.B.: Dry-transfer material should be well burnished, as badly affixed pieces tend to detach in the heat of the diazo process.

5 Aerosol spray colors can also be used to effect. After masking the edges of the area to be rendered, apply in even strokes, working approximately twelve inches from the surface. Remember that colors produce different values in diazo prints; e.g., yellow becomes black, and blue becomes almost invisible (see page 89).

6 Shoe polish is an unusually good medium for rendering large areas because it produces a fine, even range of values. Mask around the required shape and, using tissue paper as an applicator, build up to the required degree of value.

N.B.: Brown polish prints as a mid-gray value.

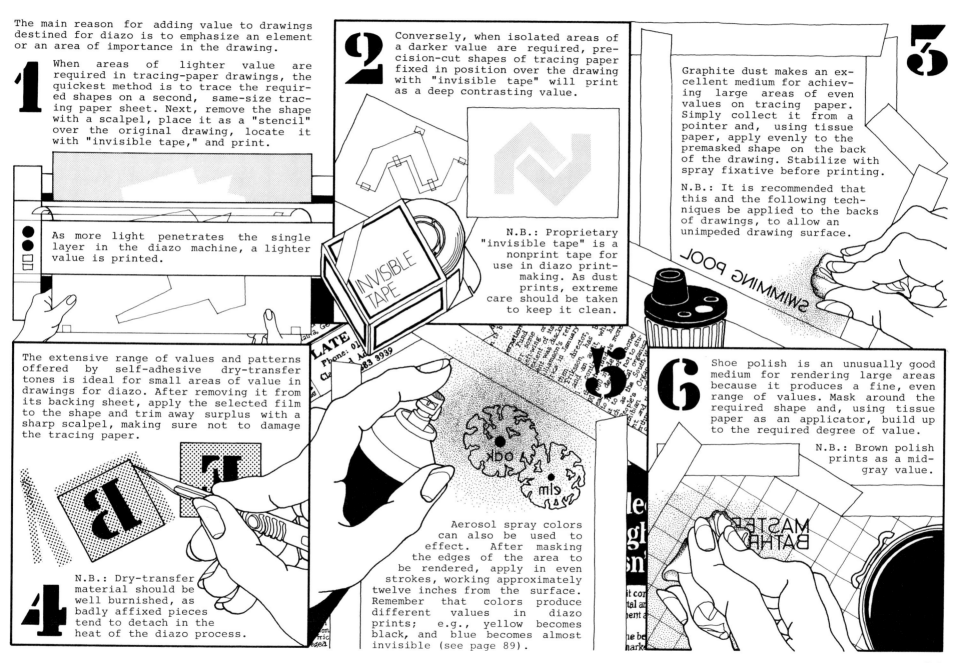

Some More Hints for Diazo Prints

1 Elevation drawings can often be improved when a sky is added. To do so, first mask around the sky area on the back of the drawing before graphite dust--collected from a pointer--is applied using a pad of soft tissue paper.

2 Cloud formations can be indicated with a soft putty-type eraser; darker areas can be added into the drawing, using a soft pencil such as a 6B.

3 The completed image should then be stabilized with fixative before printing.

4 To establish sections and elevations on the sheet, the baseline can be effectively extended by using light aerosol spray (in red or green) on the face of the sheet.

5 Titles can be integrated by trace-cutting the required lettering in frisk film overlaid on a typeface alphabet-- then positioned onto the sheet.

6 After the spray operation and prior to printing, the frisk film is removed to reveal the title against its tonal background.

Some More Hints for Diazo Prints

1 A simply achieved diazo special effect can simulate a graduated sky wash above printed elevations. This technique relies upon the negative being fed bottom-first into the diazo machine.

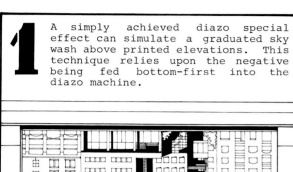

Immediately after the elevation drawing has been exposed normally, the exposure setting is speeded up to cause the area of the print above the skyline to be printed in a progressively darkening value.

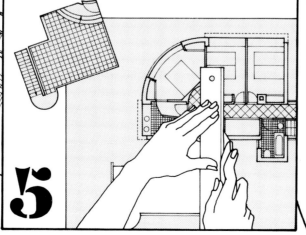

2

This trick produces a print with a diazo sky wash--the effect not only framing the drawing but also bringing additional atmosphere and apparent depth to the resulting image. **3**

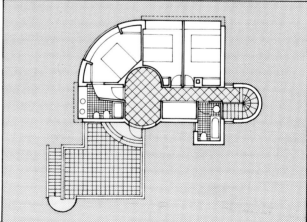

4 Another diazo technique employs a negative that is run three or four times through the diazo machine. Each print is given a different exposure speed to obtain a set of prints each in a different value.

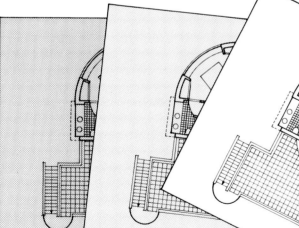

These become the basis for a composite diazo print composed of selected areas represented by different tones--the various areas being trace-cut and glued into position on a base print.

5

6 The composite image can be composed to reinforce a particular presentation message. For example, a range of tones could differentiate a hierarchy of spatial zones, or relationships between public and private spaces, etc.

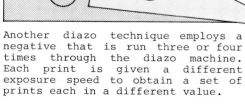

How to Enlarge a Slide into a Diazo Print

1 Pin a sheet of unexposed diazo print paper to a wall in a darkroom or darkened studio that is large enough to accommodate the required print size (with the semidry diazo process use "normal" print paper; with the ammonia diazo process use black-line, blue-line, etc.).

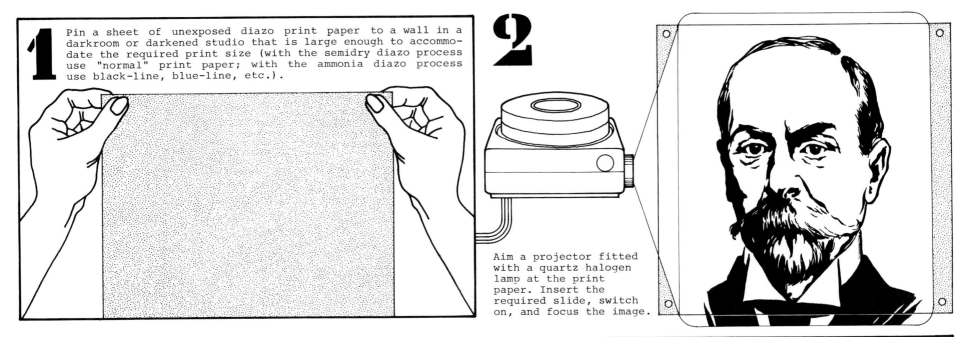

Aim a projector fitted with a quartz halogen lamp at the print paper. Insert the required slide, switch on, and focus the image.

3 An image size projected from a distance of four feet will take approximately thirty to forty minutes to expose. For larger images, the Inverse Square Law operates, i.e., doubling the image size requiring four times the exposure time. However, the progress of the exposure can be monitored by quickly switching the light in the room on and off.

4 When the exposure process is completed, protect the light-sensitive print surface until developing by diazo in the normal way. The developed print is useful in several ways, e.g., for coloring, and for integration with photomontage, collage, drawings, and so on (see facing page).

How to Diazo Print Site Perspectives

However, quite apart from the enlargement facility of this technique, diazo printing slide photographs has proved itself to be a very useful design tool, especially when used as the basis of a perspective of a design proposal shown directly in relation to its environmental context. First, aim the projector loaded with the focused slide at the diazo print paper "screen." The slide used should result from a site photograph taken from a position that provides the best vantage point from which to view and present the building design.

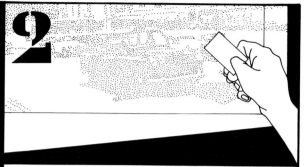

1

2

Remember that the larger the projected image, the greater the length of exposure. Apart from flicking the room light switch to check the exposure, another method of monitoring exposure is to hold a piece of already exposed diazo print paper against the screen (in the light of the projector beam). As the unexposed diazo print paper turns white when fully exposed, this color-matching check can be made in the light of the projector beam.

3

Once developed, the diazo print can now function as the setting in which a colored pencil or ink drawing of the building design can be inserted --its perspective coordinates being governed by those of the printed photographic image.

4

If the diazo-printed image of the site is weak, this can be beefed up by extending the rendering technique used for the building design into the background. This can be accomplished effectively by the singular concentration on the rendering of shade and shadow.

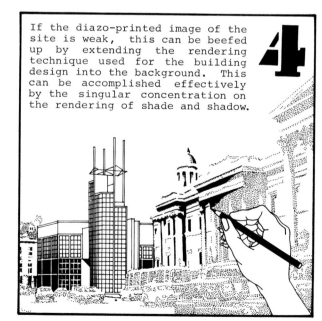

How to Diazo Print Shadows from Scale Models

By providing diazo prints that record accurately the effect of shadows cast from a model of a proposed building on its setting, this technique both replicates and extends the function of the Heliodon (an instrument for measuring shadows cast from scale models in relation to given points in the sun's azimuth).

The required equipment comprises a 500-watt tungsten spotlight to simulate the sun, and a sundial to fix its coordinates in relation to the model.

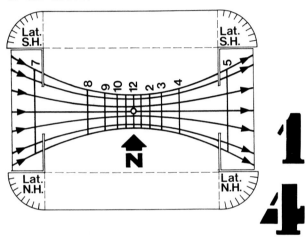

1

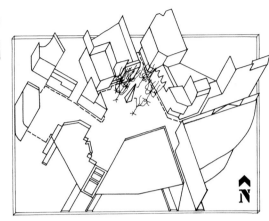

2

A scale block model of the building design should be glued to a base of clear acetate or glass. Other related vertical objects such as walls, existing buildings, or trees should be added and glued to the transparent base, which, incidentally, might also include a delineation of the surrounding layout plan.

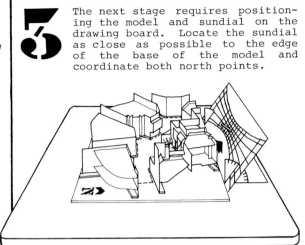

3

The next stage requires positioning the model and sundial on the drawing board. Locate the sundial as close as possible to the edge of the base of the model and coordinate both north points.

This setup is then positioned approximately 5'-0" (1.5m) below a freestanding or fixed directional spotlight.

4

Prior to exposure, it is wise to check the various shadow readings--each tracked by the sundial under the spotlight. For instance, a lateral tilting of the model will obtain various readings from the year cycle; rotating the model will find readings from the day cycle. A good starting point for a series of diazo prints would be a noon reading taken during the summer solstice, winter solstice, and equinox, as they determine extremes of shadow caused by significant points in the sun's azimuth, i.e., its highest, lowest, and midway points respectively.

N.B.: If available, the Heliodon's tilting turntable--capable of being locked into any position--can be utilized to fix the position of the model in relation to the spotlight. Otherwise, this stage relies upon jacking the model into the required position for each reading prior to subsequent exposures.

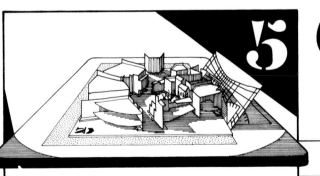

5

After the position of the model has been determined under the spotlight for the first print, switch off. Then, in a blacked-out room, carefully insert a sheet of unexposed diazo print paper between the model's transparent base and the drawing board. Then, switch on the spotlight and expose for approximately ten minutes.

N.B.: The use of an ultraviolet light would, of course, shorten considerably the length of exposure.

6

When the exposure process is completed, protect the light-sensitive print surface until developing it by diazo in the normal way.

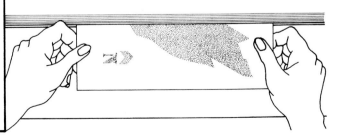

How to Diazo Print Shadows from Scale Models

Four diazo recordings of shadows taken at different points in the day and year cycles. The model from which these readings were taken was a 1:500 block model built from cardboard on an acetate base to simulate an existing Oxford city square. The study was made to test the impact of shade and shadow on the space prior to the development of design proposals for the area. This method was devised by Peter Ireland as part of a second-year architecture project.

How to Render Diazo Prints

1

The mediums employed for rendering diazo prints are governed strictly by the weight of print paper used. This is because the thinner papers tend to deform when subjected to liquid washes. In this case, the range of mediums is usually restricted to graphite, colored pencils, markers, and dry-transfer film. Of these, graphite and colored pencils are the most widely used because their sensitive application can both extend the subtle textural cast of, especially, medium-toned prints and, in the case of colored pencils, enhance the mottled tint of the print paper. Indeed, the recognition of the distinctive mottling associated with, particularly, blue-line diazo prints can encourage the creation of extremely delicate and spatially atmospheric renderings.

N.B.: Thicker papers include the high quality print papers that transform negatives into a range of tooth--from smooth to pebbled in matte or gloss finishes. Most successful for watercolor rendering are the matte-finish art papers which, when textured, can provide a diazo print on a surrogate watercolor paper.

2 The thinner print papers can receive a marker rendering--the effect of marker inks being muted on contact with the absorbent paper. Using a restricted palette, marker tips open up a whole range of graphic effects, such as the overlapping of strokes to simulate coursework, cladding, and rooftiles, etc., or the stippling of landscapes to suggest foliage.

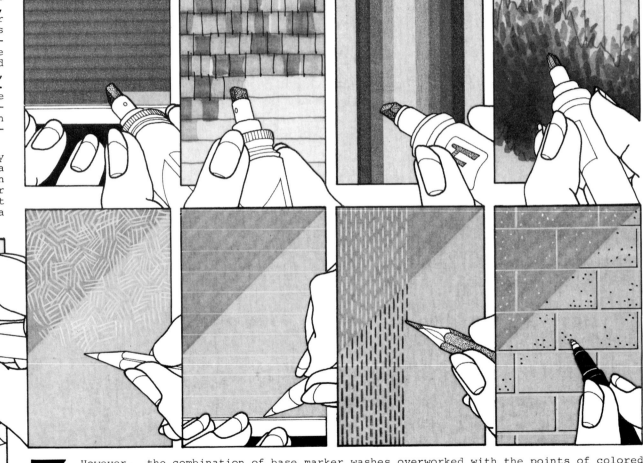

3 However, the combination of base marker washes overworked with the points of colored pencils is a technique with a myriad of possibility. In widening the opportunity for depicting all kinds of architectural surface and spatial effects, this is a highly versatile technique for rendering diazo prints which is explained fully in Michael Doyle's excellent book <u>Color Drawing</u>.

An Introduction to Photocopy Printing

1

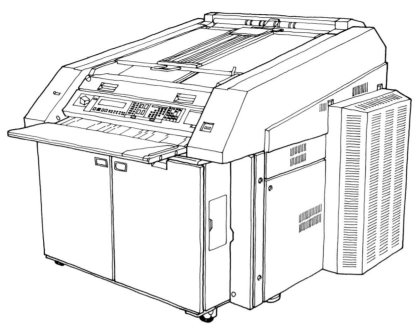

Photocopying (xeroxography) is an electrostatic print process that allows large original drawings made on both transparent and opaque materials to be printed at same-size, or be resized up to A0 (33.1 x 46.8") and beyond, or down to A4 (8.3 x 11.7") formats. Prints can be made on any kind of drawing paper up to a weight of 150gm, together with tracing paper and film. However, the facility for reproducing extremely sharp, black line prints on plain paper releases the designer to select from the full range of color-rendering mediums.

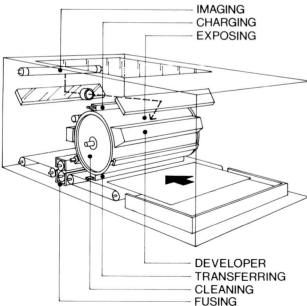

- IMAGING
- CHARGING
- EXPOSING

- DEVELOPER
- TRANSFERRING
- CLEANING
- FUSING

2

After being fed into the machine, the original is scanned by a high-intensity light. Depending upon the type of machine in use, the image is then transmitted via mirrors (when being resized) or via fiber optics (when being same-sized) onto a magnetic drum.

After receiving its magnetized version of the image the drum rotates through a chamber filled with an agitated haze of carbon dust or toner. As it passes, particles of toner are attracted to the magnetized image before being transferred from the drum to the recipient paper as it passes below.

The newly deposited image is then subjected to a fusing stage in which the toner is electronically charged for its "flash-fusion" to the paper. This process instantly fixes a dense and slightly raised black print which, when issued from the machine, can be detected with the fingertips.

3

An added bonus with the photocopying process is the ability to retrieve a print from the large commercial machines in an unfused state. This facility allows for any printed blemishes or unwanted lines in the original to be removed. This is done by carefully dusting away the toner using a putty eraser before the print is re-introduced into a separate fusing chamber.

Experimenting with the Photocopier

Access to even the smaller office photocopiers introduces the designer to some useful forms of reprography.

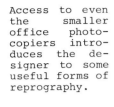

For instance, place a sheet of clear acetate film into the feeder tray of an indirect-transfer photocopier capable of processing translucent materials. The sheet size must be compatible with that acceptable to the machine.

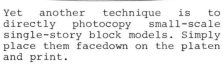

Yet another technique is to directly photocopy small-scale single-story block models. Simply place them facedown on the platen and print.

 2

Next, position the required photographic image or photomontage facedown on the glass platen and proceed with the photocopying operation.

The resultant print can now be used as a "negative" for diazo reproduction. Also, images photocopied on acetate can be used as transparencies for overhead projection (see page 214) or as overlay pages in reports (see page 212).

 Also, the development of a design idea evolving in sketch model form can be tracked in a series of prints recording strategic points along the design route, for later use in wall presentations.

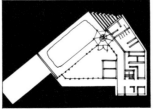
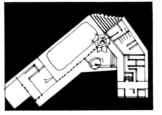

3 Another photocopy technique uses its platen as a "drawing board" on which a collection of photographic components are composed facedown to create collage print--useful for inspiring or conveying the spirit of a design concept.

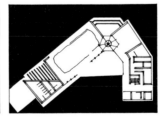

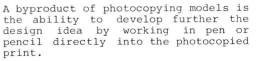

A byproduct of photocopying models is the ability to develop further the design idea by working in pen or pencil directly into the photocopied print.

6

How to Photocopy Composite Perspectives

1 A convincing graphic of a building design concept can be quickly made by introducing a drawing into a photocopy made from a 10 x 8" print of a photograph of the intended site.

2

Using scissors or a blade, first cut shaped pieces of opaque, white paper which--when glued into position on the photograph prior to photocopying--will exactly obliterate the area to be occupied by your drawing of the proposed building.

3 An alternative is to cut away the unwanted areas of the actual photograph and, before photocopying, glue the required sections to a sheet of white paper.

4 Working from memory or referring to a model if one exists, introduce the drawing of your building directly into the blanked areas of the resultant photocopy, using ink, graphite, or colored pencils, either individually or in combination.

5 Aim to coordinate your drawing to the perspective suggested by the photograph, and adopt a drawing style that encourages a visual match between the existing photocopied image and your original graphics (see pages 159-61).

6 If the finished graphic is monochromatic, it can be rephotocopied to create a second-stage print. If it is in color, the color photocopy or Cibacopy process can be used (see page 107).

How to Photocopy Composite Site Perspectives

1

Possibly the quickest and best technique for producing professional-looking site perspectives is to make traced outline drawings from photographic prints taken from key vantage points around the site. These can be worked in technical pen, black ballpoint pen, or a black fine-line marker.

Tracing begins after attaching the face of the photograph to the back of a sheet of thin tracing paper using tabs of "invisible tape." Being guided by the photograph viewed through the tracing paper, the drawing stage can allow a fairly vigorous freehand line drawing style.

2

Also, large areas of darker values can be quickly and freely introduced. Again, the complexity of their shapes will be guided by the impression of the print as seen through the tracing paper.

3

When the tracing stage is finished, place the complete assembly of tracing paper drawing and its attached photograph facedown on the platen of the photocopier and take a print.

4

The resulting photocopy will register the drawing together with evidence of the values in the photograph. It is this printed combination of freehand line and photographic halftones that provides a very attractive and convincingly "rendered" perspective drawing.

5

A variation of this technique uses a shaped white paper mask to obliterate that part of the photograph that would be occupied by a proposed building design.

How to Photocopy Composite Site Perspectives

6 After attaching the print to the tracing paper, trace in all the lines and tones of the exposed areas of the photograph surrounding the shape of the proposed building design.

7 The outline of the design proposal can now be inserted. However, make sure that its perspective coincides with that in the photograph.

8 Before photocopying, a tonal rendition using pencil or a mid- and light gray marker should be added to the drawing of the building design. This can be worked either directly on the mask . . .

9 . . . or on the tracing paper to encourage a visual match between the design and its setting.

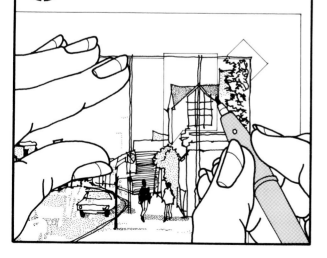

10 This site perspective was produced using this technique. Notice the way in which the photocopier has picked up the rather subtle halftones from the photograph beneath the tracing paper.

How to Make a Photocopy Transfer Print

1

The photocopy transfer technique is ideal for presenting design drawings describing dramatic themes. It begins with the preparation of a baseboard cut to the same format as the print to be transferred. In this case, the baseboard is Masonite--its textured face being subjected to an atmospheric color or monochrome rendering in acrylic paint. As this rendering will function as the background to the subsequent "print," two points should be considered: first, the painted background should be light enough in value to maintain a visible contrast for the ensuing transfer; second, a predetermined visualization of the relationship between the background rendering and that of the ensuing transfer print will avoid any compositional conflict.

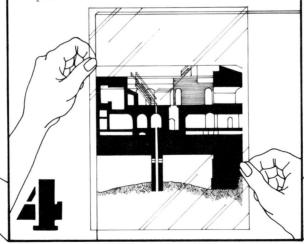

2 The next step sees a photocopy print made on acetate from the original design drawing to be transferred. This is printed to produce a handed, or back-to-front image.

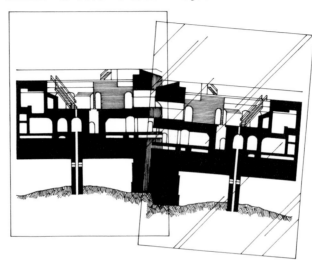

4 Place the acetate print facedown, i.e., the side carrying the fixative, onto the rendered baseboard. The tacky nature of the fixative will help to hold the print in place.

Next, the side of the acetate print carrying the deposited photocopy image is sprayed evenly with fixative.

N.B.: As the fixative acts as a solvent in the next stage of the process, it is important to use the appropriate brand. Students have found Rowney Spray Fix matte to be ideal for the transfer process.

3

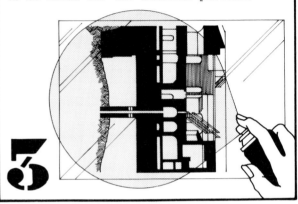

5 Working from the middle outward, now begin to transfer the photocopy onto the baseboard. Two intensities of transfer can be achieved: a light print resulting from rubbing down with a finger; a darker print resulting from rubbing down with a soft pencil point.

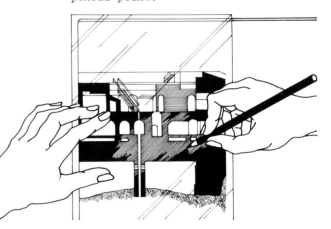

How to Make a Photocopy Transfer Print

During his development of this technique for a large drawing, fifth-year architecture student Steve Warburton first made a full-size photocopy print of his drawing on tracing paper using a commercial copier. He then cut the print into small sections before reprinting each in turn as handed prints on acetate using a regular office photocopier.

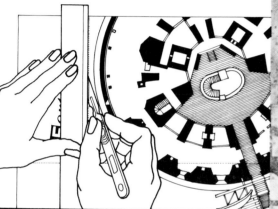

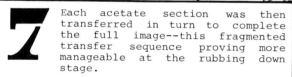

7 Each acetate section was then transferred in turn to complete the full image--this fragmented transfer sequence proving more manageable at the rubbing down stage.

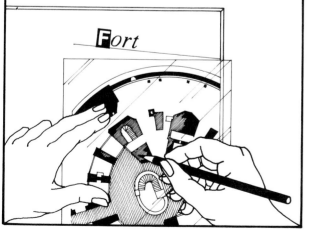

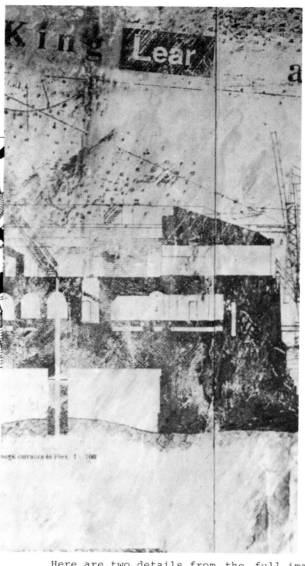

8 Here are two details from the full image as transferred in sections by Steve. The drawing is part of a larger display showing his sketch design for the conversion of a Napoleonic estuary fort into a theater. His preparatory acrylic rendering is reminiscent of the atmospheric backgrounds found in William Turner's paintings and its fusion with the textured quality of the transferred photocopy produces a print with a period charm appropriate both to the fort's history and setting and, indeed, to its new function.

How to Combine Positive and Reversed Photocopies

1 The recent revival of reversed printing is a recycling of a technique popular in the sixties. The technique involves the transformation and, if required, resizing of positive (black-on-white) originals into reversed, or negative (white-on-black) prints. The reversal print technique is particularly useful when depicting night views exploring lighting effects in exterior perspectives and elevations or large interior spaces, such as auditoriums (see facing page and pages 108-9).

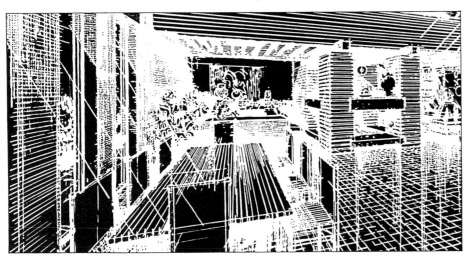

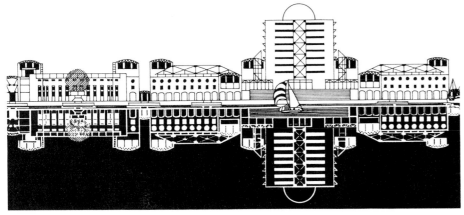

3 Another application of this print combination technique is seen in this waterfront elevation from the office of Avery Associates Architects. Here, the combination of a positive print of the facade and an inverted, reversed print of the same drawing to represent a reflection extends the elevation drawing into a quasi-perspective.

2 However, here are two ways of combining positive and reversed prints. This is a technique that results from the introduction of elements from a positive print into selected areas of a reversed print, or vice versa.

For example, this axonometric was photocopied as a reversed print before parts from a second, positive print of the same drawing were trace-cut and heat-mounted into their equivalent position on the reversed print. This print combination has many applications but is used here to focus on the cutaway interior views and also to receive some selective color rendering.

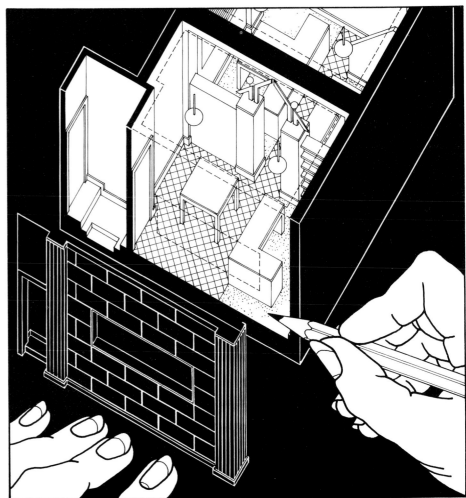

Other Photographic Resizing Processes

1

High-quality photographic reversed prints can, at a price, be commercially made from drawings by specialized print shops. This process involves a film negative produced by a process camera before being hand-touched under a magnifying glass to remove any blemishes. The negative is then printed to any given size (a do-it-yourself version of this process is explained on pages 108-9).

N.B.: The negative can also provide a PMT (photomechanical transfer), which gives a positive photographic image suitable for reproduction (see page 196).

2

There are two basic methods of color printing offered by print shops: color photocopying and Cibacopy printing.

Color photocopying using the laser printer process is comparatively cheap and colored originals can range from rendered artwork to 35mm transparencies. Smaller color photocopiers can reduce A3 (11.7 x 16.5") originals to A4 format (8.3 x 11.7") or enlarge to A2 (16.5 x 23.4"). The new machines have gradually increased the size of same-size printing and enlargement to A1 format (23.4 x 33.1") and beyond. However, larger format prints can be achieved on the smaller machines. To do this, the machine is computer programmed to make copies from the original in a precisely matching sequence of enlarged and segmented prints. These are then reassembled and mounted into overall formats of mural size.

3

Being a positive-to-positive system, the Cibacopy print process achieves a higher quality of color reproduction than color photocopying. However, like color photocopying, this process produces resized or same-size prints on a while-you-wait basis on matte or glossy photographic paper or plastic film. Most machines accept A1 size originals for reduction only to A4 or A3 size and, sometimes, A5. Same-size prints can be made at the smaller sizes. Major city center print shops, however, can Cibacopy 35mm slides and also produce extra-large originals-- but this process can be expensive. The expense involved makes Cibacopy printing a special event with students who reserve this process for reducing prestigious color-renderings for use in presentation, exhibition, portfolio, and for making high-quality second-stage prints from mixed-media originals.

How to Make a Do-It-Yourself Reversed Print

1

Thrifty students who wish to improve on the lack of contrast often provided by photocopied white-on-black prints, and who wish to bypass the expense associated with commercially reversed photographic prints turn to the following do-it-yourself reversal print techniques.

The original is drawn in black ink on Mylar or thick tracing paper. However, during the line drawing process care must be taken to keep the artwork surface flat and impeccably clean. To achieve this degree of cleanliness, students will often wear a pair of thin gloves to avoid fingerprinting the drawing surface.

2

The next stage occurs in a darkroom where the completed line drawing is placed right-way-up onto a same-size sheet of gloss- or pearl-finish photographic print paper, such as high-contrast paper grade 3 or 4, or a multigrade print paper.

3

Prior to exposure, this assembly is then placed onto a drawing board before being covered with a sheet of clean, dust-free glass. To achieve the immaculate quality of transparency required, gloves should also be worn at this stage.

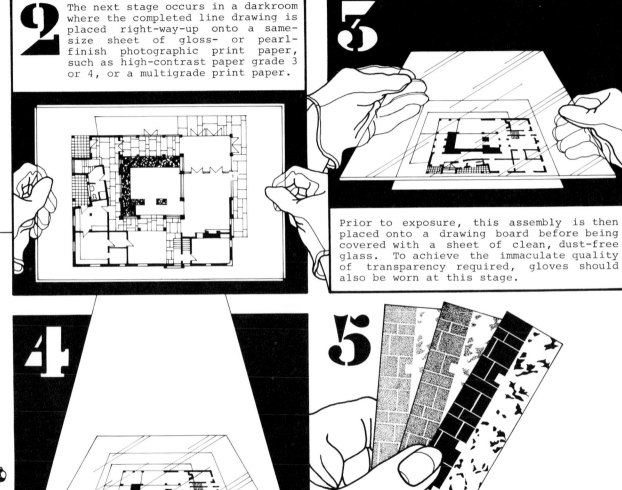

4

Now set the enlarger high enough so that the entire surface of the artwork will be exposed evenly to light.

5

Using a high-contrast filter in the enlarger, now expose the artwork. An exposure time of seven to ten seconds should be sufficient for those print papers specified here, but for the best result make a preliminary series of trial exposures using test strips of the print paper of your choice.

How to Make a Do-It-Yourself Reversed Print

6 Another way of making a do-it-yourself reverse print begins by making a photocopy of the drawing to be reversed onto acetate.

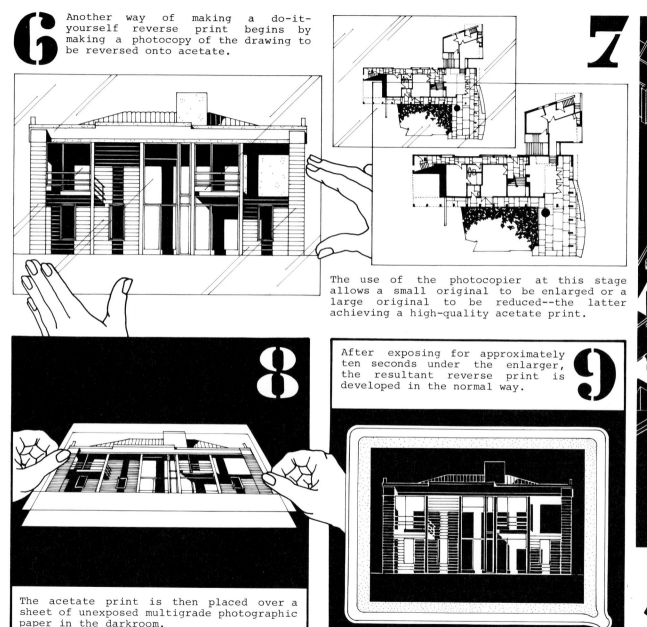

7 The use of the photocopier at this stage allows a small original to be enlarged or a large original to be reduced--the latter achieving a high-quality acetate print.

8 The acetate print is then placed over a sheet of unexposed multigrade photographic paper in the darkroom.

9 After exposing for approximately ten seconds under the enlarger, the resultant reverse print is developed in the normal way.

10 This is a detail from a reversed print quickly produced by fifth-year architecture student Stuart Adlam to use in a presentation of his design proposal that refurbished an underground level of Oxford University's Particle and Nuclear Physics Laboratory.

How to Transfer-Print Magazine Photographs

An impressive way of incorporating figures, skies, trees, and other entourage into design drawings is their direct transfer from newly printed monochrome or color magazine photographs. This transfer printing process is easily achieved, the only consideration being the scale, appropriateness, and compatability of the transfer technique to that of the rendering technique used elsewhere in the recipient drawing.

To make a photo-transfer, first cut around the area of the selected image.

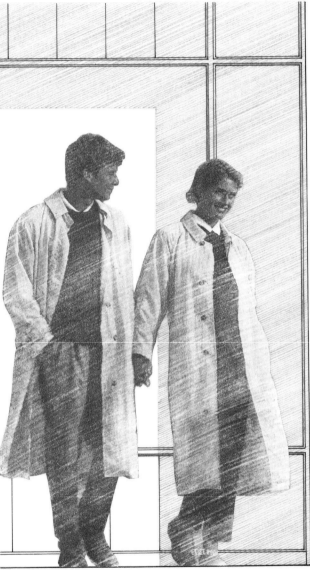

2 Next place it facedown on a clean sheet of paper. Then coat the image liberally with a solvent, such as turpentine, white spirit, acetone, or methylated spirits.

N.B.: Sometimes the photographs found in glossy magazines are more difficult to transfer, but trial transfers will identify the best solvent for the photo-print process.

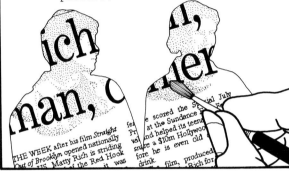

3 When thoroughly soaked, place the photo facedown onto the appropriate area of the recipient drawing, cover it with a sheet of paper and, holding it in position, rub briskly and firmly over the back with the point of a pencil or ballpoint pen.

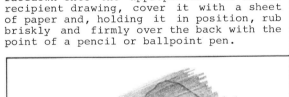

4 Carefully peel back one edge of the photo to check if the image has been successfully transferred. Each line of pressure exerted when rubbing should result in a corresponding line of released printing ink. If sections of the image are a bit patchy, reposition the edge of the photo and repeat the rubbing process.

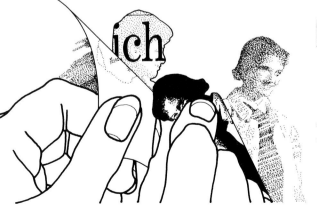

5 Finally, peel back the entire photograph to reveal the complete image.

5 PERSPECTIVE PROJECTION

An Introduction to One-Point Perspective

1

One-point perspective is much more employed for depicting interior spaces, but certain types of external views of objects and collections of forms can be constructed using the plan-projection method.

In one-point perspective a set of planes is parallel to the picture plane, i.e., located at right angles to the observer's line of sight, and the set retains its orientation and original shape. However, the horizontal edges of planes perpendicular to the picture plane converge on the single vanishing point.

N.B.: The plan-projection method of perspective drawing essentially functions as a presentation device rather than a design tool because it relies upon the provision of accurate plan and elevation, in other words, a predesigned form.

2 When visualizing spaces that exist only in the mind's eye, the following method is fast and easily applied to different kinds of graphics.

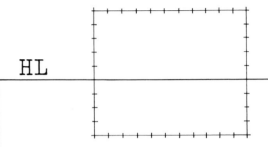

HL

Select a scale and draw a "picture frame" on the drawing board. Mark off increments of equal measure around its edge. Next, draw in the eye level (horizon line)--this is assumed to be 5'-3" (1600mm) above the base line.

The vanishing point controls the direction of view. Position this on the horizon line to promote the best view--off center, if possible, to achieve a more dynamic drawing. Then, project radiating lines from the vanishing point through each of the baseline increments. **3**

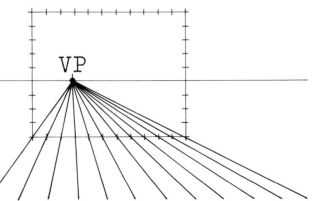

VP

An Introduction to One-Point Perspective

4

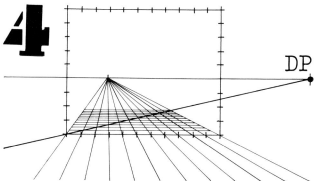

Locate a diagonal point outside the picture frame on the horizon line--its distance from the vanishing point representing that of the viewer from the picture-frame plane, i.e., the nearer its position to the vanishing point the more acute the foreshortening. Next, project a line from the diagonal point to the farther, lower corner of the frame. Where this crosses the radiating lines it establishes the equal units of measure as diminishing in depth.

7

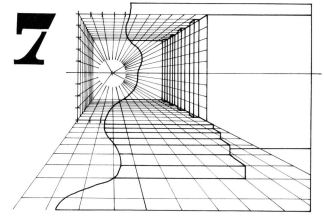

After connecting the upper corners of the frame to the vanishing point together with the radiating lines on the remaining three sides of the space, the horizontal depth measurements can be extended around the framework to complete the grid. This can now act as an underlay guide from which the size and location of the components of an interior or exterior perspective can be scaled.

At this point it is worth pausing to examine the role of the diagonal point. This diagram demonstrates that it is, in fact, the station point found in the plan-projection method. However, in the grid method it has moved to the horizon line. Its distance from the vanishing point still represents that of the observer from the object but also acts as the point from which to measure degrees of depth.

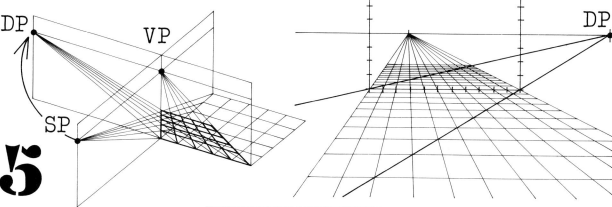

5

8

Perspective drawings worked from construction to final rendering on one drawing surface have to cope with the removal of initial and redundant construction lines. For this reason they often retain a constructed quality, appearing wooden and devoid of any atmosphere. On the other hand, the underlay process separates the construction from the rendering stage, thus allowing a concentration on the introduction of tone, texture, color, and light, shade, and shadow.

One-point grids can be used to convert orthographic drawings into convincing perspectives. It is to their use in orthographic transformation that we now turn.

6

The units of equal measure can also be projected in front of the picture frame by taking a line from the diagonal point through the nearer, lower corner of the frame.

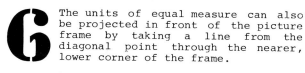

How to Convert Elevations into Perspectives

1

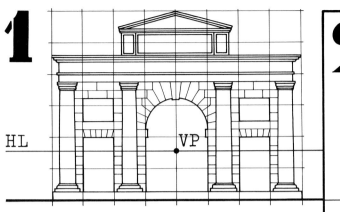

HL · VP

To convert an exterior or interior elevation into a perspective, first superimpose a lightly drawn grid over the facade. Then insert a horizon line (HL) at a scaled eye level height above the ground line. A vanishing point (VP) that will concentrate the resultant angle of view on an important feature should now be spotted on a point on the horizon line, such as a main entrance.

2 Next, project lines from the vanishing point that radiate out toward the viewer, making sure that they each intersect the points at which the vertical grid lines superimposed on the elevation touch the ground line.

3 By extending the units of measurement represented by the vertical grid lines on the ground line out to either side of the elevation, the entire width of the foreground plane can be filled with lines of convergence.

4

DP

Now locate a diagonal point (DP) on the horizon line out to the extreme right or left of the elevation. The distance of this point from the vanishing point should be at least one and a half times the width of the elevation. Strike a line from the diagonal point so that it bisects the nearest, lower corner of the facade on the ground line.

5 The points at which this diagonal line intersects the foreground radiating lines fixes scaled units of depth that increase as they approach the viewer. These can be extended horizontally to complete the measured plane of the foreground perspective grid.

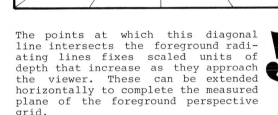

6

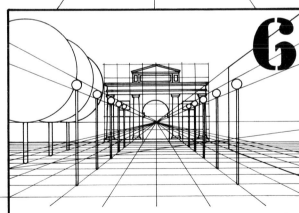

The foreground grid will now guide the accurate location and delineation of objects that occupy the illusion of space between viewer and facade. Heights in this perspective are easily found by projecting lines out from the vanishing point and through the appropriate scaled point on the original facade grid.

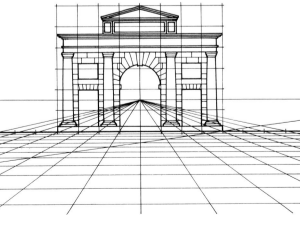

114

How to Convert Sections into Perspective Sections

1

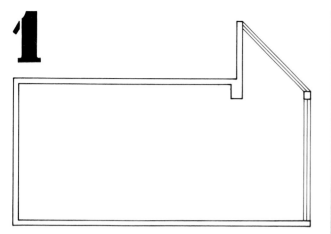

The conversion of a section into a perspective section simply applies the basic principles of one-point perspective construction. It begins with a basically drafted scaled section--the location of its cut having responded to your predetermined idea of the view to be realized.

2

The section drawing functions as the picture plane, i.e., a true-to-scale framework through which the perspective will be projected and viewed. First, establish the horizon line (eye level) and the vanishing point (angle of view). Remember that a horizon line raised above scaled eye level will give added prominence to floor planes. Conversely, lowering the horizon line below scaled eye level will emphasize ceiling planes.

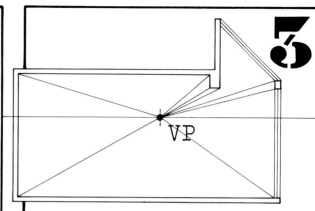

3

The vanishing point (VP) should be positioned on the horizon line to obtain the best possible angle of view. For instance, try locating the vanishing point off center so that an important wall is emphasized. Once established, project lines from the vanishing point back to the inside corners of the section.

4

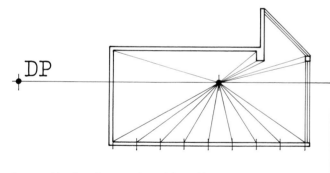

One method of constructing the perspective without the aid of a plan is to mark off increments of equal measure around the inner edge of the section and connect those on the floor plane back to the vanishing point. Then locate a diagonal point (DP) on the horizon line just outside the section.

N.B.: The distance between the diagonal point and the vanishing point should be at least as great as the width of the section.

5

The diagonal point represents the distance of the viewer from the picture plane (or section). The nearer its location to the vanishing point, the more acute the foreshortening in the resultant perspective. Now strike a line from the diagonal point to the farther, lower corner of the inside of the section.

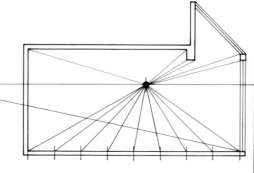

6

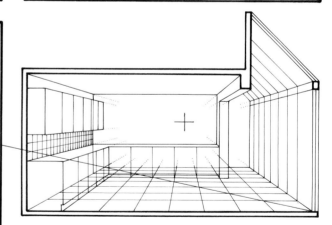

Where the diagonal line crosses the radiating floor plane lines it establishes equal units of measure as diminishing in depth. These can now be easily projected around the walls and ceiling to guide the accurate location of the rear wall together with openings and objects in the interior space.

115

How to Convert Plans into Bird's-Eye Perspectives

1

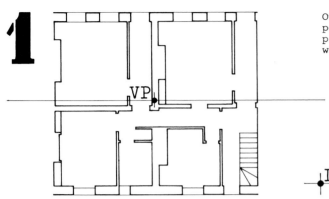

Here is another, more elegant method of measuring depth, this time in transforming a plan into the "three dimensions" of a more realistic, overhead view. After drafting the plan, position a vanishing point (VP) in a central position. This will direct the resultant angle of view. Then rule a horizontal line through the vanishing point and out to either side of the plan.

Outside the plan, next locate the diagonal point (DP)--its distance from the edge of the plan being at least as great as the overall width of the plan.

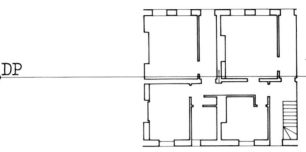

2

3

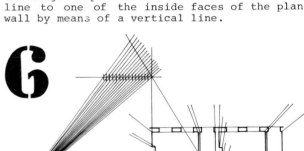

Now draw a horizontal measuring line (ML) above or below the area between the plan and the diagonal point. Connect the end of this line to one of the inside faces of the plan wall by means of a vertical line.

4

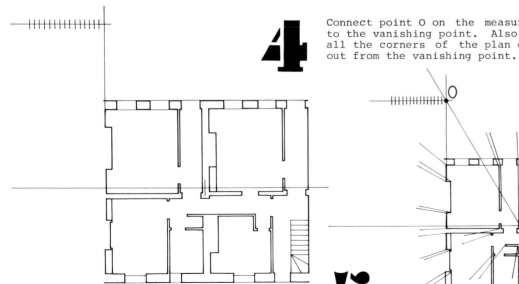

From the point where it intersects the vertical line, next mark off a series of scaled units along the measuring line.

Connect point O on the measuring scale back to the vanishing point. Also, at this stage all the corners of the plan can be projected out from the vanishing point.

5

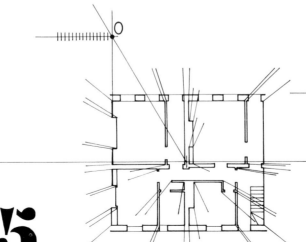

6

Now project a series of radiating lines from the diagonal point so that they each cut successive units along the measuring line. The points at which these radiating lines bisect the diagonal connecting the vanishing point with the measuring line represent units of perspective depth.

How to Convert Plans into Bird's-Eye Perspectives

7

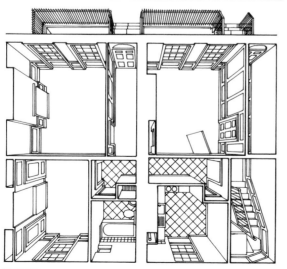

The perspective scale on the diagonal line can now be projected around the walls of the plan to find ceiling level and other scaled heights.

Furthermore, the heights of any objects that occur within the space defined by the plan can also be found by transferring the perspective depth scale from a convenient point.

Finally, draw in the details and remove any superfluous construction lines.

This simple perspective plan projection can be used to look upward into a worm's-eye view of interior spaces. As the features shown on the plan will be retained in the front plane of the image, it is simpler to project into the plan rather then outward as in the overhead view. This is achieved by drawing the measuring line over the plan. Remember to flip the plan over in order to produce the "right-way-round" view from below.

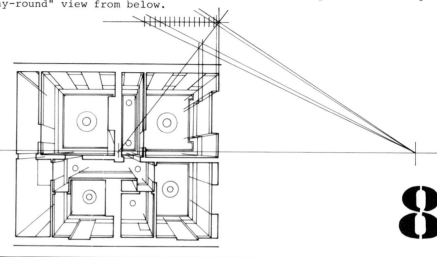

8

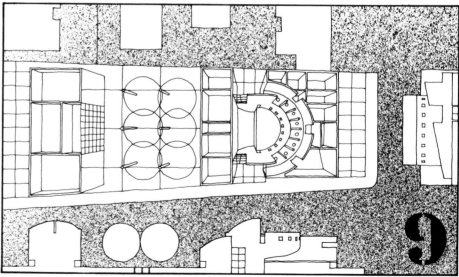

9

The worm's-eye viewpoint is especially useful when showing more complex ceiling forms, such as in this drawing of a new church.

Three-Dimensional Orthographics in Action

These three perspectives--each developed from a plan, elevation, and section respectively--employ the construction methods previously described. However, as with all perspective projections the trick is to leave behind the construction lines before the rendering stage. For example, for a freehand sketch perspective, the construction process can be worked in blue dropout pencil and, after inking in the required lines of convergence, this can be transformed into a same-size or resized photocopy print (which reproduces only the ink lines). However, when making a fine-line perspective, the more common method involves tracing-off the required perspective lines before making a photocopy print.

N.B.: Notice that, in the plan projection drawing illustrated here, the vanishing point is placed outside the interior space for a better view of the featured walls.

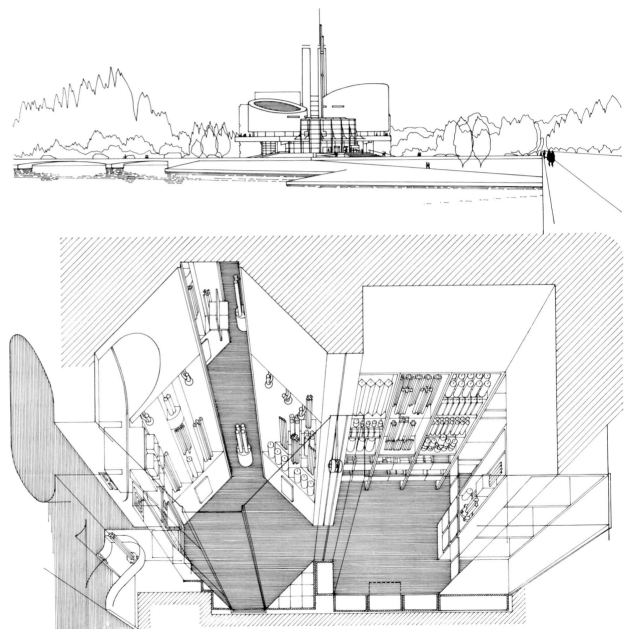

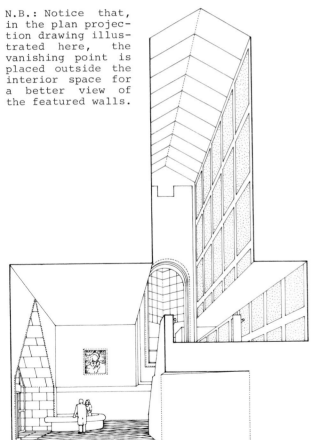

An Introduction to Two-Point Perspective

One of the fastest ways of understanding the mechanics of two-point perspective is to re-trace the coordinates over a photograph showing two faces of a cubic building.

Using a ruler and a pen, project all horizontal edges. Where these lines converge to the left and right of the form are the vanishing points. If these are connected, the horizon line (eye level) is established. This is a horizontal line corresponding to the height of the observer's eye from the ground.

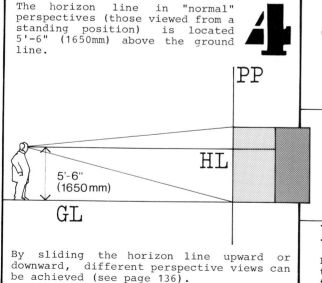

1

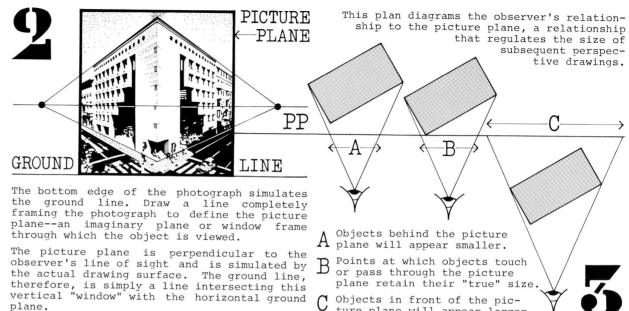

2

The bottom edge of the photograph simulates the ground line. Draw a line completely framing the photograph to define the picture plane--an imaginary plane or window frame through which the object is viewed.

The picture plane is perpendicular to the observer's line of sight and is simulated by the actual drawing surface. The ground line, therefore, is simply a line intersecting this vertical "window" with the horizontal ground plane.

This plan diagrams the observer's relationship to the picture plane, a relationship that regulates the size of subsequent perspective drawings.

3

A Objects behind the picture plane will appear smaller.

B Points at which objects touch or pass through the picture plane retain their "true" size.

C Objects in front of the picture plane will appear larger.

4

The horizon line in "normal" perspectives (those viewed from a standing position) is located 5'-6" (1650mm) above the ground line.

By sliding the horizon line upward or downward, different perspective views can be achieved (see page 136).

5

The station point simulates the observer's location, i.e., the distance between the viewer and that which is viewed. It also controls the relative position and proximity of the vanishing points to the object.

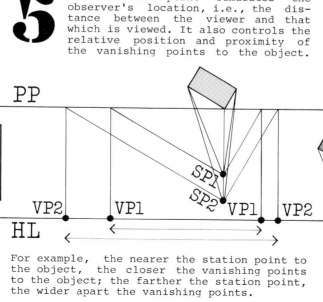

For example, the nearer the station point to the object, the closer the vanishing points to the object; the farther the station point, the wider apart the vanishing points.

6

The orientation of the object in relation to the station point determines the angle of vision. For instance, if the object presents two equal faces to the observer, they will appear equally foreshortened. If the object is rotated to present two unequal faces, the faces will vanish at different rates.

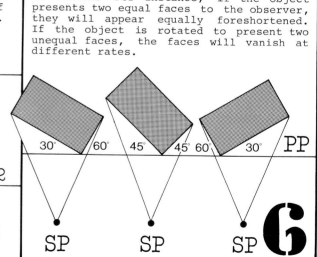

How to Construct a Two-Point Perspective

The plan-projection method of perspective described here is a means of translating accurately the dimensions of a plan and elevation into a three-dimensional illusion of a building.

1 Draw the line of the picture plane and, in relation to it, establish the plan.

N.B.: Remember that at this stage you are determining the relative size of the building and, indeed, the size of the ultimate perspective drawing in relation to the plan.

2 Select and locate the station point (viewing position) at right angles to the picture plane.

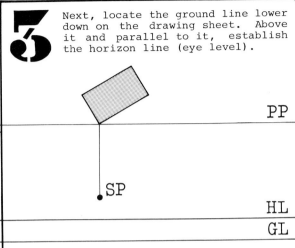

N.B.: Remember that the amount of distance between the station point and the plan regulates the acuteness of the angles of perspective convergence.

3 Next, locate the ground line lower down on the drawing sheet. Above it and parallel to it, establish the horizon line (eye level).

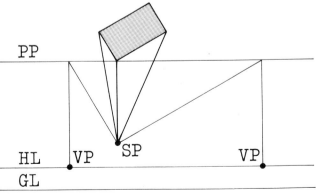

N.B.: In this instance, the horizon line represents a scaled version of the "normal" viewing height, i.e., 5'-6" (1650mm) above the ground line.

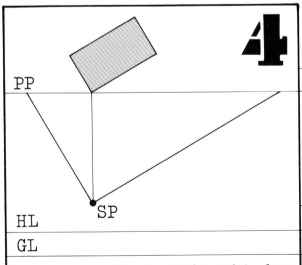

4 Project lines from the station point, drawn parallel to the two faces of the plan, so that they intersect the picture plane.

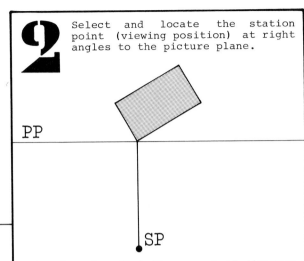

5 Then transfer vertically each intersection down to the horizon line. This establishes the vanishing points for the two-point perspective.

6 Project lines from the station point to all "visible" corners of the plan. The points at which these projections intersect the picture plane establish the further limits of the receding sides of the building.

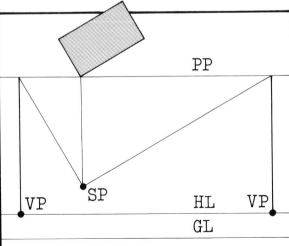

N.B.: In representing the angle of vision, these lines also correspond to our cone of vision, which is between 40 and 60 degrees.

How to Construct a Two-Point Perspective

7 Transfer the corner of the plan that is opposite the station point down to the horizon line and ground line.

N.B.: Because this line is a bisection of the angle of vision, it is called the center of vision.

8 As, in this case, the plan actually touches the picture plane, the "true height" of its projection from the ground line can be conveniently determined via the elevation.

N.B.: For plans occurring in front of or behind the picture plane, see page 122.

9 Project lines from the top and bottom of this front edge so that they converge at the vanishing points.

10 In order to establish the further, vertical edges of each receding plane, transfer the points at which the angle of vision intersects the picture plane down vertically to the horizon line.

11 The point at which these intersect the vanishing lines completes all the coordinates for the three-dimensional reconstruction of a building design from its plan and elevation.

12 The completed perspective drawing now acts as the basis for a rendering technique of your choice.

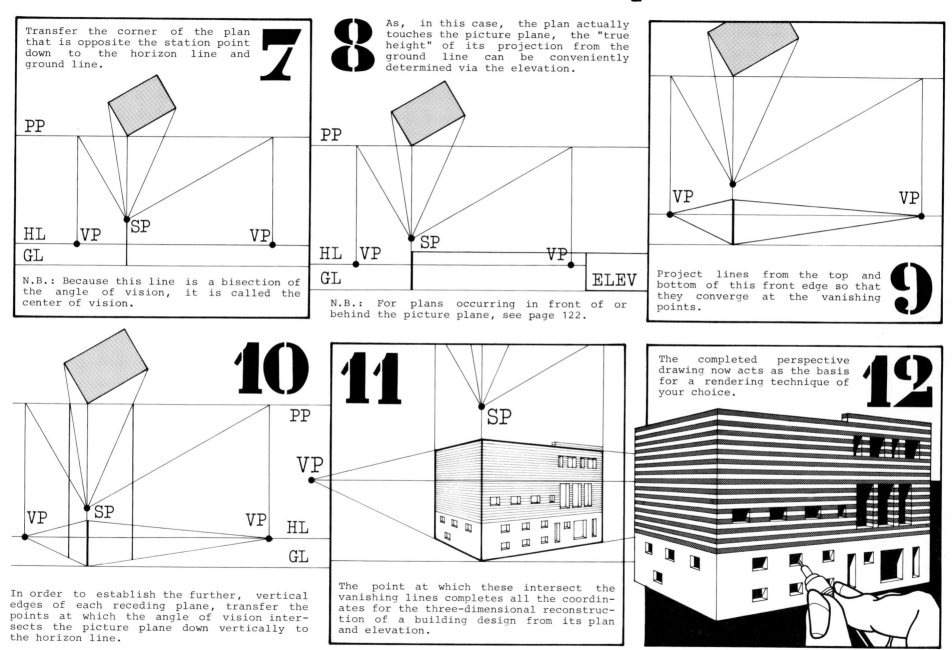

How to Animate Perspective Coordinates

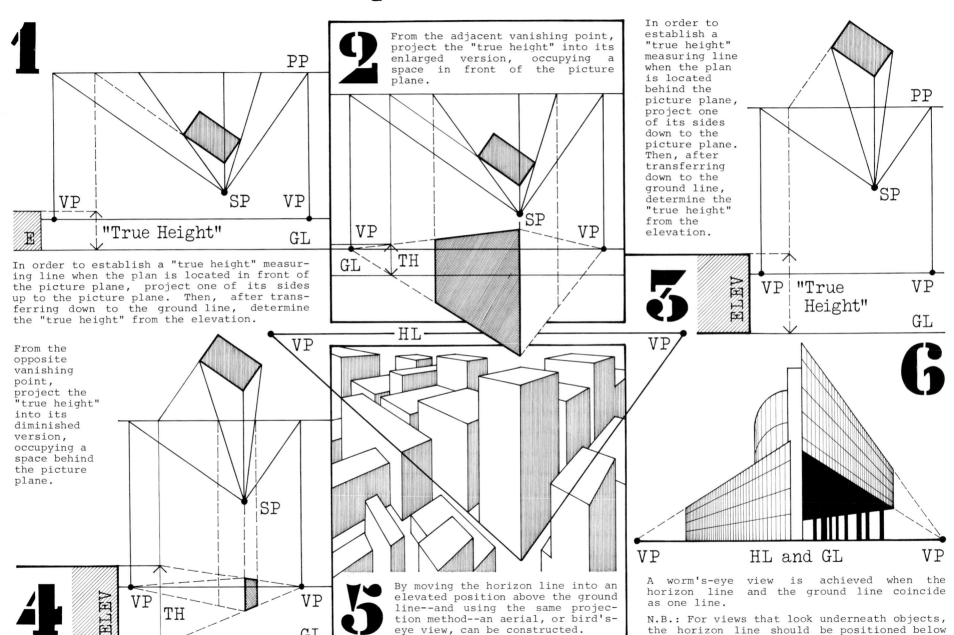

1 In order to establish a "true height" measuring line when the plan is located in front of the picture plane, project one of its sides up to the picture plane. Then, after transferring down to the ground line, determine the "true height" from the elevation.

2 From the adjacent vanishing point, project the "true height" into its enlarged version, occupying a space in front of the picture plane.

In order to establish a "true height" measuring line when the plan is located behind the picture plane, project one of its sides down to the picture plane. Then, after transferring down to the ground line, determine the "true height" from the elevation.

4 From the opposite vanishing point, project the "true height" into its diminished version, occupying a space behind the picture plane.

5 By moving the horizon line into an elevated position above the ground line--and using the same projection method--an aerial, or bird's-eye view, can be constructed.

6 A worm's-eye view is achieved when the horizon line and the ground line coincide as one line.

N.B.: For views that look underneath objects, the horizon line should be positioned below the ground line.

How to Animate Perspective Coordinates

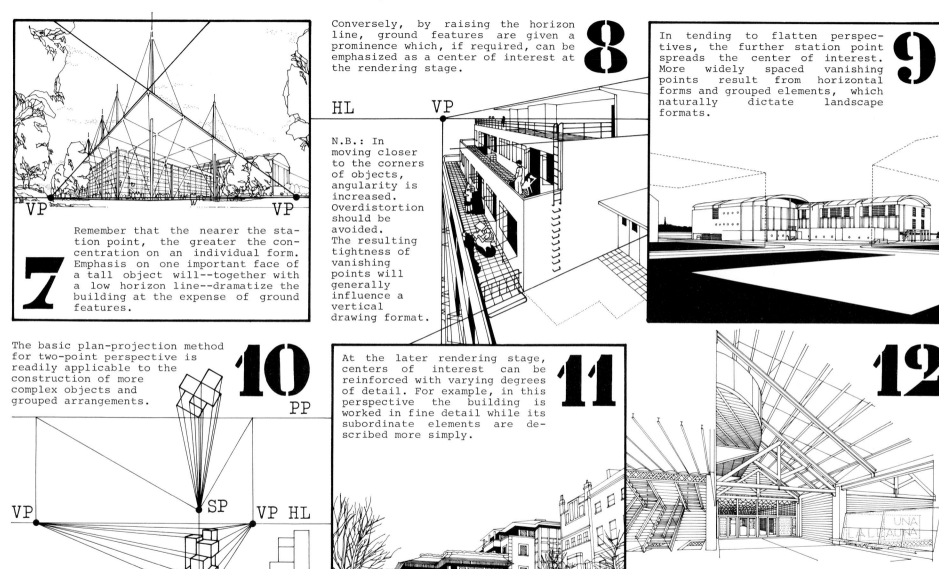

8 Conversely, by raising the horizon line, ground features are given a prominence which, if required, can be emphasized as a center of interest at the rendering stage.

7 Remember that the nearer the station point, the greater the concentration on an individual form. Emphasis on one important face of a tall object will--together with a low horizon line--dramatize the building at the expense of ground features.

N.B.: In moving closer to the corners of objects, angularity is increased. Overdistortion should be avoided. The resulting tightness of vanishing points will generally influence a vertical drawing format.

9 In tending to flatten perspectives, the further station point spreads the center of interest. More widely spaced vanishing points result from horizontal forms and grouped elements, which naturally dictate landscape formats.

HL   VP

10 The basic plan-projection method for two-point perspective is readily applicable to the construction of more complex objects and grouped arrangements.

PP

VP   SP   VP HL

GL

N.B.: Remember to make thumbnail diagrams prior to construction in order to predetermine the best viewpoint-composition-center of interest relationship.

11 At the later rendering stage, centers of interest can be reinforced with varying degrees of detail. For example, in this perspective the building is worked in fine detail while its subordinate elements are described more simply.

12 When drawing details of objects, make sure that the central reason for producing the graphic is evident. For example, the aim of this vignette is to illustrate "approach" and "entrance." Thus the door becomes the center of interest, the eye being led toward it via the structure of the drawing.

Office Method Perspective Construction

1 Described over the next nine pages is a fast and accurate method of angled perspective known as the "Office Method." Unlike the previously explained plan-projection method, this method does not require the plan to be tilted. It begins with the roof plan of the building fixed square-on near to the top of the drawing board.

2 Next tape a sheet of tracing paper over the plan. As the tracing paper will carry the station point and, if possible, the vanishing points, it should be considerably larger than the drawing of the plan.

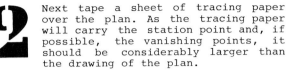

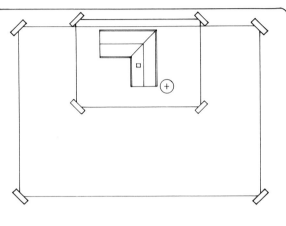

3 Then trace the plan and include any surrounding details, such as trees, pathways, and so on.

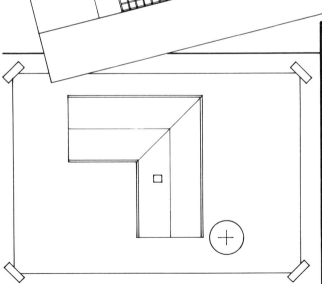

N.B.: It is a good idea to keep the referent elevation close at hand as this will act as a useful guide when tracing information.

4 The location of all windows and doors that will be seen in the finished perspective, together with any projections, such as balconies, piers, chimneys, and so on, should also be marked on the tracing.

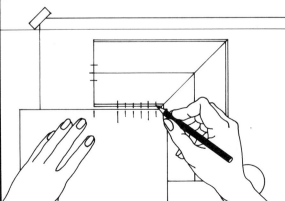

5 If the building comprises two or more stories, then it is advisable to trace the features of each floor, or roof, in different colored pencils or inks.

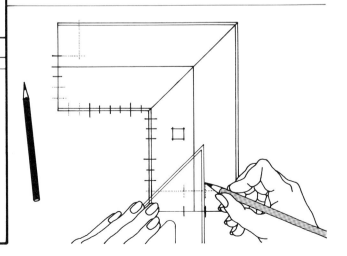

How to Establish the Direction of View

1

The exact viewpoint from which the building will appear to the spectator when drawn should now be established. This necessitates the location of the station point, i.e., the distance between the viewer and the building.

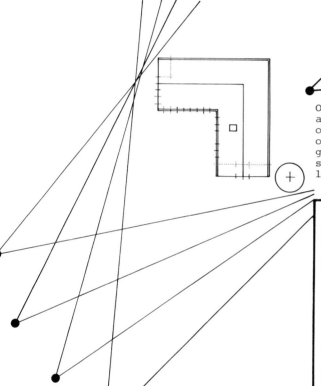

A factor in locating the station point is the extent of the arc of vision, i.e., the angle formed by two lines that radiate from the station point to determine the extreme edges of the picture.

2

ARC OF VISION 40°

Obviously, if the spectator is standing only a few feet away from the building, the angle of vision would be so wide as to place most of the picture out of focus. Therefore, it is generally agreed that the angle of vision should not be more than 60 degrees and not less than 40 degrees.

When positioning the station point, a general rule is that the spectator should be at a distance of about three times the height of the building.

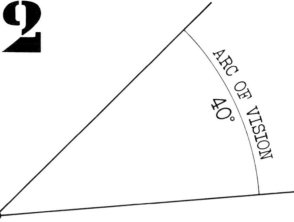

3

4

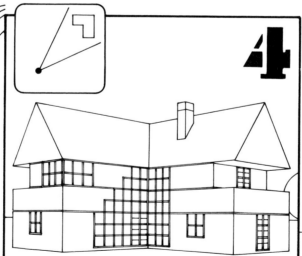

When working with square or rectangular buildings, avoid placing the spectator in a position from which a symmetrical view with equally foreshortened planes is given.

5

Aim instead for the interesting variety of two side planes with differing angles of perspective.

How to Establish the Picture Plane

1

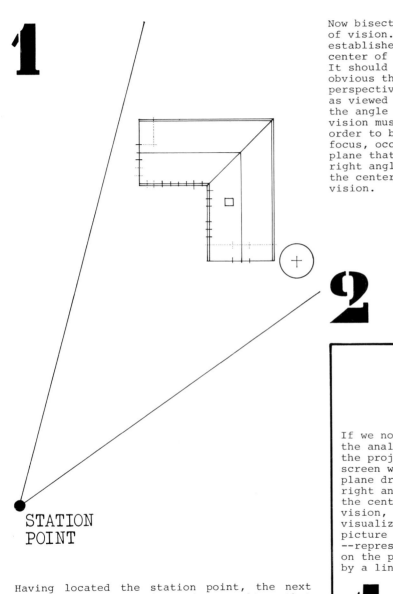

STATION
POINT

Having located the station point, the next operation is to project the two lines that describe the arc of vision so that they determine the outer edges of the desired picture. Any object that falls outside these lines will not appear in the final drawing.

126

Now bisect the angle of vision. This line establishes the center of vision. It should now be obvious that the perspective image as viewed within the angle of vision must, in order to be in focus, occur on a plane that is at right angles to the center of vision.

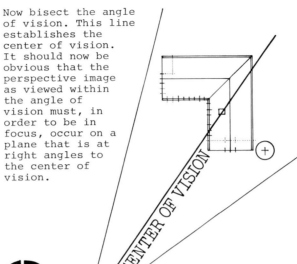

CENTER OF VISION

2

If we now replace the analogy of the projector screen with a plane drawn at right angles to the center of vision, we visualize the picture plane --represented on the plan by a line.

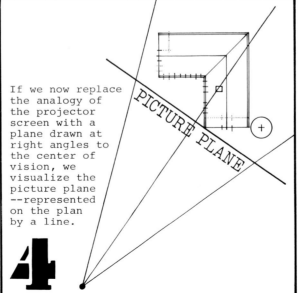

PICTURE PLANE

4

For example, imagine a slide projector: the center of vision represents the direction in which it is beamed; the two extremity lines represent the arc of its projected rays of light. To achieve a true projected image, the screen must be at right angles to the direction in which it is pointed.

If we move this "screen," or picture plane, away from or nearer the station point, and keep it at right angles to the center of vision, we can either reduce or enlarge the image. This is an important aspect for consideration when locating the picture plane.

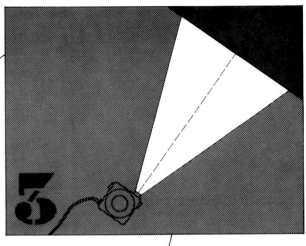

5

The Function of the Picture Plane

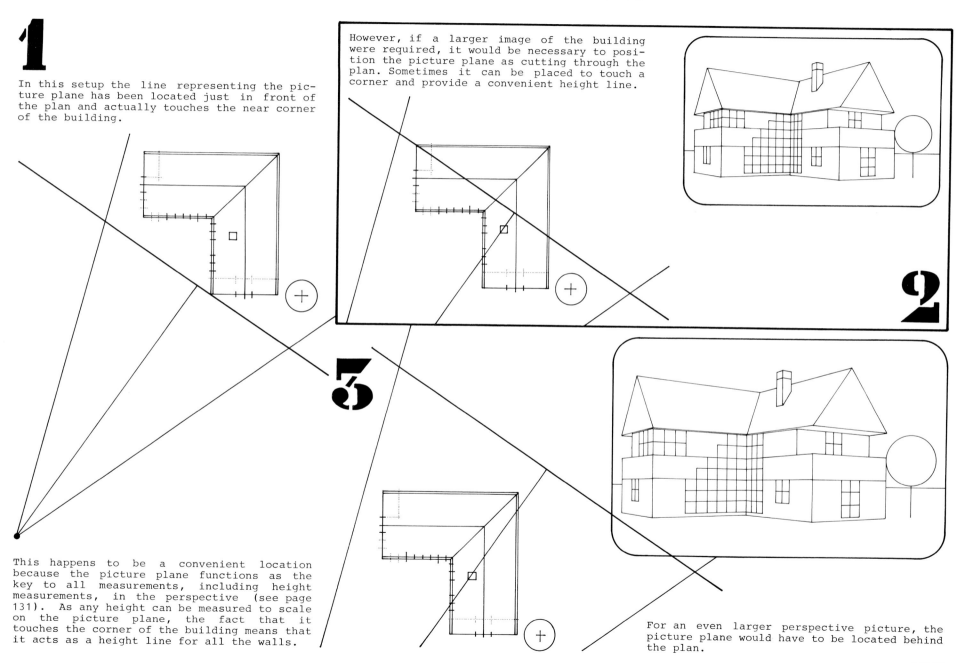

1

In this setup the line representing the picture plane has been located just in front of the plan and actually touches the near corner of the building.

However, if a larger image of the building were required, it would be necessary to position the picture plane as cutting through the plan. Sometimes it can be placed to touch a corner and provide a convenient height line.

2

3

This happens to be a convenient location because the picture plane functions as the key to all measurements, including height measurements, in the perspective (see page 131). As any height can be measured to scale on the picture plane, the fact that it touches the corner of the building means that it acts as a height line for all the walls.

For an even larger perspective picture, the picture plane would have to be located behind the plan.

How to Establish the Vanishing Points

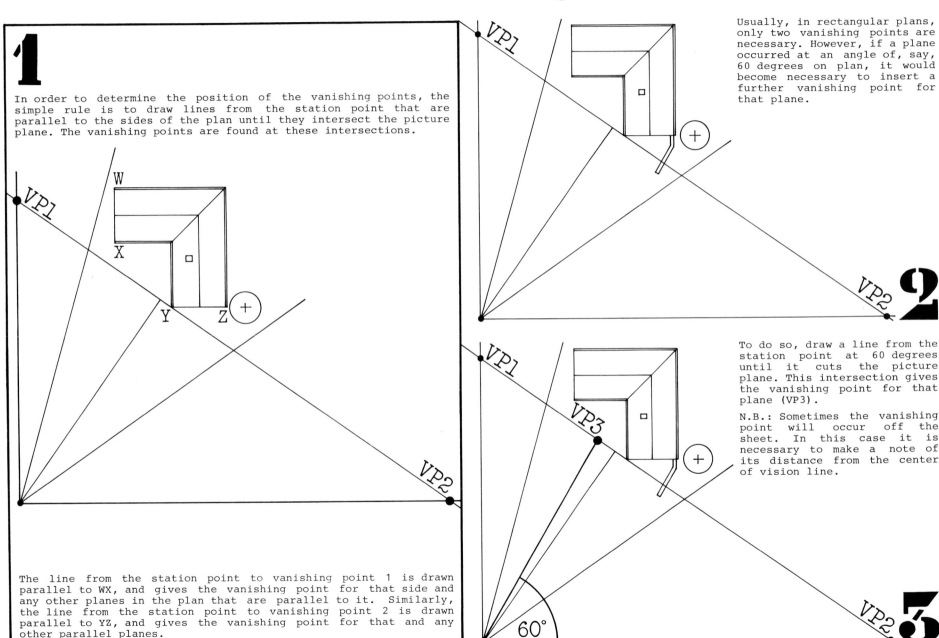

1

In order to determine the position of the vanishing points, the simple rule is to draw lines from the station point that are parallel to the sides of the plan until they intersect the picture plane. The vanishing points are found at these intersections.

The line from the station point to vanishing point 1 is drawn parallel to WX, and gives the vanishing point for that side and any other planes in the plan that are parallel to it. Similarly, the line from the station point to vanishing point 2 is drawn parallel to YZ, and gives the vanishing point for that and any other parallel planes.

2

Usually, in rectangular plans, only two vanishing points are necessary. However, if a plane occurred at an angle of, say, 60 degrees on plan, it would become necessary to insert a further vanishing point for that plane.

3

To do so, draw a line from the station point at 60 degrees until it cuts the picture plane. This intersection gives the vanishing point for that plane (VP3).

N.B.: Sometimes the vanishing point will occur off the sheet. In this case it is necessary to make a note of its distance from the center of vision line.

How to Establish Widths and Heights

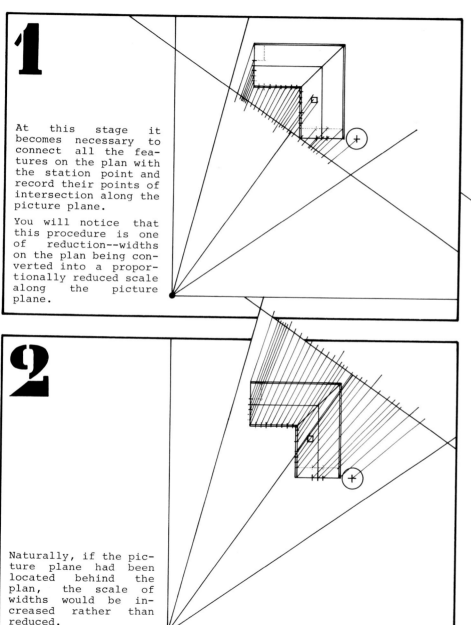

1

At this stage it becomes necessary to connect all the features on the plan with the station point and record their points of intersection along the picture plane.

You will notice that this procedure is one of reduction--widths on the plan being converted into a proportionally reduced scale along the picture plane.

2

Naturally, if the picture plane had been located behind the plan, the scale of widths would be increased rather than reduced.

3

Also at this stage, height lines should be determined so that scaled heights can later be measured. To establish the height lines, draw a line from the point for which a height measurement is required parallel to one of the planes for which you already have a vanishing point. Project this line until it cuts the picture plane. The resulting intersection gives the position of the height line.

As all the other heights can be achieved directly from the point at which the near corner of the building touches the line of the picture plane, the remaining heights required at this stage are those for the ridge, chimney, and tree.

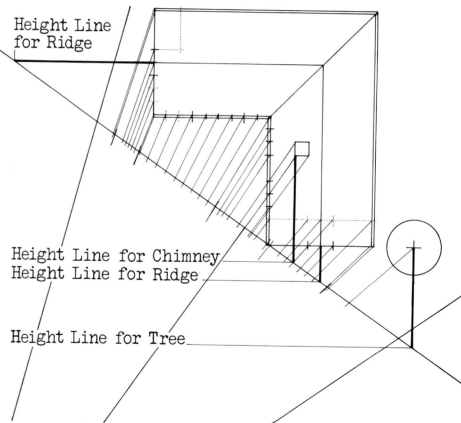

Height Line for Ridge

Height Line for Chimney
Height Line for Ridge

Height Line for Tree

Two important points emerge at this stage: first, everything converges on the picture plane; second, all information required for the perspective has been achieved without the awkward tilting of the sheet. The next stage sees the removal of the original plan from the drawing board, its replacement by a clean sheet of drawing paper, and use of the tracing as a measuring guide.

How to Transfer the Perspective Coordinates

1

Remove the tracing and the original plan drawing from the drawing board and replace with a clean sheet of drawing paper.

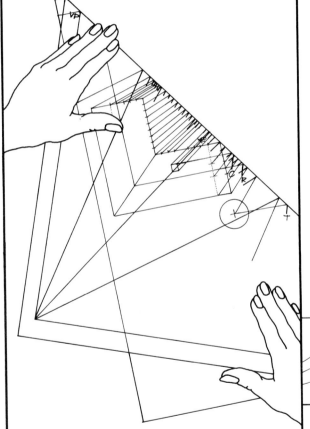

Next fold the tracing paper along the line of the picture plane, making sure that the point where the center of vision cuts the picture plane is clearly marked. This point will function as a check during the transfer of the traced measurements.

2

Now draw a horizon line across the lower part of the drawing paper. This line is the datum line for height measurements and is usually taken to be the ground line on a level site.

N.B.: Any line can represent the datum line provided that every measurement taken from it is first taken from a corresponding datum line on the elevation.

4

EYE LEVEL

On the other hand, if the ground falls away rapidly from the building, a more convincing perspective impression of the building, or group of buildings, will necessitate the lowering of the eye level below the ground line. In this event a certain amount of the form will be lost behind the rising foreground of the worm's-eye perspective view.

The next decision involves the location of the eye level, or horizon line. Normal eye level is usually 5'-6" (1650mm) or so above ground level. However, if the nature of the landscape is to feature in the final drawing, or a more general view of a group of buildings is required, it would be necessary to raise the eye level. For example, a bird's-eye view is achieved when the level is elevated to a height of 30 or 40 feet above the ground line.

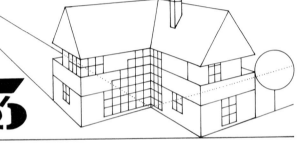

EYE LEVEL

3

In any event, whether the eye level is placed above or below the ground line, its ultimate location does not affect the system of working. However, a golden rule is to avoid placing the eye level line at the same height as any significant horizontal line on the building, such as the eaves or other projection. This is because it will exist simply as a line in the finished perspective and thus lose its sense of projection.

EYE LEVEL

5

130

How to Set Up the Perspective Drawing

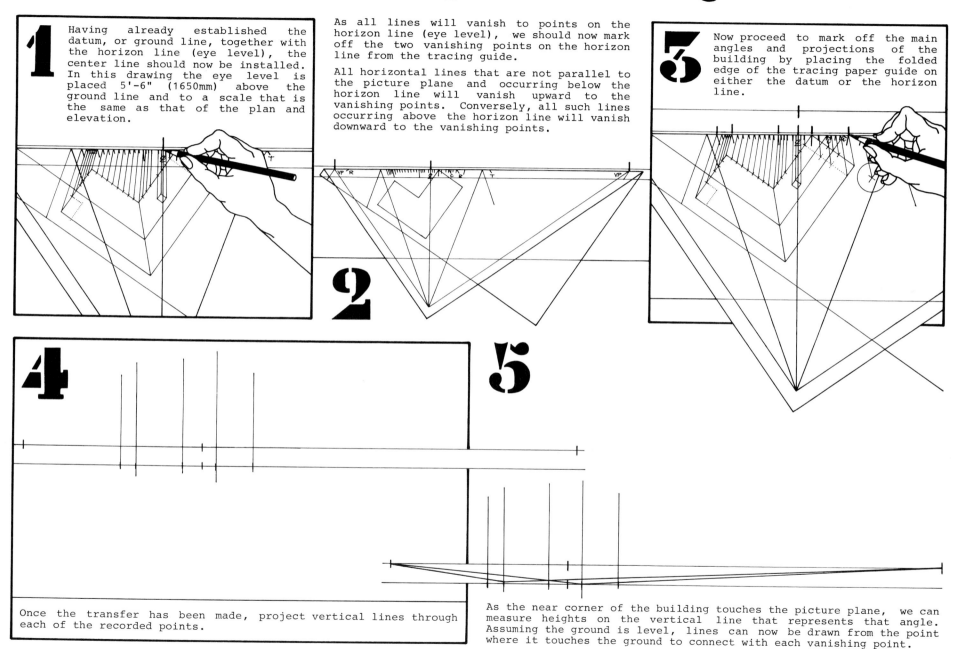

1 Having already established the datum, or ground line, together with the horizon line (eye level), the center line should now be installed. In this drawing the eye level is placed 5'-6" (1650mm) above the ground line and to a scale that is the same as that of the plan and elevation.

As all lines will vanish to points on the horizon line (eye level), we should now mark off the two vanishing points on the horizon line from the tracing guide.

All horizontal lines that are not parallel to the picture plane and occurring below the horizon line will vanish upward to the vanishing points. Conversely, all such lines occurring above the horizon line will vanish downward to the vanishing points.

3 Now proceed to mark off the main angles and projections of the building by placing the folded edge of the tracing paper guide on either the datum or the horizon line.

2

4

5

Once the transfer has been made, project vertical lines through each of the recorded points.

As the near corner of the building touches the picture plane, we can measure heights on the vertical line that represents that angle. Assuming the ground is level, lines can now be drawn from the point where it touches the ground to connect with each vanishing point.

How to Set Up the Perspective Drawing

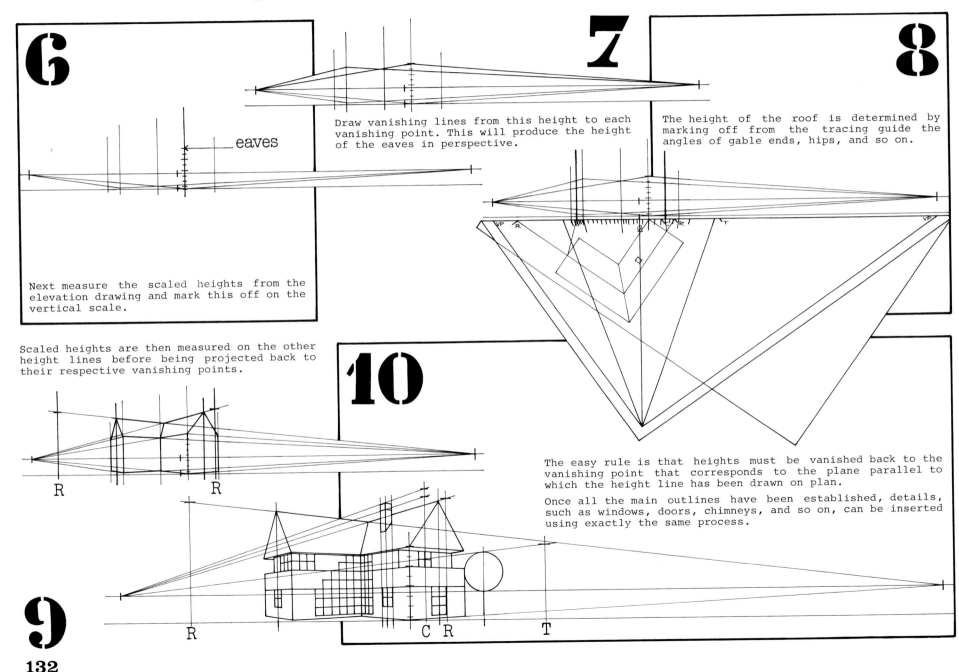

6 Next measure the scaled heights from the elevation drawing and mark this off on the vertical scale.

eaves

7 Draw vanishing lines from this height to each vanishing point. This will produce the height of the eaves in perspective.

8 The height of the roof is determined by marking off from the tracing guide the angles of gable ends, hips, and so on.

Scaled heights are then measured on the other height lines before being projected back to their respective vanishing points.

10

The easy rule is that heights must be vanished back to the vanishing point that corresponds to the plane parallel to which the height line has been drawn on plan.

Once all the main outlines have been established, details, such as windows, doors, chimneys, and so on, can be inserted using exactly the same process.

9

How to Construct a Two-Point Interior Perspective

1

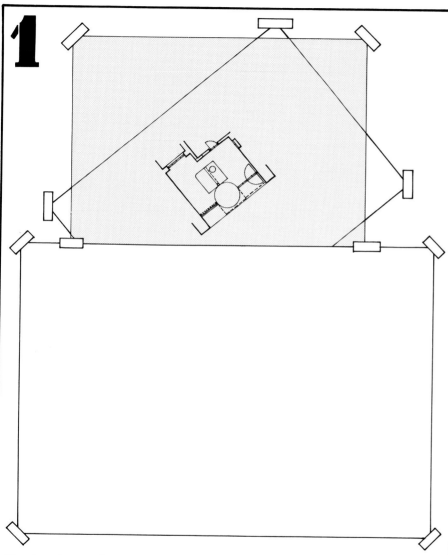

First rotate the plan of the room to be transformed into a perspective drawing into a position from which the best view of the interior is seen directly from below. Tape the plan to the top of the drawing board with a clean sheet of paper attached to the lower section of the board. Before proceeding, overlay a sheet of tracing paper on the plan.

2

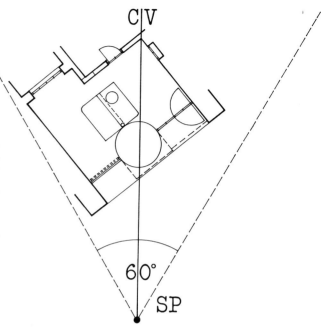

Working on the tracing paper, begin by recording the required position of the station point (SP) together with its attendant cone of vision and line of center of vision (CV).

N.B.: Remember that the station point represents your vantage point in relation to the interior of the room.

Now insert a horizontal line that will represent the picture plane (PP). This has been drawn here so that it cuts the farther angle of the room--a ploy that will later enable vertical measurements to be related to the height of the room. Finally, record each vanishing point (VP1 and VP2) by projecting lines out from the station point and parallel to the angles of the near walls of the plan.

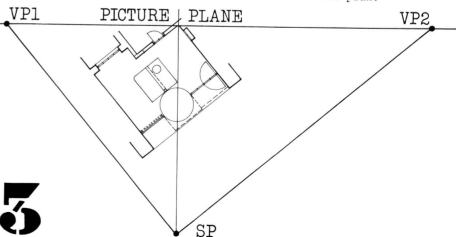

3

How to Construct a Two-Point Interior Perspective

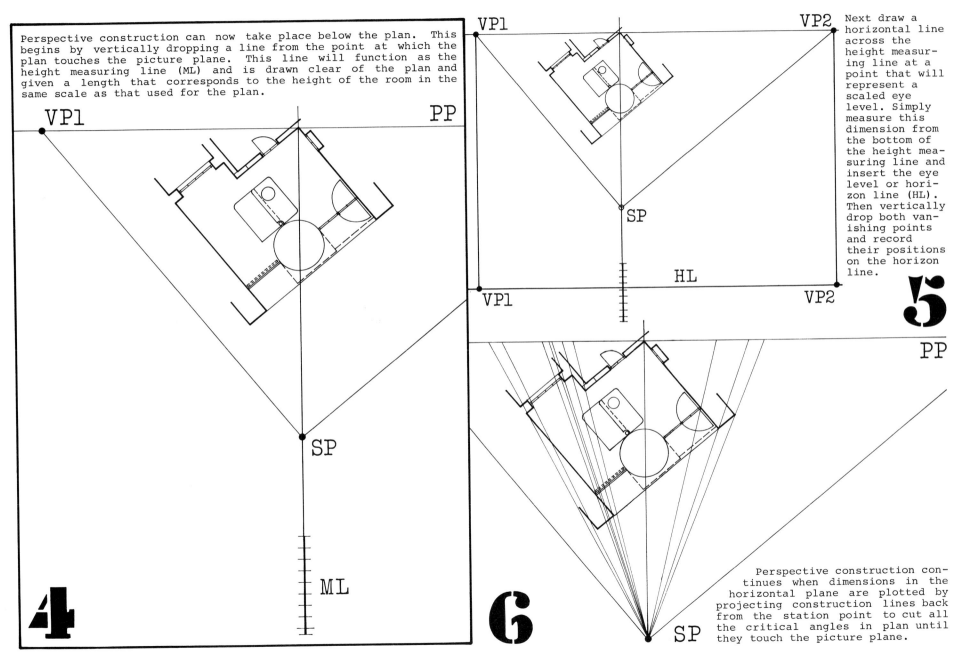

Perspective construction can now take place below the plan. This begins by vertically dropping a line from the point at which the plan touches the picture plane. This line will function as the height measuring line (ML) and is drawn clear of the plan and given a length that corresponds to the height of the room in the same scale as that used for the plan.

VP1

PP

VP1

SP

ML

4

Next draw a horizontal line across the height measuring line at a point that will represent a scaled eye level. Simply measure this dimension from the bottom of the height measuring line and insert the eye level or horizon line (HL). Then vertically drop both vanishing points and record their positions on the horizon line.

VP1

VP2

SP

VP1

HL

VP2

5

PP

6

Perspective construction continues when dimensions in the horizontal plane are plotted by projecting construction lines back from the station point to cut all the critical angles in plan until they touch the picture plane.

SP

How to Construct a Two-Point Interior Perspective

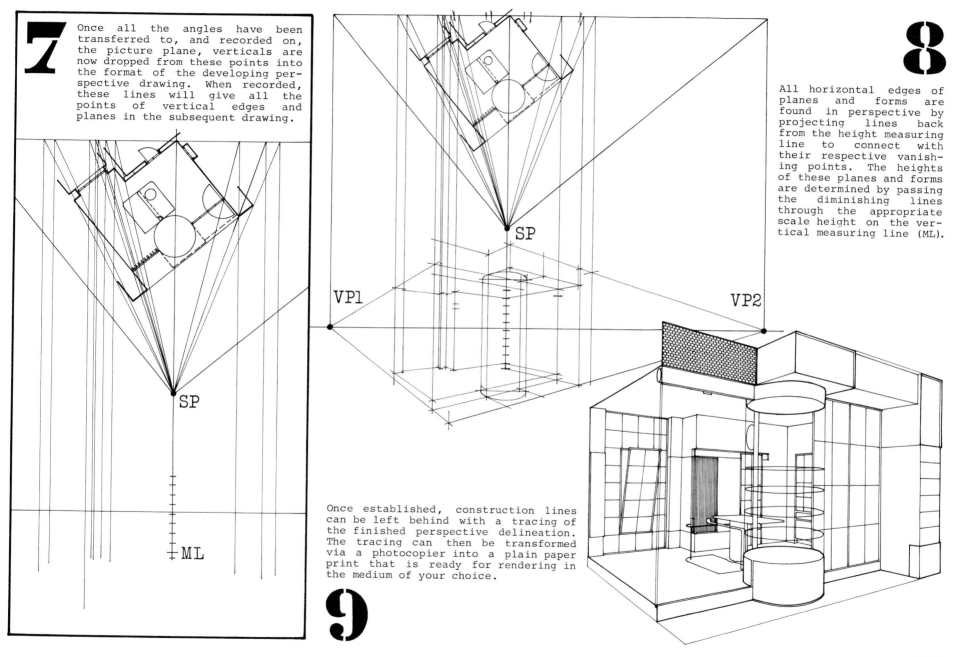

7 Once all the angles have been transferred to, and recorded on, the picture plane, verticals are now dropped from these points into the format of the developing perspective drawing. When recorded, these lines will give all the points of vertical edges and planes in the subsequent drawing.

8 All horizontal edges of planes and forms are found in perspective by projecting lines back from the height measuring line to connect with their respective vanishing points. The heights of these planes and forms are determined by passing the diminishing lines through the appropriate scale height on the vertical measuring line (ML).

SP

VP1   VP2

SP

ML

Once established, construction lines can be left behind with a tracing of the finished perspective delineation. The tracing can then be transformed via a photocopier into a plain paper print that is ready for rendering in the medium of your choice.

9

An Introduction to Three-Point Perspective

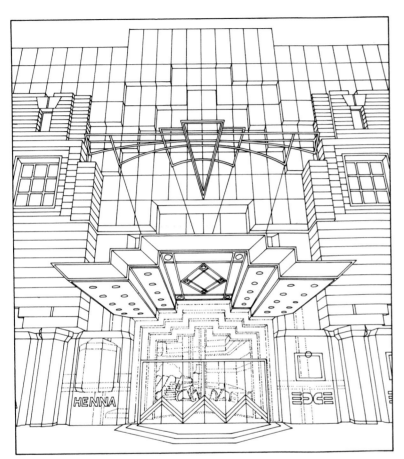

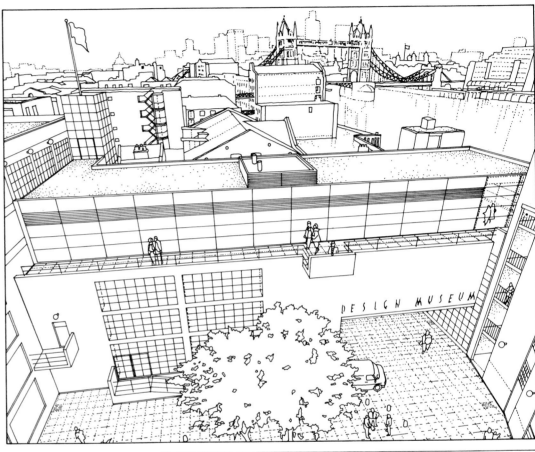

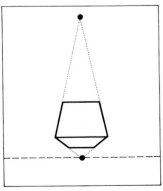

Whenever we look up or down at an object, the resulting view is a three-dimensional perspective. Therefore, when we look up from the road at a tall building, or down from, say, an airplane, we view architecture as it would appear in three-point perspective. However, the drawing on the left uses only two vanishing points: a central vanishing point on the horizon line (eye level), with a second vanishing point located skyward to introduce the illusion of vertical convergence. Unlike this drawing, the plane of building facade in the drawing on the right is not parallel to the picture plane--an oblique view requiring three vanishing points. Horizontal convergence is controlled by two vanishing points located on its elevated horizon line; vertical convergence is controlled by a third vanishing point located below ground level.

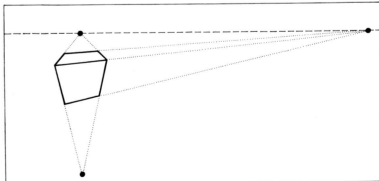

How to Construct a Three-Point Perspective

1

VP above

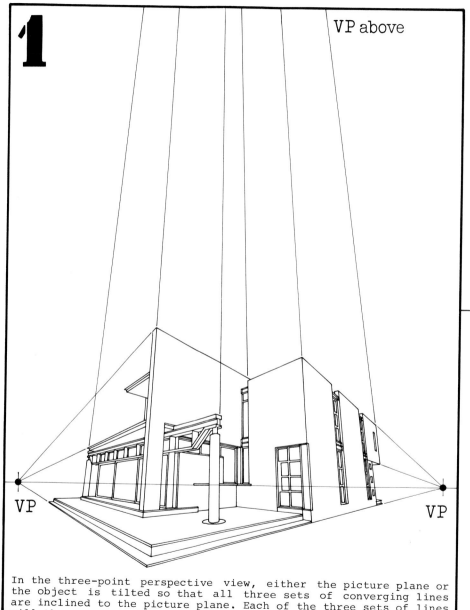

VP

VP

In the three-point perspective view, either the picture plane or the object is tilted so that all three sets of converging lines are inclined to the picture plane. Each of the three sets of lines will then converge to their respective vanishing points.

2

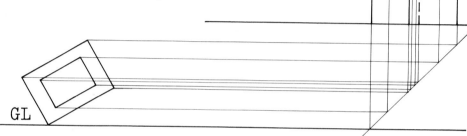

Possibly, the best means of understanding the basic principles of three-point perspective construction is the plan-projection method using an auxiliary elevation. This method relies upon a working knowledge of the form to be projected and begins by rotating the plan to find the best viewing direction. Once established, the near corner of the plan is positioned on a ground line (GL), and a scaled elevation looking parallel to the ground line is then drafted from the plan.

GL

The location of the station point (SP1) is then selected with reference to the elevation and, from this, the line of center of vision (CV) drawn to represent the upward viewing direction--in this case, toward the middle of the elevation. The line of the picture plane (PP) is then drawn at right angles to the center of vision line through the elevation at point GL, the ground line.

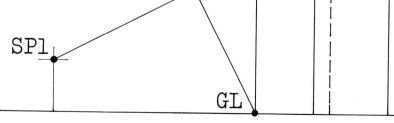

PP

CV

SP1

3

GL

How to Construct a Three-Point Perspective

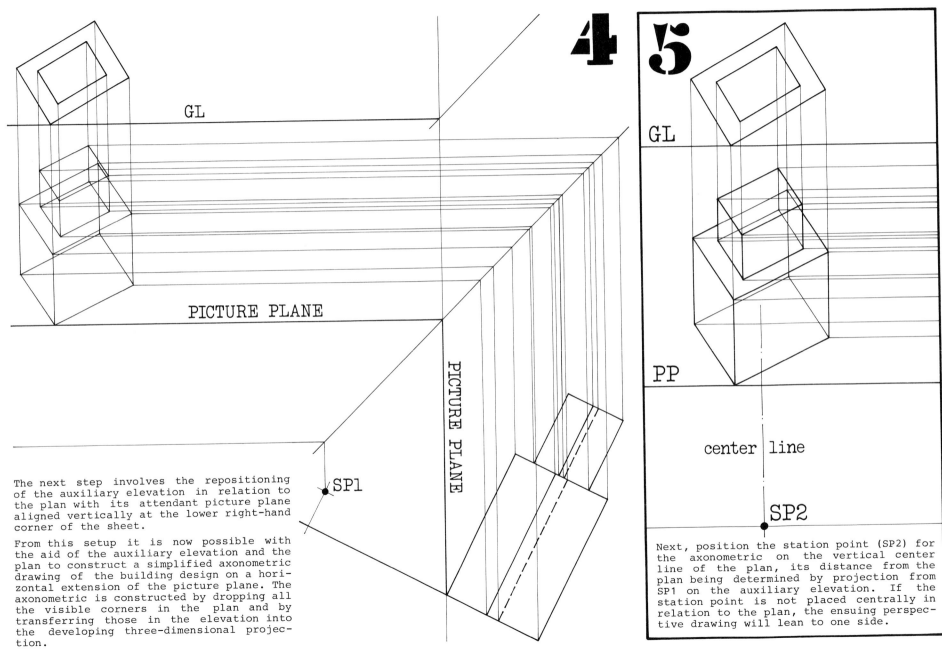

GL

PICTURE PLANE

PICTURE PLANE

SP1

4 **5**

GL

PP

center line

SP2

The next step involves the repositioning of the auxiliary elevation in relation to the plan with its attendant picture plane aligned vertically at the lower right-hand corner of the sheet.

From this setup it is now possible with the aid of the auxiliary elevation and the plan to construct a simplified axonometric drawing of the building design on a horizontal extension of the picture plane. The axonometric is constructed by dropping all the visible corners in the plan and by transferring those in the elevation into the developing three-dimensional projection.

Next, position the station point (SP2) for the axonometric on the vertical center line of the plan, its distance from the plan being determined by projection from SP1 on the auxiliary elevation. If the station point is not placed centrally in relation to the plan, the ensuing perspective drawing will lean to one side.

How to Construct a Three-Point Perspective

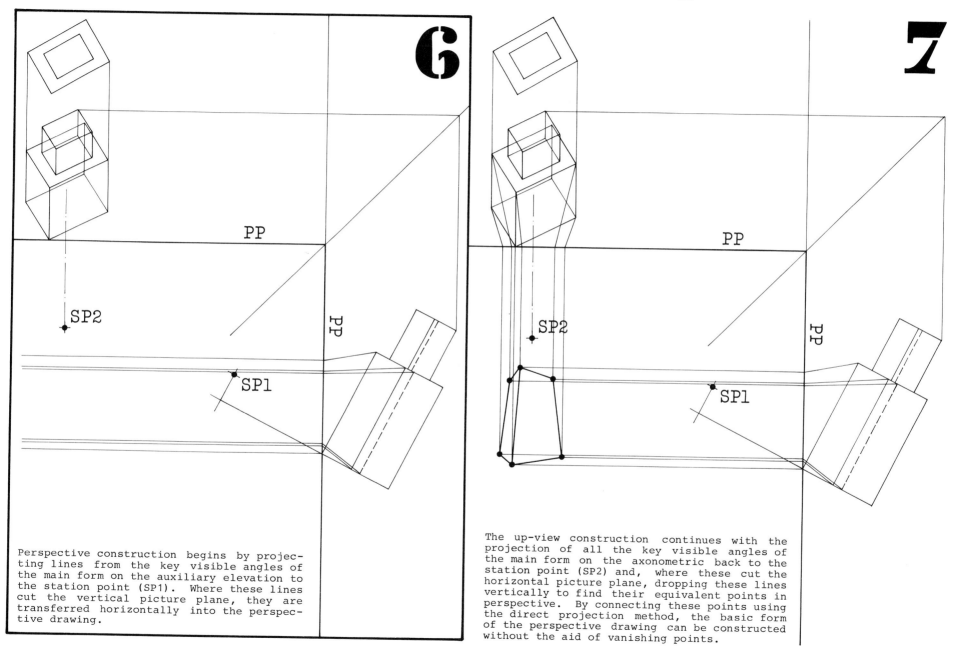

6

PP

dd

SP2

SP1

Perspective construction begins by projecting lines from the key visible angles of the main form on the auxiliary elevation to the station point (SP1). Where these lines cut the vertical picture plane, they are transferred horizontally into the perspective drawing.

7

PP

dd

SP2

SP1

The up-view construction continues with the projection of all the key visible angles of the main form on the axonometric back to the station point (SP2) and, where these cut the horizontal picture plane, dropping these lines vertically to find their equivalent points in perspective. By connecting these points using the direct projection method, the basic form of the perspective drawing can be constructed without the aid of vanishing points.

How to Construct a Three-Point Perspective

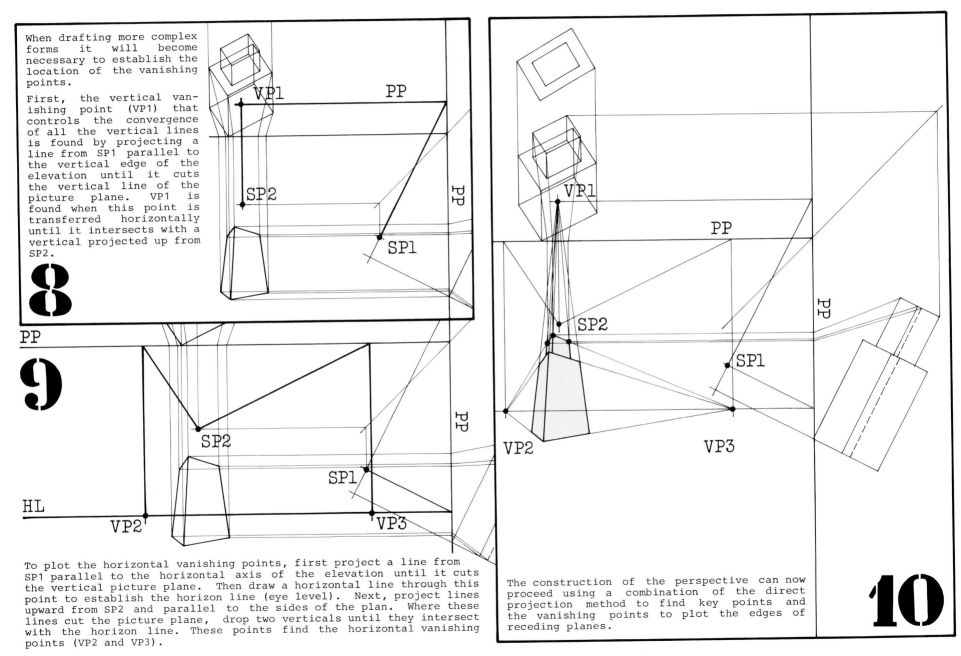

When drafting more complex forms it will become necessary to establish the location of the vanishing points.

First, the vertical vanishing point (VP1) that controls the convergence of all the vertical lines is found by projecting a line from SP1 parallel to the vertical edge of the elevation until it cuts the vertical line of the picture plane. VP1 is found when this point is transferred horizontally until it intersects with a vertical projected up from SP2.

8

9

To plot the horizontal vanishing points, first project a line from SP1 parallel to the horizontal axis of the elevation until it cuts the vertical picture plane. Then draw a horizontal line through this point to establish the horizon line (eye level). Next, project lines upward from SP2 and parallel to the sides of the plan. Where these lines cut the picture plane, drop two verticals until they intersect with the horizon line. These points find the horizontal vanishing points (VP2 and VP3).

The construction of the perspective can now proceed using a combination of the direct projection method to find key points and the vanishing points to plot the edges of receding planes.

10

An Introduction to Computer-Generated Perspectives

1

In order to circumvent the time spent in manually constructing individual perspective views of building designs, many students have turned to the ease and speed of computer-generated three-dimensional views. This technology has made it possible to generate rapidly a multitude of perspectives without any previous knowledge of perspective construction. Once the building information, such as walls, windows, doors, etc., is entered into computer memory, a perspective image can be generated on the monitor screen in an instant. Station points and angle of view can be changed on command, making it possible to rotate the perspective, or simulate a walk through and around a building concept.

Designated points, such as the ends of lines, and the positions of objects or elements, are fixed in three-dimensional space using one of a series of pointing devices. Pointing devices include the digitizing tablet stylus, the multibutton cursor (sometimes called a "puck" or a "mouse"), and the keyboard. Push-button commands on cursor or keyboard move, modify, add to, and subtract from the developing perspective drawing. Furthermore, the computer memory can contain thousands of standard details and architectural elements, such as staircases, windows, roof types, etc., etc., that can be called up in an instant, sized, and moved into position in a developing drawing.

However, when a perspective drawing is to be "drafted" into the computer from scratch, i.e., without any previous existence on paper, the designer should have in his or her head a basic visualization of the form and volume to be depicted. In some systems, such as AutoCAD, the process begins by first entering the scale and size of the drawing.

Computer drawings usually begin with a plan view. The most common method of drafting is to select the appropriate wall type, such as cavity or solid, from the menu and draw in the footprint of the design.

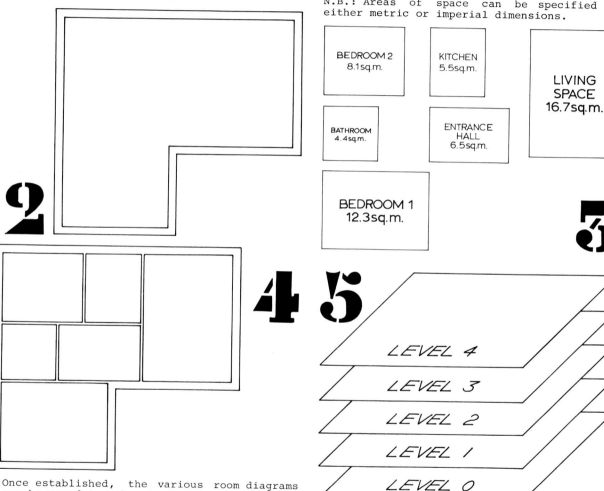

An alternative method is to record the plan as a collection of separate single-line diagrams. Various rooms can be depicted and, if required, given annotated names.

N.B.: Areas of space can be specified in either metric or imperial dimensions.

BEDROOM 2
8.1sq.m.

KITCHEN
5.5sq.m.

LIVING SPACE
16.7sq.m.

BATHROOM
4.4sq.m.

ENTRANCE HALL
6.5sq.m.

BEDROOM 1
12.3sq.m.

LEVEL 4

LEVEL 3

LEVEL 2

LEVEL 1

LEVEL 0

Once established, the various room diagrams can be moved together to form an overall plan before being converted into their appropriate wall types and thicknesses.

N.B.: Prior to conversion into a three-dimensional image, wall heights should be declared. These can be entered or changed at any point during the planning phase.

Once designated, the levels of a multistory building design can be selectively turned on or off. In other words, this "leveling" facility can slice horizontally through a design to focus exclusively on an isolated floor, or selected groups of floors.

An Introduction to Computer-Generated Perspectives

All the different elements of a building design, such as walls, windows, furniture, dimensions, etc., exist in computer memory on different and definable layers. The layering option allows the designer to switch these layers on or off, permitting isolated layers or combinations of layers to be displayed either in plan or in three dimensions. For instance, here we illustrate a layered view that focuses exclusively on the structural components of a developing design.

N.B.: Meanwhile, the status of walls, i.e., width, height, etc., can on command, be changed at any time, and windows and doors can be moved, rotated, or handed.

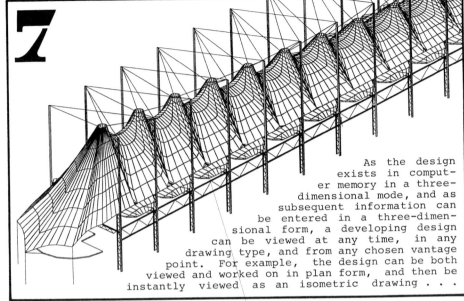

7

As the design exists in computer memory in a three-dimensional mode, and as subsequent information can be entered in a three-dimensional form, a developing design can be viewed at any time, in any drawing type, and from any chosen vantage point. For example, the design can be both viewed and worked on in plan form, and then be instantly viewed as an isometric drawing . . .

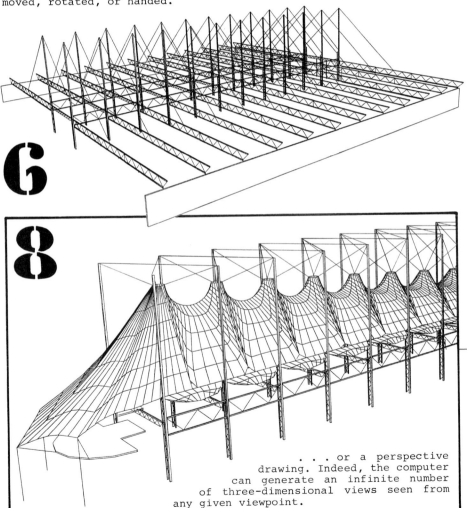

6

8

. . . or a perspective drawing. Indeed, the computer can generate an infinite number of three-dimensional views seen from any given viewpoint.

9

PERSPECTIVE

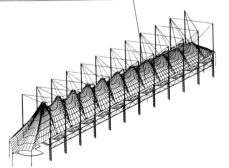

A further facility enables two or more three-dimensional views to appear simultaneously on the monitor. This feature allows the impact of any modifications made to one drawing to be seen instantaneously on the others.

ISOMETRIC

An Introduction to Computer-Generated Perspectives

10

Whichever view has been selected for a printed perspective, the image will first exist as a "wireframe" drawing, i.e., with the outlines of planes and objects in the background being visible through the outlines of planes and objects in the foreground.

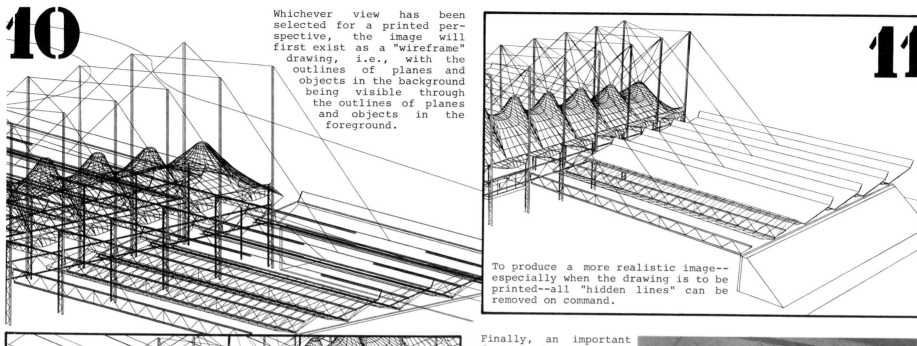

11

To produce a more realistic image--especially when the drawing is to be printed--all "hidden lines" can be removed on command.

12

When the design is ready for the printout stage, a wide variety of choice becomes available. For instance, apart from removing hidden lines, establishing the printout scale to fit the size of print paper, and allocating line weight, a whole range of specialized drawing types can also be produced from the information that has been entered. For example, by removing various layers, structural diagrams can be printed, and by using different edit commands, cutaway views of the design can be achieved, etc., etc.

Finally, an important feature of, particularly, the AutoCAD system, is the ability to shade a three-dimensional object or a building design. Called "Autoshade," and based on a filmmaking analogy, this feature results from specifying point or directed light sources in three-dimensional space, specifying a target point and viewpoint from one of several cameras (that represent a choice of different views), and defining a scene which may include as many lights as you wish.

13

N.B.: Only three-dimensional planes can be color-rendered, i.e., not individual lines. Colors are dictated by the hue assigned to the different layers, quality of image on the screen, and the quality of printout and the print paper used.

An Introduction to Computer-Generated Perspectives

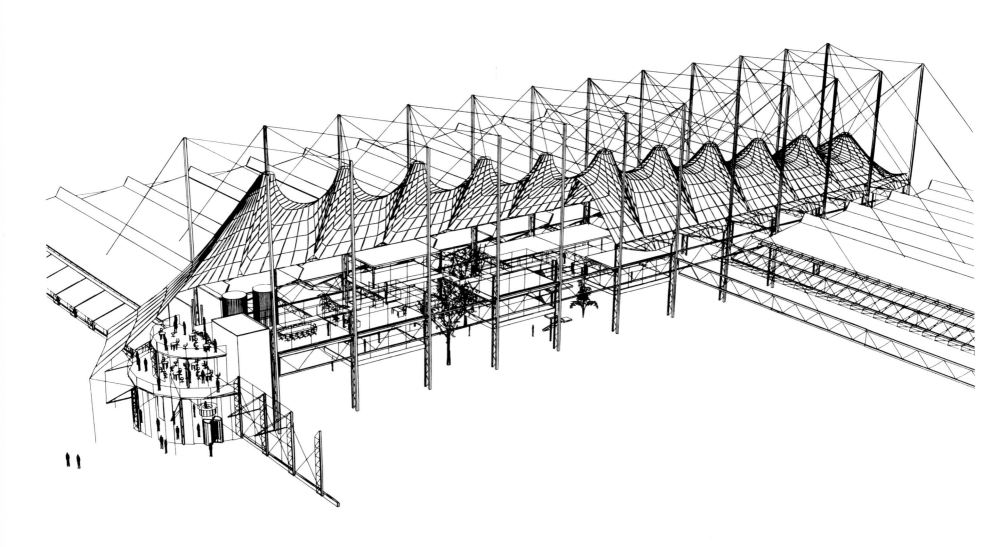

This cutaway perspective of an industrial tile factory is part of the first-prize winning submission for the British Gas Energy Awards competition by fifth-year students David Downing, Iain Bramhill, and D. Mark Grayson. The drawing was generated on an IBM 386 PC using AutoCAD Release 10 with AutoCAD Release 2.

6 PHOTO-TECHNIQUES

An Introduction to the Camera as a Design Tool

1 The camera is a primary design aid. It is essential to the analytical recording of environment, as a support to drawing techniques, the documenting of completed projects, and--in conjunction with a slide projector--the transforming, rescaling, and presenting of pictures from artwork and models. The most practical camera for all these design functions is the single-lens reflex, as it allows a virtually identical viewfinder preview of the ultimate image.

The single-lens reflex camera is also ideal for all kinds of daytime studio and fieldwork without the need for auxiliary lighting. When buying new or secondhand, make sure that the camera body will accept interchangeable lenses.

A recommended general-purpose lens for most outdoor and indoor design photography is an f/2.8, 50mm Macro lens. Additional recommended lenses are 28mm wide-angle lens for interiors, eye-level views, models, and photography in tight spaces; 135mm telephoto lens for the long-distance avoidance of warped perspectives on details and large elevations.

a

b

2 The creative use of the camera can begin on the site of a potential building design where, in preparation for later composite perspectives combining drawings and photographs, representative shots are taken from vantage points around the area to be occupied by the design (a). Also, shots of surrounding views can be taken from inside the predicted area to be occupied by the building design (b). These shots provide useful pictorial material for introducing into composite interior perspectives (see page 156).

An Introduction to the Camera as a Design Tool

3 A comprehensive site appraisal can also be systematically documented with the camera. First, photograph the long-distance implications of the site from vantage points such as tall buildings or hillsides (c). Next shoot all access routes and visual links--sneak glimpses, views, etc.--from around the immediate site periphery looking in (d).

4 Conversely, the on-site shots should record spatial links from inside out: routes and shuttered, filtered, framed, sneak, and panoramic views into surrounding space.

c

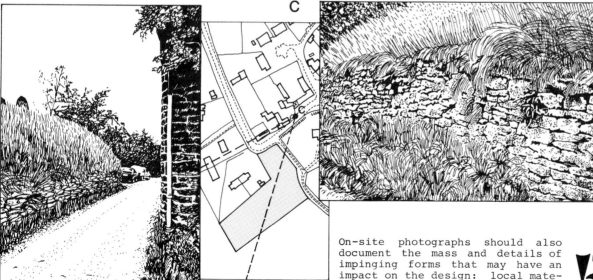

On-site photographs should also document the mass and details of impinging forms that may have an impact on the design: local materials, openings, architectural features, textures, colors, etc.

5

d

6 At the later presentation stage, such photographs, especially when accompanied by annotated sketches that analytically describe your impressions of the recorded quality of the site, become valuable design tools.

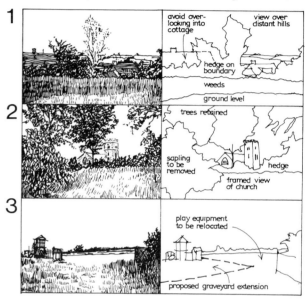

1 — avoid over-looking into cottage; view over distant hills; hedge on boundary; weeds; ground level

2 — trees retained; sapling to be removed; hedge; framed view of church

3 — play equipment to be relocated; proposed graveyard extension

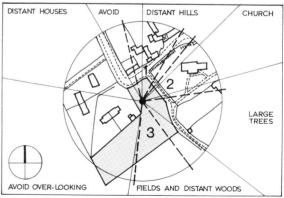

DISTANT HOUSES · AVOID · DISTANT HILLS · CHURCH · LARGE TREES · AVOID OVER-LOOKING · FIELDS AND DISTANT WOODS

N.B.: Photographs should be coordinated with a key site plan showing both the position of each shot and the direction of view. This annotation aids orientation during both the design and communication stages.

147

How to Make "Joiner" Photographs

A version of the photographic technique much used by architects has been elevated into an art form by the artist David Hockney. Known as "joiner" photography, this technique uses a montage of multiview prints to record events that occur over time and also outside a single and fixed field of view.

1

This technique uses the camera to simulate head and eye movements to produce more comprehensive images that, albeit distorted, come much closer to the way we actually perceive visually the world around us. The technique begins the moment we take a series of photographs to record the broader implications of a scene, such as this first-year architecture student's panoramic montage of shots to show the context for his design of a freestanding Oxford tourist information unit.

2

Therefore, the technique abandons the single glimpse represented by the conventional perspective view in favor of a whole series of different angles of viewpoint. In other words, in mirroring eye movement, the camera is used to "paint in" the complexity of the view. The resultant prints are then assembled loosely to reconstruct the multiview image before being glued into their respective positions.

3

4

This is a "joiner" photograph produced by first-year architecture student Andrew Murphie.

148

How to Develop Analytical Photo-Sketch Techniques

1 Using a gridded-up photograph as a guide, several freehand drawing techniques can be developed for use in presenting analytical aspects of, for example, a site appraisal.

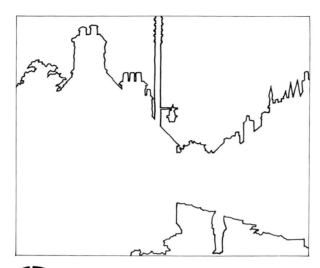

2 In this drawing, only the massing has been isolated through a selective delineation of skyline and base line.

3 Another analytical drawing method is the translation of the tonal range in the photograph into a system of four tones--plus the white of the paper--in the drawing.

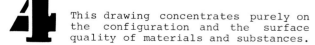

4 This drawing concentrates purely on the configuration and the surface quality of materials and substances.

5 This is a drawing of space; a delineated study of the shape of sections of space between objects--rather than outlines of form.

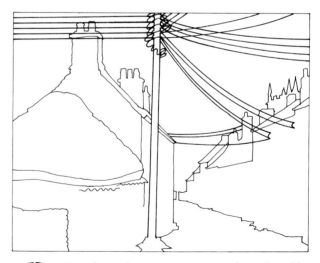

6 Drawing is a means of visually analyzing and recording aspects of our visual experience; each drawing should, therefore, make a specific point and communicate it clearly.

149

How to Develop a Photo-Realist Rendering Technique

Working from photographs as drawing sources can prove beneficial to beginners. The following technique introduces another version of analytical drawing which can be useful in design drawing.

1 After selecting the source material, superimpose its image with a grid. A duplicate grid should then be drawn to the required scale in light graphite on the drawing board.

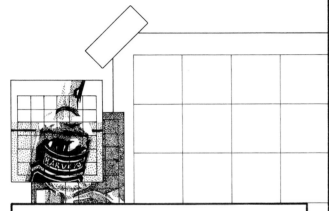

Different grades of graphite and drawing pressures will achieve the required range of values when rendering in pencil. Make sure, however, that a structured application of graphite carefully establishes the character (i.e., the hardness or softness) of the edge of each shape. **4**

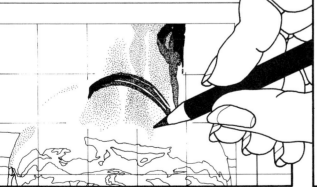

2 A close inspection of any photograph will reveal its formation as a pattern of subtle, obvious, and complicated abstract shapes. In monochromatic photographs, these shapes are defined by changing values, whereas in color photographs the shapes are determined by changes in hue. The secret of producing convincing photo-realist artwork is to recognize these shapes and transfer them meticulously and accurately in line to the artwork, regardless of their apparent insignificance.

This stage, then, involves the transfer in pencil line of the precise outline of each value- or color-shape, into its appropriate rescaled linear "container" on the artwork grid.

N.B.: Avoid outlining obvious forms, as is done in conventional line drawings. A useful way to encourage concentration on the abstract pattern of shapes is to have both the source image and the artwork in an upside-down position as you work with them.

3 After completion, each shape can now be filled with its corresponding value or color. As the linear network of transferred shapes simultaneously embraces all visual cues in the original image, an even, flat application of medium should be attempted.

More diffuse edges of darker values can be achieved by a controlled rubbing of the graphite with the finger or a wad of cotton wool. An alternative method of structuring "out-of-focus" zones is to use a series of ascending tonal bands. **5**

How to Develop a Photo-Realist Rendering Technique

When working in color, use an opaque paint such as gouache as the medium. In this case, each color-shape seen in the source image is in turn translated into carefully matched mixtures of pigment. Each color mix is then applied to the artwork in a layer thick enough to obliterate both the guideline pencil drawing and the paper support.

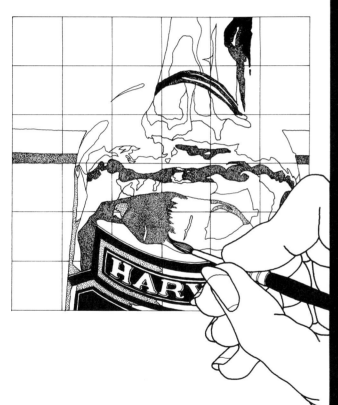

This study of reflections in glass and ice was entirely produced from magazine ads and painted in precise patches of gouache over a meticulous pencil line drawing. It is interesting to note that this first-year student's painting's reappearance as a photographic print transforms it back into its original mode of representation.

How to Trace Perspectives from Photographic Prints

Photographs are useful as sources for perspective drawings, especially when presenting "before" and "after" impressions of modifications to an existing architecture. First find the horizon line (eye level) by aligning a ruler against the edge of all receding planes, such as window-sills, that appear as horizontal in the photograph and mark this in the margin to either side of the print.

Now tape the print to the drawing board and overlay this with a taped sheet of tracing paper.

1

Next slip a sheet of white paper between the tracing and the print. Using the perspective coordinates established from the photograph, project the outlines of the addition using proportional cues, such as the size of doors and the modules of building materials, to establish its scale in relation to the existing form. The addition can now be detailed in the manner used for recording the existing building.

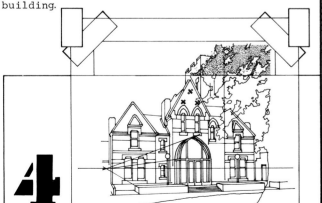

4

2 Using a pencil, extend the horizon line across the overlay and, with reference to the existing building, project the main lines of convergence to find the vanishing points. If the vanishing points occur off the overlay, simply mark these onto a strip of masking tape fixed into position on the board.

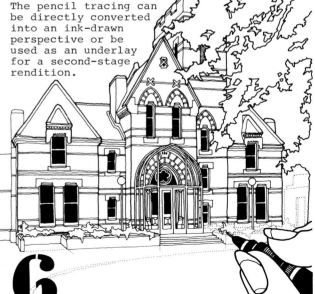

5 Remove the paper underlay and complete the drawing by inserting any detail of the existing building that may be seen through the new addition.

Trace the main outlines of the existing building, leaving the approximate area that will be occupied by the architectural addition. All areas of the existing building that will appear in the final drawing can be confidently detailed at this stage.

3

The pencil tracing can be directly converted into an ink-drawn perspective or be used as an underlay for a second-stage rendition.

6

How to Make a Do-It-Yourself Slide-Copy Table

A simple and efficient demountable slide-copy table can be quickly assembled from 2 x 1" (50 x 25mm) timber, 1/4" (6mm) square beading, a 26 x 26" (700 x 700mm) sheet of thick glass, a 30 x 36" (750 x 900mm) sheet of 1/2" (12mm) plywood, and a 2 x 3' (600 x 900mm) bathroom mirror. First, make a timber frame that will support the sheet of glass. Form a rebate around the inside edge with the beading. This is glued and pinned into position so that, when inserted, the glass sheet is level with the upper face of the frame.

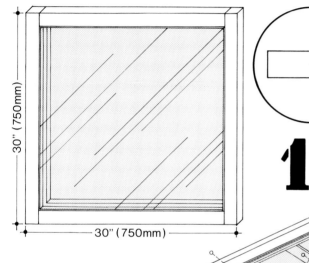

Next, construct two 30 x 30" (750 x 750mm) side frames and brace each with two diagonal struts, predrilled at their centerpoints. Glue and pin the struts into position.

Then mount the mirror centrally on the sheet of plywood. Drill two holes on each side of the plywood sheet, spaced the same distance apart as the holes drilled in the struts.

N.B.: An alternative version of the framed mirror is constructed in the same manner as the glass frame explained in Frame 1.

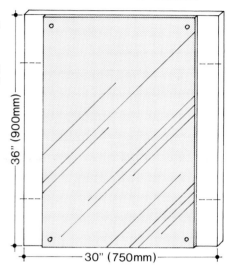

After drilling two holes on either side of the top bar of the side frames and matching holes in the corresponding faces of the frame containing the glass sheet, the unit can be assembled as shown--with the mirror plane resting at 45 degrees.

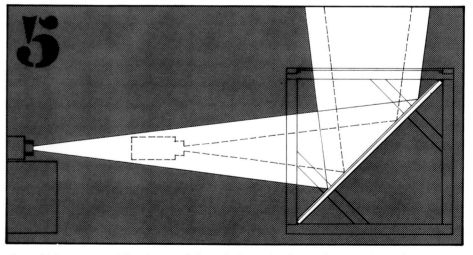

The slide-copy table is used by aiming the beam from a loaded projector horizontally at the mirror--its deflected image being reprojected up and onto the horizontal glass plane. Using tracing paper or acetate, the deflected image can be traced--the size of the drawing being regulated by the distance of the projector from the mirror.

How to Trace Panoramic Perspectives from Slides

1

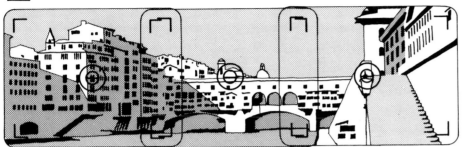

The easiest shortcut to producing perspective drawings of existing spaces is via the tracing of projected photographic prints or slides onto a "screen" of drawing paper.

A development of this technique is the panoramic perspective derived from two or more projected sections. For this technique the original photographs should be taken with care, each shot in the sequence allowing some overlap so that, at the drawing stage, the second and third projected slide can readily be connected to the drawn sections.

2 After pinning the drawing paper to the wall, the first slide is inserted into the projector and its projected image adjusted so that it corresponds to its allocated size and location on the drawing paper "screen."

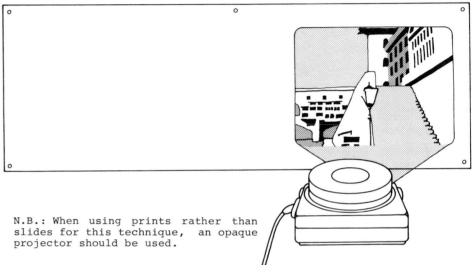

N.B.: When using prints rather than slides for this technique, an opaque projector should be used.

3 The drawing is then built up section by section by tracing each projected image in turn. Between each drawing the position of the projector is adjusted so that each subsequent slide in the panoramic series is locked onto the end of the corresponding drawn section.

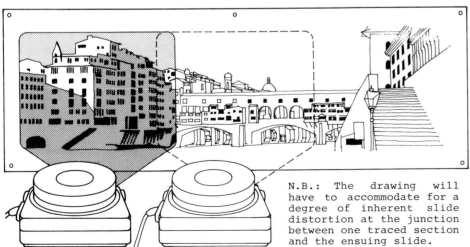

N.B.: The drawing will have to accommodate for a degree of inherent slide distortion at the junction between one traced section and the ensuing slide.

4

Discrimination of the traced line in the beam of the projected slide image can often prove difficult during the drawing stage. However, a good tip is to periodically intercept that part of the beamed image being drawn by placing the hand forward of the drawing paper. This action "removes" the projected image and allows a direct check on the progress of the drawing.

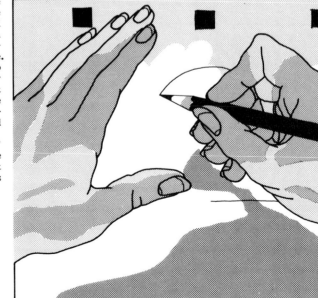

How to Trace Panoramic Perspectives from Slides

5 When drawing in the beam from projected slides, two basic approaches can be made. One approach is to simply produce a trace-drawing that selectively delineates the main outlines of space and form. Such drawings can be worked in pencil, fiber-tipped pen, or technical pen, and are useful when communicating site analyses.

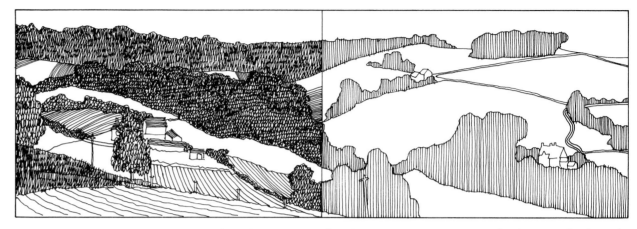

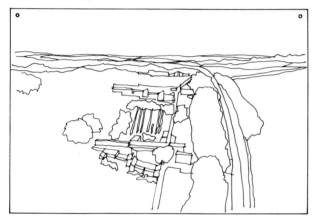

A tonal version can also be extracted. However, a more convincing rendering is achieved when the areas of value are structured into an open system of directional tone (see pages 10-11) so that visual contact with the projected image is maintained. **6** It is always wise to translate the projected image into the kind of drawing dictated by its ultimate purpose in communication. This drawing represents two interpretations of the same image. The section on the right is as equally effective as its counterpart, but its selectivity of detail corresponds to a drastic reduction in the amount of time spent in drawing.

7

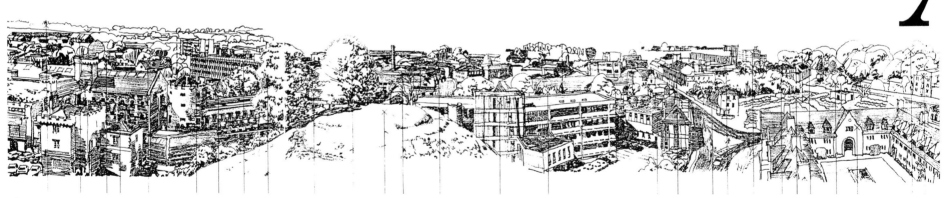

This perspective pencil drawing was produced using the slide projector method. Its author, John Cadell, a first-year architecture student, "assembled" the drawing from right to left using three source slides. Its roofscape detail was traced meticulously using a combination of silhouette line and simple hatching to translate each successive slide into drawn areas of form and value. Hand-written notes were then added above and below the drawing to develop the issues of a project that studied urban use along a stretch of the River Thames at Oxford. Although this example of the technique was produced on two sheets of A2 size paper (approximately half imperial), there is no limit to the size of a projected image. For example, wall painters often project slides of mural designs onto the sides of large buildings as a means of transferring and rescaling accurately their outlines before painting.

How to Produce Rapid Interior Perspectives

A quick and easy method of producing a perspective image that conveys the relationship between inside and outside space is to incorporate on-site photographs with either simple outline drawings or found photographic images. This is a technique much used by architects and it relies upon shooting views from site vantage points to simulate an outlook as it would be seen from within the proposed building (see page 146).

For example, this collage was quickly produced by fifth-year student Sarah Kearns. The collage began with a color print of the main site prospect taken from an adjacent existing building to simulate the vista from the upper level of her design for a tower coffee shop for Oxford's High Street. The sensation of being "inside" is given by the addition of found magazine photographs of plants applied to simulate indoor planting and to frame the view through the window.

An extension of this technique is the addition of a line drawing. This method begins with a one-point perspective constructed in outline and with a vanishing point that coincides approximately with any major glazed connection to outside space.

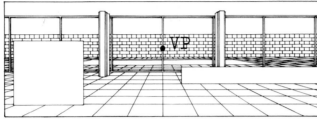

This can then be ink-drawn before cropping the appropriate site photograph to fit the shape of the view as defined by the windows.

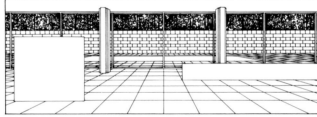

When the photographs are glued or heat-sealed into position, the result is a convincing image. Its effect is extended by the insertion of selected surface finishes and the addition of trace-cut figures found in photographs.

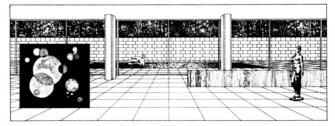

There are many uses for this technique, such as in interior wall elevations or, indeed, any drawing that relates layers of architectural space with an existing setting.

A variation on this technique is to slide a site photograph under a perspective drawn on tracing paper and to trace off the image in the style of the drawing. This may be used to show an existing view from part of a proposed building (a) or the effect of a proposed design on the view from an existing building (b).

How to Produce Perspectives Using Found Images

Composite perspectives can be quickly constructed from the assembly of found images and drawings. For example, this well-known graphic--adapted from the work of Aldo Rossi--fuses a line and hatched perspective drawing with a backcloth created from an engraving of trees and rock formations. The result is convincing--the mechanical hatching of shade and shadows on the architectural form being completely in sympathy with the texture of engraved foliage. To complete the spatial illusion, Rossi has also introduced starkly drawn shadows, cast from the stilted forms, to trace the contours of the foreground plane.

The insertion of found photographic elements into the foregrounds, middlegrounds, and backgrounds of perspective drawings is a fast and efficient means of assembling convincing graphics. Occasionally, this technique of image-building demands that a number of the found graphic components be resized in order to achieve their scaled fusion with the parent image. Resizing can be done instantly on a photocopier--the same reprographic process also being used to transform the completed original into the final fusion of a second-stage photocopied print.

This combination of an engraving with a line drawing is adapted from the work of Leon Krier. It makes an interesting comparison with Rossi's because, here, an engraving is used to provide a dramatic foreground space as a contextual setting for a building design. However, there is a further development in this composite image that is worth noting. A greater fusion of the two elements has been encouraged by the insertion of a group of drawn figures clad in modern dress who now occupy the street space with their engraved and period-costumed counterparts. Also, in the background zone, and behind the message area, further contextual buildings have been included that echo--both in design and drawing technique--those in the engraved foreground.

Composite Photographs from Models and Slides

1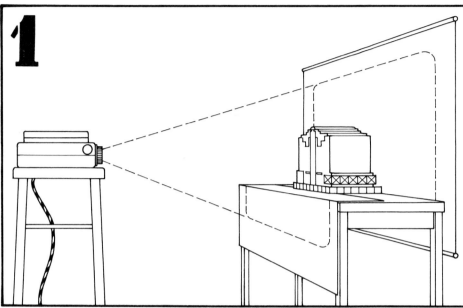

The photographed combination of a model against its intended setting represented by a projected 35mm slide of the site can produce an exciting perspective preview of a building design both for its designer and for the client. The setup is basic. First place the model on a table in front of a large projection screen, or a backdrop of white paper, or a white painted wall. Then tape a sheet of folded white paper to the top of the table so that its large side drapes over the front facing the projector.

2 Insert the site slide into the projector and beam its image at the model, backdrop, and foreground white paper screen. Maneuver both projector and model until the scale and positioning of the model and the beamed image are synchronized.

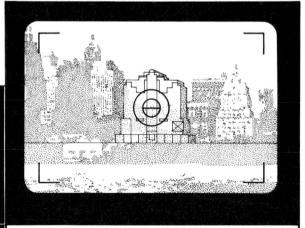

3 The combined model-slide image can now be photographed in a darkened room using a camera with a Macro lens and fitted to a tripod for a long exposure.

4 Here are two prints made from 35mm color slides using the technique described here. The three-dimensional quality of the model appears to survive being "washed" by the front-projected slide image and, in the lower example, "foreground" information seems separated from "background" information. This layered effect results from the positioning of the two screens--one picking up the projection forward of the model and the other picking up the image behind the model. The slides were taken by Sonny Ching, a sixth-year architecture student, using a 1:200 scale model of his design for a Computer Research and Development Center sited hypothetically in Hong Kong.

How to Produce Drawing-Photograph Composites

1

The following version of a composite perspective is based on a student's combination of a single print of a site photograph used as the recipient for a drawing of a proposed design.

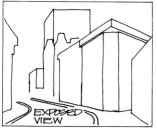 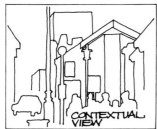

The site photograph need not show a totally exposed view, but can exist as a convincing glimpse of the proposed building seen within a framed or partially screened context.

4

If it is planned not to produce a second-stage photograph from the artwork, the next phase is all-important. The quality and degree of rendering should be guided exclusively by a constant reference to the visual character of the site print. For example, a sharp and strongly contrasting image will dictate a similar graphic for the design, possibly employing a crisp pen technique. Conversely, a more diffuse or grainy print might suggest soft graphite or a wash rendering.

2

Photograph the site and develop as large a print as possible of the selected view.

N.B.: Several photographic agencies offer a cheap super-enlargement to poster size from prints. Although not of high quality, such prints are ideal for this form of graphic.

5

By taking advantage of the available possibilities for a greater fusion between the appearance of the drawing and the parent site print (correct angle of light, shadows cast by objects in the print onto planes in the drawing, nearer forms in the print overlapping the drawing's edge, etc.), a greater degree of realism will be achieved.

Next, place tracing paper over the print and, in response to its perspective, sketch the basic form of the building design. When satisfied as to its appropriateness, transfer it via tracing onto the drawing board.

N.B.: Perspective coordinates for proposed buildings are easily found by projecting lines back from rectilinear forms in the site photograph to their vanishing points.

3

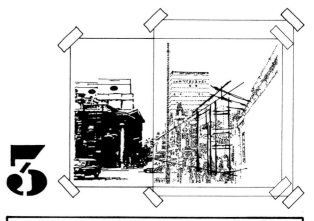

6

Finally, cut out the drawing and spray mount it onto its print support or insert it, using the photomontage method described on pages 162-63.

Photoperspectives: Drawing-Photograph Combinations

A further stage in the combination of drawings with other graphic material is represented by this image, which integrates a delineated perspective drawing of a proposed building design with a montage of photographic prints of the site.

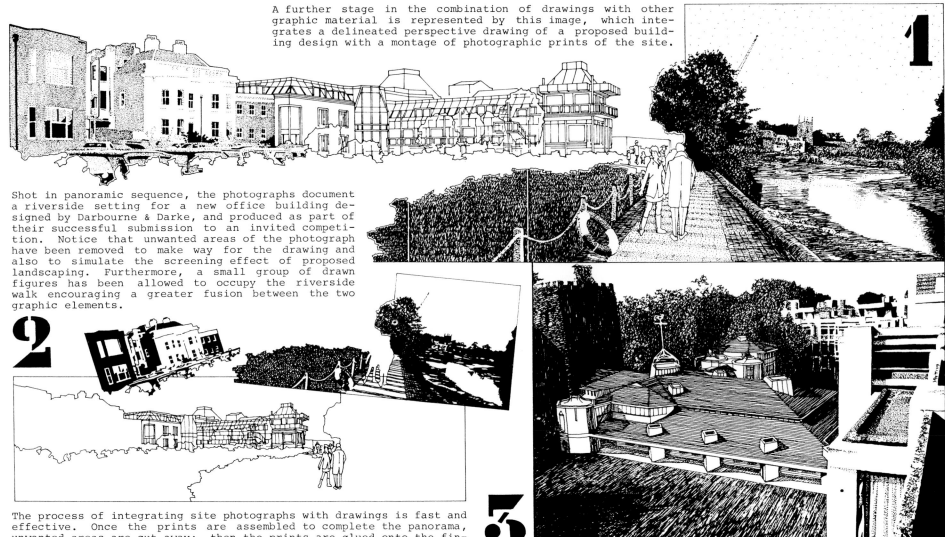

Shot in panoramic sequence, the photographs document a riverside setting for a new office building designed by Darbourne & Darke, and produced as part of their successful submission to an invited competition. Notice that unwanted areas of the photograph have been removed to make way for the drawing and also to simulate the screening effect of proposed landscaping. Furthermore, a small group of drawn figures has been allowed to occupy the riverside walk encouraging a greater fusion between the two graphic elements.

The process of integrating site photographs with drawings is fast and effective. Once the prints are assembled to complete the panorama, unwanted areas are cut away; then the prints are glued onto the finished line drawing. An alternative method is to first glue-assemble the prints intact to receive a direct application of the shaped and drawn elements. Perspective coordinates that guide the line drawing are established from the photographs by tracing the lines of convergence and locating the vanishing points (see page 119). The line drawing is then worked on a tracing paper overlay and, once visually integrated with the photographic elements, is finally transferred into a composite form via photocopying or photography.

In simulating the tonal quality, light direction, and textural grain of its parent site photograph, the drawing technique of this building design attempts a closer visual match with the print of its intended setting. The quest for higher levels of reality in this instance stems, possibly, from the fact that its designers, Saunders Boston, propose a new college facility in the historic and highly sensitive campus at Cambridge University, England.

Photoperspectives: Drawing-Photograph Combinations

If the montage of drawing and print is to be transformed into the overall fusion of a second-stage photograph, more license can be taken with the drawing. For example, even a basic line drawing will appear convincing in the final print.

4

5 When dealing with more complex buildings, a large drawing of their design can be photographed for reduction into a print and subsequent introduction to the site photograph via the photomontage technique described on pages 162-63.

Two photoperspectives by Paul Chemetov.

This direct combination of a pencil drawing and a photographic print was produced by Gary Jemmett, a fifth-year architecture student, to assess the impact of his design for a picture gallery and restaurant on a site adjacent to the National Gallery in Trafalgar Square, London.

How to Produce a Photomontage

An excellent method of communicating a highly realistic impression of a building design in context with its proposed location is to introduce a photograph of a model to a photograph of the site.

1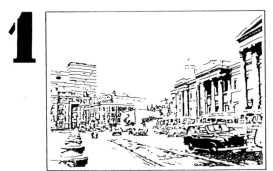

Depending upon what the image is intended to convey, and after reviewing all possible vantage points, take a photograph of the site, allowing plenty of foreground detail.

N.B.: The print should not be smaller than 10 x 8" (250 x 200mm).

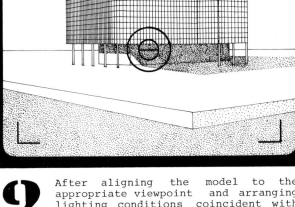

2 After aligning the model to the appropriate viewpoint and arranging lighting conditions coincident with that of the site print, photograph the model.

3 Next, place a sheet of tracing paper over the developed site print and make a sketch outlining the predicted shape of the building's proportions in relation to the proportions of its setting.

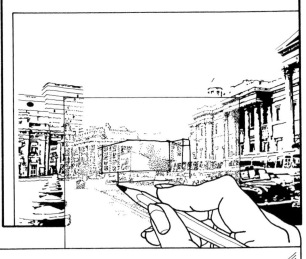

4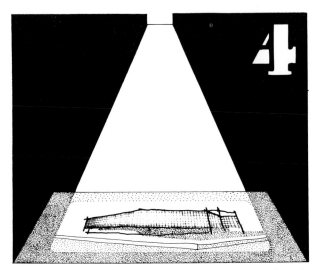

When placed on the enlarger easel, the sketch acts as a template against which the projected size of the model on the negative is determined before exposure.

Using a sharp scalpel, trace-cut the photograph of the model from its print. Leave an area below the building image, which will later act as a tab when gluing the photo into the site print. **5**

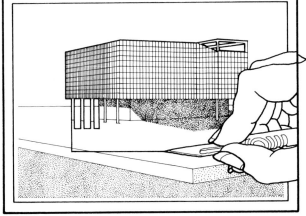

6 Finally, trace-cut the baseline and any vertical forms that will surround and overlap the image of the building on the site print. Insert the model image and carefully glue the tab to the back of the site print together with any other overlapping edges.

162

How to Produce a Second-Stage Photomontage

Here is an investigation via photomontage of the impact of a building design on a site adjoining Trafalgar Square. Produced from site and model prints by John Stewart, a fifth-year architecture student, each original montage was rephotographed to achieve the fusion of a second-stage print. These were then used as presentation graphics in a design competition.

N.B.: A useful tip to improve the impression of the photomontage illusion is to lightly sand the back edges of overlapping areas on both model and site prints with fine-grade glasspaper prior to gluing. The resultant reduction of the print paper's thickness helps to increase the visual integration of the two images.

How to Use a Modelscope: Triple Exposures

Achieving a photograph of an architectural model that will give an impression of how the project will ultimately appear to an observer standing in its precincts can present a number of problems. For example, the camera is usually too bulky to be accommodated within the confines of the model, its focal axis being difficult to position at the scale of simulated eye level. Also, normal lenses do not provide an adequate depth of field in such short-focus situations.

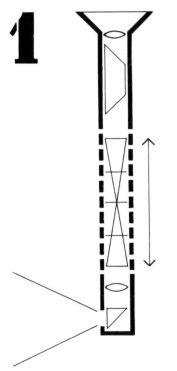

1

eyepiece

erecting prism

multiple lens system varying with length and diameter of instrument

wide-angle object lens

right-angled prism

SCHEMATIC ARRANGEMENT OF A MODELSCOPE OPTICAL SYSTEM

These problems can be overcome by attaching a modelscope, or periscope, to the camera. However, modelscope photography can also introduce its own difficulties. These include poor light transmission combined with picture distortion and a falling-off in sharpness toward the edge of the circular pictures. The following tips and techniques therefore are offered as a means of achieving the best possible results.

2 When purchasing a modelscope instrument for photographic use, evidence of its capabilities should always be obtained in the form of test pictures. Here is such a test picture. The numbers represent distances in centimeters from the viewing point.

4 It is important to note that the angle of field, that is, the amount of information viewed, covered in a picture is determined by the optical characteristics of the modelscope. Alternative lenses in the camera will only spread or diminish the size of image produced on the film. Although modelscope manufacturers often provide long-focus (telephoto) lenses to achieve greater coverage of the normal picture format, this is achieved only at the expense of image brightness, necessitating excessively long exposure times. Modelscopes, however, provide a very simple means of achieving wide-angle coverage. Richard Abbott has devised an interesting technique comprising three or more overlapping exposures that can be trimmed into a rectangular image. Although originally designed for his Execuscope instrument, the technique is applicable to other types of modelscope.

Modelscopes coupled directly to the front of a camera will normally project onto the film a circular image with a diameter equal to one-fifth the focal length of the camera lens. Thus, a 35mm camera with a standard 50mm lens will give a .4 inch (10mm) diameter image. If fine-grain photographic materials are used, the basic image will enlarge comfortably by ten diameters.

3

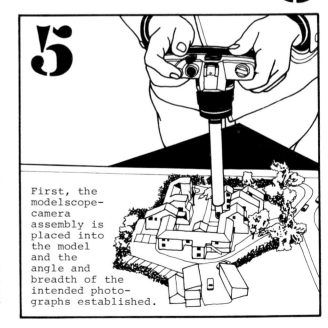

5 First, the modelscope-camera assembly is placed into the model and the angle and breadth of the intended photographs established.

How to Use a Modelscope: Triple Exposures

A cardboard platform graduated in 25-degree intervals is next placed into the model at the point at which the modelscope head will be positioned for shooting. Each gradation in turn will control the precise angle of each shot in the sequence.

N.B.: The gradations are positioned behind the modelscope head, each angle being aligned to a mark on the back of the modelscope head before each shot.

6

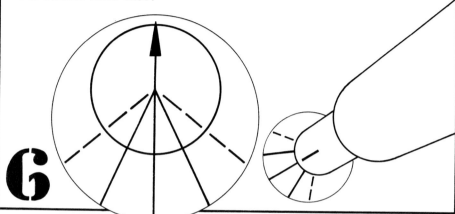

Now, take the first shot and rotate the modelscope 25 degrees after each exposure. If the camera is tripod mounted, movement between exposures can usually be made by rotating the modelscope in its mounting, without disturbing the camera. If the camera is hand held, a check on the vertical alignment of the modelscope before each shot can be made with a small spirit level placed on the back of the camera.

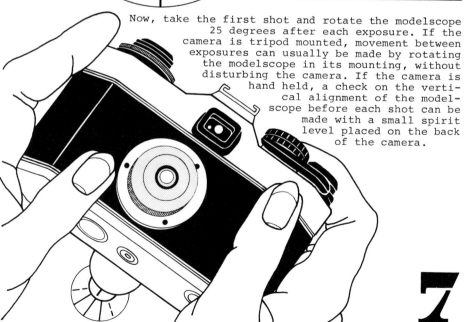

7

8 Provided that lighting levels, camera settings, and film processing remain constant, little difficulty will be experienced in matching the three individual prints that, allowing for overlap, will provide a field of view of approximately 90 degrees. The three exposures also provide a "wide screen" impression of a far greater reality than do single exposures and can give a composite processed picture of up to 12.6 x 9.8 inches (320 x 250mm).

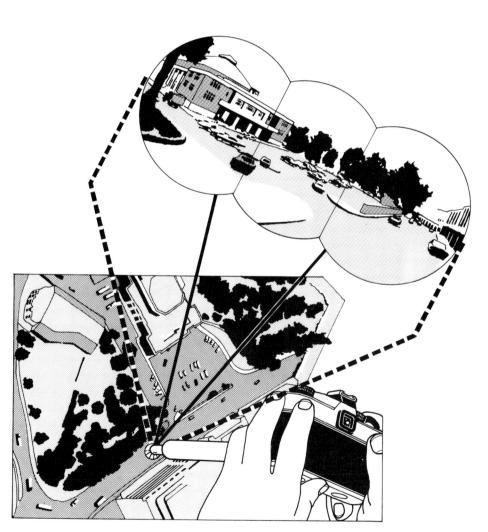

165

Modelscope Triple Exposures

Both of these triple-exposure photographs were achieved in the following manner. The three circular modelscope pictures were first trimmed carefully to achieve an accurate joining into a composite panorama, then dry-mounted in position on a paper backing sheet. The skyline profile was then trace-cut with a sharp knife to remove the background behind the model.

Next, a photographic print of a natural backdrop, that is, of a sky or treescape (taken especially for this role), was inserted above and behind the skyline. The montage of four prints was finally cropped into the rectangular format, in readiness for reshooting as a second-stage print.

1 These are two examples of the triple-exposure technique described on pages 164-65. The photographs, taken by Richard Abbott of a 1:100 scale model (top) and a 1:200 scale model (bottom), illustrate how his technique can be used on both large and small projects.

N.B.: When required, a fourth exposure can be made to extend the width of the field of view.

7 LETTERING TECHNIQUES

An Introduction to Lettering

1

Rather than invent a debased form of lettering for design drawings, it is better to base freehand letter forms on the integrity of a recognized source. Also, when selecting lettering, excessively modish styles should be avoided. Instead, choose typefaces that will communicate clearly without imposing their own design or style statements. Timeless examples include Helvetica Medium, Microgramma Medium Extended, Roman, Clarendon, and the box stencil letterforms popularized by Eileen Gray and Le Corbusier.

Plan Elevation Se

Perspective Axono

Plan Elevation Sec

Perspective Axono

PLAN ELEVATION SE

PERSPECTIVE AXON

PLAN ELEVATION S

PERSPECTIVE AXON

PLAN ELEVATION S

PERSPECTIVE AXON

A good and economical way of collecting alphabets is to photocopy sheets or catalogues of dry-transfer lettering. These can then be enlarged or reduced on a photocopier before being used as tracing guides for lettering titles in drawings on transparent materials.

N.B.: When working on opaque materials, letter forms can be trace-transferred using carbon paper or by rubbing graphite over the back of each character. Larger lettering can be projected into position for tracing using an episcope.

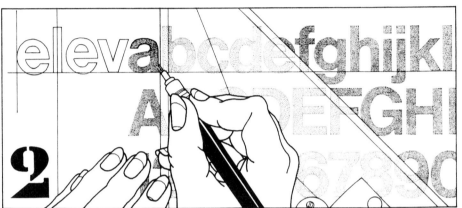

2

Lettering can, by itself, become a powerfully descriptive graphic element. The double function of lettering as both printed word and pictorial image can result from selecting letter forms sympathetic to the message, and the relationships of their spacing in word formation. A good way of approaching lettering in design is to consider it in this dual role of symbol and of form. In this manner, letter forms become building blocks in the structuring of drawings and of overall presentation layouts.

Two forms of letter spacing are in common use: mechanical and optical ("eyeballed"). Optical spacing involves the arrangement of letters by eye, a positive-negative exercise creating visually unified elements. Mechanical spacing refers to sheets of instant lettering and some stencils that incorporate registration marks that regulate the distance between letters.

60pt GARAMOND *instant letteri*

1

Conversely, when letters that include large areas of space as part of their construction come together, such as two T's, the other letters in the word should be spatially eased in compensation.

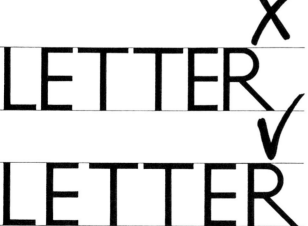

2 However, as the eye reads the gaps between letters as space and not as distance, it is essential that a word, in order to appear as a unit, embodies balanced areas of space between its letters. This is impossible to achieve when letters are equally spaced.

MINIMUM ✗

MINIMUM ✓

Spacing problems lurk where certain letter forms are brought together; for example, when closely related sequences of upright strokes occur. In such events more space should be allowed, to retain an even pattern.

3 Beware of the potential spatial "hiccup" that can occur when vertical letter forms are followed by oblique or rounded letters.

4 ATTAR

LILY

N.B.: When such letters as TA and LY come together in a tight formation, they can be allowed to spatially overlap slightly.

5 odvepnlry

1 1 -1 2 2 3 3 0

Uptown

3 0 0 -1   1

Broadway

2 0 1 2 1   -1 -1

These are examples of a spacing system devised for New York's Metropolitan Transit Authority. They illustrate a "mechanical" spacing method that takes into account the various spacing requirements of different types of letter form when juxtaposed in words. The top line illustrates units of spacing required by letters when those of similar and dissimilar character become neighbors. The second and third lines exemplify this spacing system applied to typical words used in subway signs.

How to Use Lettering in Design Drawings

1

When combined with drawings, lettering should be integrated carefully as a design component into display layouts. As we have mentioned, the selection of simple and efficient letter forms used in a consistent fashion will aid clarity in communication, with degrees of importance in their message being achieved by variations in size, boldness, color, and location in the layout.

An efficient method of annotating drawings is to stack written information into two blocks, either above and below or to either side of the drawn image. Labels can then be clearly keyed in to their graphic counterparts without making the drawing confusing.

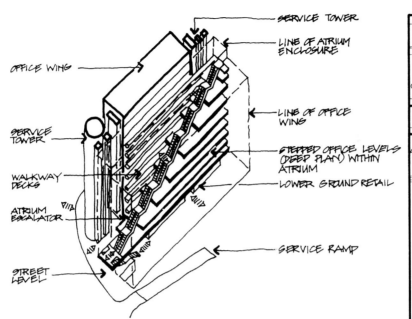

SERVICE TOWER
LINE OF ATRIUM ENCLOSURE
OFFICE WING
LINE OF OFFICE WING
SERVICE TOWER
STEPPED OFFICE LEVELS (DEEP PLAN) WITHIN ATRIUM
WALKWAY DECKS
LOWER GROUND RETAIL
ATRIUM ESCALATOR
SERVICE RAMP
STREET LEVEL

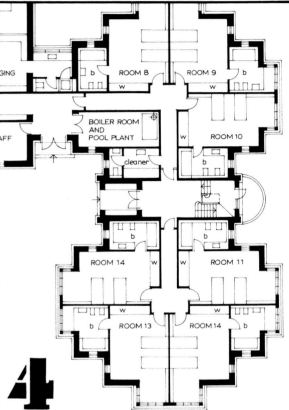

ROOM 8   ROOM 9
GING   b   b
BOILER ROOM AND POOL PLANT   ROOM 10
AFF
cleaner   b
ROOM 14   w   w   ROOM 11
ROOM 13   ROOM 14
b   w   w   b

2

① BOILER ⑤ PORCH ⑨ DRYING
② SHELVES ⑥ FOOD CBD ⑩ WARDROBE
③ MICROWAVE ⑦ SINK ⑪ BED
④ FRIDGE ⑧ WASHING ⑫ STORAGE

Another method is the annotation of drawings with numbers. These refer the viewer to a legend which, within the overall sheet layout, is located clearly in relation to the drawing.

When annotating directly an element of a drawing, aim to create compact blocks of information. Also, when labeling areas, as in plans, choose a lettering size that sits comfortably inside the space. For instance, when lettering irregular shapes, position labels at their visual centers or in a position that remains consistent throughout the drawing.

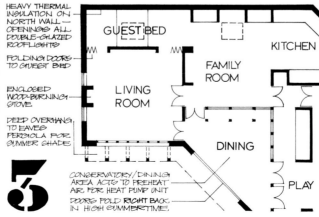

HEAVY THERMAL INSULATION ON NORTH WALL — OPENINGS ALL DOUBLE-GLAZED ROOFLIGHTS

FOLDING DOORS TO GUEST BED

ENCLOSED WOOD-BURNING STOVE

DEEP OVERHANG TO EAVES PERGOLA FOR SUMMER SHADE

3

CONSERVATORY/DINING AREA ACTS TO PREHEAT AIR FOR HEAT PUMP UNIT

DOORS FOLD RIGHT BACK IN HIGH SUMMERTIME

GUEST BED   KITCHEN
FAMILY ROOM
LIVING ROOM
DINING
PLAY

4

Complicated drawings will require that lettering be organized both inside and outside the drawn image. They also benefit from a hierarchy of letter sizes, each layer of written information functioning in different ways and being read at different distances from the drawing. In such drawings, main titles should be read in conjunction with the whole sheet. Subtitles (type of drawing, name, scale, etc.) should be legible without interference with the drawing; labels (functions of various spatial zones, etc.) should be clearly perceived as part of their drawn zones; and captions (references, details, construction information, etc.) should be clearly related or keyed in with their drawn counterparts.

How to Use Lettering in Design Drawings

5 When approached as a design component, lettering can perform several functions in an architectural presentation. For example, titles can act as visual "plinths" or . . .

BLETCHINGDON PARK
WEST ELEVATION
1:200

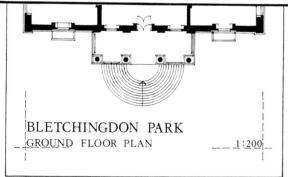

BLETCHINGDON PARK
GROUND FLOOR PLAN   1:200

7 Furthermore, a good method of juxtaposing titles with drawings is to design the titles so that their blocks either begin or end in direct relationship to the main edge of the drawing. This use of lettering to "frame," or visually restrain, is simple to use and works well on layouts comprising different drawings.

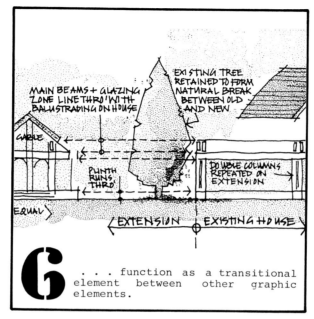

6 . . . function as a transitional element between other graphic elements.

Lettering should also find its own scale in layouts without appearing either too mean or assuming an over-sized proportion that might distract from the attendant drawing. One way to select size is simply to see how a particular letter form reads when viewed from the predicted distance between drawing and viewer.

8

plan actual size

plan seen from 6´ (1.8M)

plan seen from 20´ (6M)

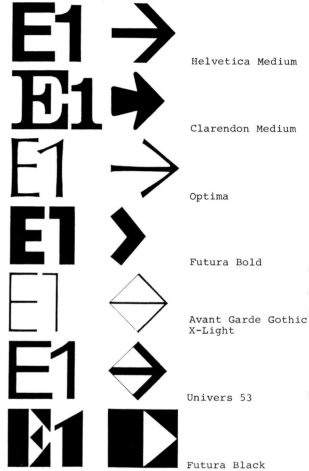

Helvetica Medium

Clarendon Medium

Optima

Futura Bold

Avant Garde Gothic X-Light

Univers 53

Futura Black

9 Continuity between lettering and other graphic elements, such as the northpoint, is a stylistic issue raised by Professor Sarah Recken of Washington University. She proposes that, since well-designed alphabets are hallmarked by a recognizable consistency of form, boldness, and style, the selected letterform for headings and titles, etc., should dictate the design of the arrow. She illustrates this quest for graphic consistency in the examples shown here.

An Introduction to Freehand Pen Lettering

1

Very often, hand lettering is used to annotate, identify, and clarify information that is carried in a design drawing. It is also used because it is sometimes faster, more convenient, and more economical than drawing by mechanical means, such as instant lettering and stencils. However, when hand-lettered information is badly formed, it can appear the weakest element in a design presentation, with its malformation distracting the viewer from the message it conveys.

As the central function of lettering is that of communicating information quickly, it is crucial that the designer develop a legible style. For example, in architectural design, production drawings usually include written notes that communicate directly with those who will construct the building. In this context, hand lettering will be hampered by clever or overstylized treatments. Therefore, the simpler and clearer the formation of letters and words, the more legible the means of communication.

Although the following alphabet is based on the use of a lettering pen, it is a good idea for the beginner to approach hand lettering as an extension of normal handwriting. Initially, a pencil, fountain pen, or technical pen can be used in the practice of basic letter formation. Once a degree of control has been established, the lettering pen technique should then be attempted.

ABCDEFGHIJKLMNOPQRS
TUVWXYZ 1234567890
abcdefghijklmnopqrstuvwxyz

N.B.: Don't worry too much about early mistakes. Practice sessions aiming at the achievement of individually proportioned letters should progress to speed tests in which letters are drawn with the minimum number of strokes.

2

The following alphabet results from the use of a lettering pen such as a Graphos, and a chisel- or square-cut nib.

First, remove any protective lacquer from a new nib by immersing it briefly in boiling water. Pens not fitted with an integrated ink-feeding system are loaded by drawing an ink-loaded brush over their upturned reservoir.

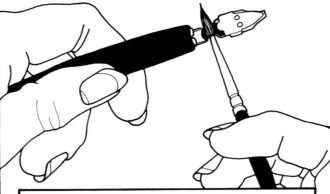

3

Throughout the drawing action, the pen should be held in a relaxed manner and at a constant angle of 45 degrees to the line of lettering, with the entire edge of the nib in contact with the paper.

N.B.: Avoid working on textured paper, as this can both inhibit spontaneity and clog the nib.

4

An oblique-cut nib is available for left-handed calligraphers. However, in both left- and right-handed drawing positions, a comfortable drawing hand position should be found, with the unused fingers curled to act as a rest on the paper.

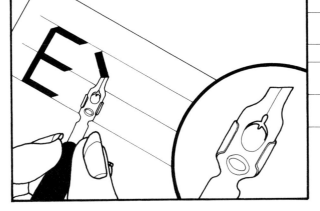

5

As an aid to accuracy, beginners should use lightly penciled guidelines. These should be of a height equal to seven or eight times the thickness of the lettering nib in use.

EXHIBI

A further aid is preliminary plotting of proportions using penciled dots. However, as the ultimate goal is a spontaneously formed letter, this practice should be abandoned when confidence is gained.

An Introduction to Freehand Pen Lettering

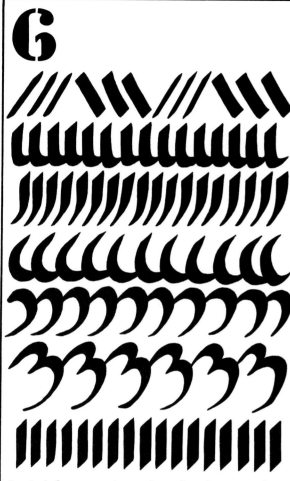

6

A trial exercise in forming various strokes will develop sensitivity toward the mark-making ability of the pen as well as find the best position in which to hold it. Initial experiments in making continuous strokes should be followed by exercises in forming individual strokes that practice the presentation and removal of the nib in a clean, decisive manner.

N.B.: Make deliberate strokes, always drawing toward yourself. Never exert pressure--allow the pen to do the work.

7

Once you have established a degree of familiarity with the pen, attempt the alphabet. Aim for simple, well-formed letters, remembering to draw them by using the slightest of pressure and holding the pen at a constant 45-degree angle. Also, aim to make each letter form distinct, with no chance of its being mistaken for another.

Each of the above capital and lowercase letters is shown with a suggested order and direction of pen-stroke. Some letters can be formed in several ways. After much practice you will be able to form them using fewer strokes.

N.B.: This alphabet can be drawn using a technical pen or a pencil, in which case the drawing instrument should be held in the upright position.

How to Construct a Sans Serif Alphabet

1 The construction of the following alphabet is based on the proportion of the square. It is sans serif, i.e., without serifs, and can be quickly drafted using a T square, set square, and a pair of compasses with pencil or pen. Its main construction is based generally on Roman lettering (see pages 178-93). This accounts for adjustments to its relationship with the square as reductions in the overall width of some of its full letters respond to the existence of serifs in the original. The thickness of the strokes is shown as one-ninth that of the letter height. However, depending on its design application, letter thickness can be reduced for delicacy or made heavier or bolder for added emphasis.

N.B.: When making letters bolder than those shown here, the extra thickness should be added on the inside of the strokes.

2 The letters I, L, F, and E are the simplest forms to construct. Apart from the upright stroke that represents the letter I, each occupies a half square. When constructing letters it is wise always to create the upright first.

N.B.: To avoid a top-heavy appearance on the letters E and F, their central bar should be positioned slightly higher than halfway. Also, the lower bar of the letter E should slightly overreach the upper two bars.

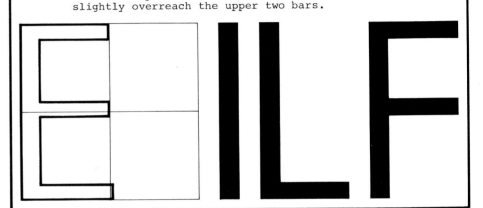

3 The letter T fills the square, its crossbar being reduced to four-fifths the width of the square to avoid top-heaviness.

N.B.: Another optical refinement is a slight reduction of thickness in the crossbar, which can be applied to all horizontal strokes in the alphabet.

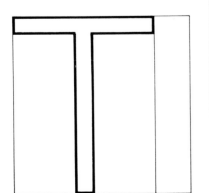

4 The letter H fills the square, its overall width reduced to four-fifths the width of the square. Apart from the slight reduction to its thickness, the crossbar should be positioned slightly higher than halfway to compensate for an optical effect of top-heaviness if the crossbar is drawn centrally.

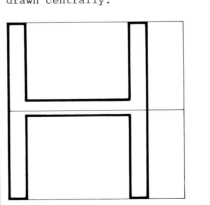

5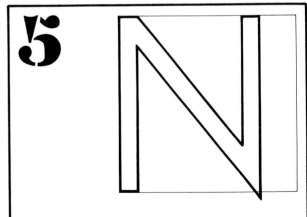

The letter N occupies the same width as the letter H. Notice that the upper intersection of the diagonal is blunted while the lower intersection is pointed--the latter sitting just below the baseline.

174

How to Construct a Sans Serif Alphabet

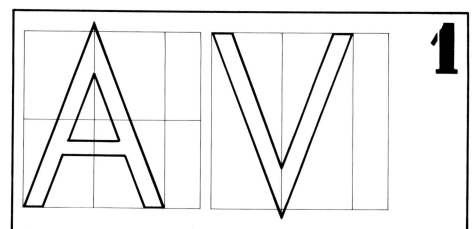

1

The form of the letter A occupies the square reduced to four-fifths the square's width. The crossbar is inserted last and, to avoid weakening this letter form, is set below the halfway line.

The letter V is simply an inverted letter A minus the crossbar. In some alphabets, however, the letter V is sometimes further condensed in width.

In its double role when forming the letter W, the V does become condensed, with the two V's occupying 1 1/4 squares. A proportional adjustment should be made when constructing this letter so that the central, triangular space is made slightly smaller than its outer and inverted counterparts. This optical adjustment is achieved by giving the central triangle a narrower base when constructing the two outer strokes.

N.B.: This letter can be constructed with pointed intersections if required. When they are used, however, the points should sit just above and below the line.

2

3

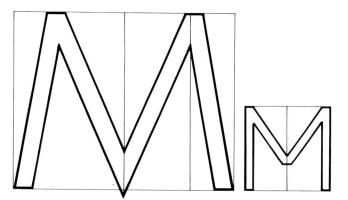

4

The letter M also fills the 1 1/4-square format, reversing that of the letter W but with a different optical adjustment. In this letter the central, inverted triangular space is drawn as slightly larger than its outer counterparts, which have narrower baselines.

N.B.: This letter can also be made to fit the square, but this contraction necessitates the introduction of rather ugly, shortened center strokes to avoid an appearance of being overcrowded.

The upper arm of the letter K extends approximately two-thirds the width of the square. Draw the upright first and then add the upper diagonal stroke so that its left-hand edge penetrates halfway into the upright on the center line. An optical adjustment that makes this form appear more balanced is to allow the lower stroke to overreach the limits of its overhead counterpart slightly.

The letter X occupies the square minus the width of one stroke. Its center of balance can be raised to avoid a squat appearance by slightly reducing the upper triangular space.

How to Construct a Sans Serif Alphabet

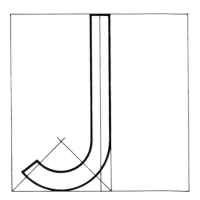

1

The arms of the letter Y extend to within two stroke widths of the full square. Construct the inverted triangle first so that the arms make their connection with the upright just below the halfway line.

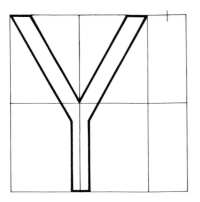 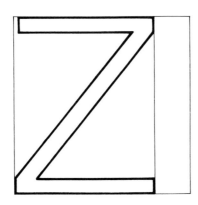

The letter Z extends to four-fifths the width of the square. First construct the diagonal, then add the horizontal bars. Top-heaviness is avoided by slightly shortening the upper bar.

The letter J fills just over half a square. Follow the construction of the loop with that of the upright, the former being drawn from the center of the lower quarter square. **2**

N.B.: Be careful to avoid ugly junctions between curve and upright during construction.

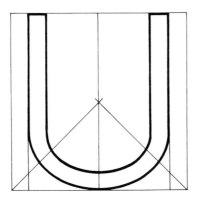

The letter U occupies the square reduced by one-fifth of its width. Once again, it is better to draw the curve first and then add the two upright strokes.

176

3

The letters C, Q, and G are all relatives of the letter O and each occupies the full square. If required, the upper and lower curves of the letters C and G can be softened as shown by the dotted lines. The letter G can be constructed from a variety of extensions, each used as a means of eliminating any confusion with the letter C.

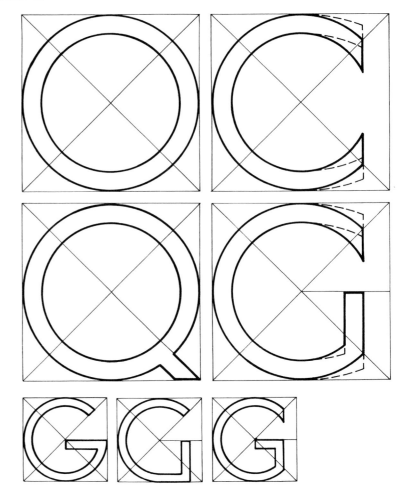

How to Construct a Sans Serif Alphabet

The letter D fills the square minus the width of one stroke. First construct the upright. The center of the square locates the semicircles that, when inscribed, merge the curve into the upper and lower horizontal sections.

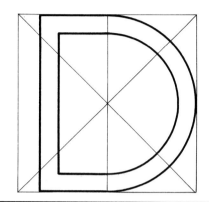

1

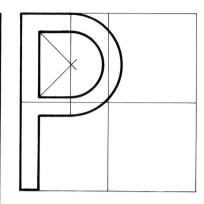 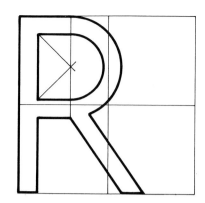

2

The letters P and R have a common loop whose belly extends out just beyond the half square, its lower section connecting back with the upright slightly below the halfway line. The inside edge of the letter R's diagonal leg begins on the loop's underside at a point immediately below the center for the semicircles.

N.B.: The diagonal leg extends out beyond the loop by approximately the thickness of its stroke.

If constructed of two equally sized loops, the letter B can appear unbalanced and top-heavy. In order to compensate for this optical illusion, the upper loop is reduced in size to allow a larger, lower loop that extends out just beyond the limits of the upper loop.

3

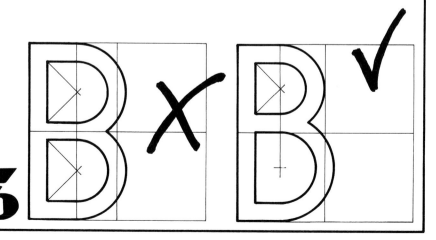

4

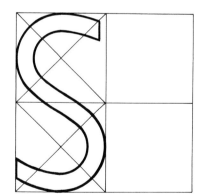 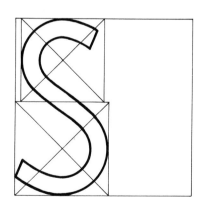

The letter S is formed by two circles occupying a half square. Again, rigid use of these guidelines to form this letter can result in a mechanical appearance not in character with this letter form.

It is better to use the basic construction as a framework on which to build up this letter. In doing so, it should not be necessary to make part of the line straight when changing from one circle to the other. Each end should break away slightly from the circle and follow a graceful line that allows the lower section to be slightly larger than the upper one.

177

How to Construct Roman Lettering

1

Roman lettering provides a most beautiful alphabet whose formation comprises optically adjusted and elegant forms. The following pages explain the construction of the individual letters, their proportions being based on L. C. Evett's classic 1938 interpretation of the Trajan Column. They are presented in order of ease of construction, in four groups: the uprights, the obliques, the curves, and the loops.

The drawing instruments required are a T square, an adjustable set square, and a set of compasses. Guidelines should be drawn lightly with hard graphite, with a softer graphite used for drawing curves. Once constructed, the letters can be brush-painted solid with India ink after outlining them with a technical or ruling pen.

N.B.: Inking mistakes can be retouched with white paint or typewriter correction fluid.

2

Apart from an upper guideline and a baseline, a halfway guideline should be used in the construction of such letters as F, H, Y, and K. However, an optical adjustment is made to the crossbar of the letter A and the middle arm of the letter E. Also, depth-of-loop lines for the letters R, P, and B deviate from the halfway line (see pages 190-92).

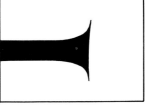
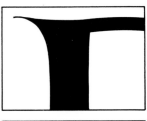

3

Serifs act to finish each stroke and also to help the eye pass along the line. There are several variations, but each should always extend the letter form, that is, appear to grow from the letter so that no hint of junction is evident.

4

Extended flourishes, or tails, occur on the letters Q, R, J, and K. Apart from that on the letter K, these swing below the baseline, with the extra-long version on the Q acting as a visual connection between it and U, its following letter.

The letter I is the easiest Roman letter form to construct. It is represented by a full-width upright stroke, its thickness being one-tenth of the chosen height of the letter size.

N.B.: All other stroke thicknesses are multiples of this width.

5

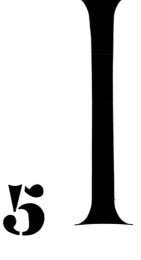

Two important optical effects that modify the appearance of the I and, indeed, all other full-stroke uprights in this alphabet, should be introduced. The first is the entasis, or slight concavity, of its sides, achieved by changing the drawing angle of the pencil against the raised edge of the ruler during construction. The second effect is a slight concavity of the face of each serif as it touches the upper and lower guidelines.

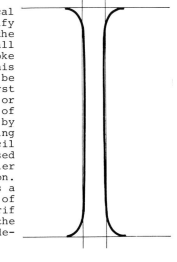

178

How to Construct the Uprights: T, H

The length of the upper crossbar on the letter T is determined by the letter's height less two upright stroke thicknesses. The thickness of the crossbar is just over half that of the upright.

Bisect the crossbar to center the position of the upright.

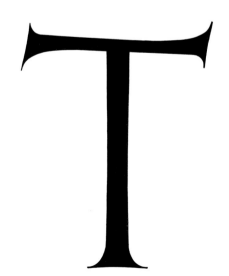

1

Although some designers prefer to draw the crossbar serifs so that they are symmetrical with the upright, a further refinement is to angle them along an 80-degree slope to vertical. Yet another refinement is the subtle elongation of the lower, left-arm serif and the upper, right-arm serif.

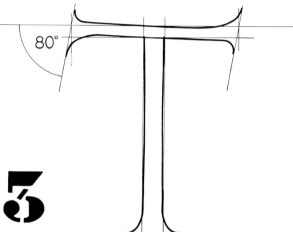

80°

3

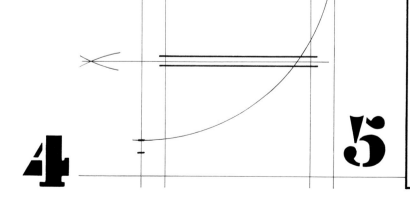

2

Notice that the crossbar is slanted slightly from left to right. This brings movement to the form and helps the eye read this letter in context with others. Having both a shortened and a slanted crossbar also avoids a potential top-heaviness commonly associated with this letter form.

The result is an elegant and dynamic form, and one more easily spaced when forming words, by first locating the crossbar.

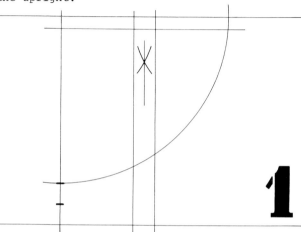

The width of the letter H is determined by the letter's height less the thickness of one and a half upright strokes.

5

6

Essentially, the H is constructed like two letter I's connected by a central crossbar just over one-third the thickness of the upright.

How to Construct the Uprights: L, E, F

To construct the letter L, first establish its full-width upright. One-half its height gives the extent of its arm, the thickness being roughly half that of the upright. This thickness is maintained for all the arms in the letters E and F.

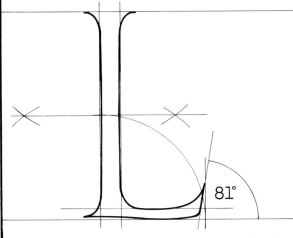

Notice how the base of the upright is raised with a subtle curve along the baseline, and also note the inclination of the serif's face.

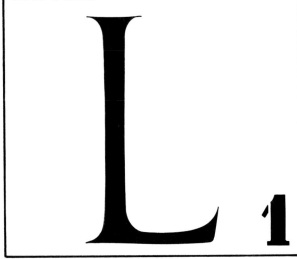

2 The letter E extends the construction of the letter L. Its middle arm is centered on a line bisecting the top guideline and a line formed one-half of a full-width stroke above the baseline. This dimension also gives the length of the base arm, the extent of the top arm being found by measuring back one-half of a full-width stroke.

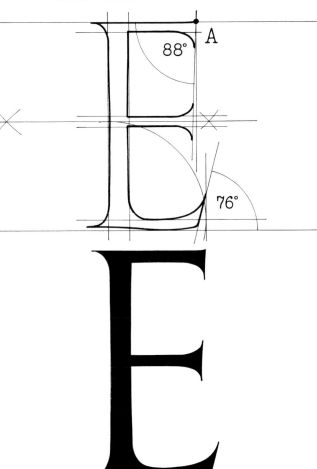

Note that the inclination of the serifs on the upper two arms is described by a line projected from **A** at 88 degrees to the horizontal.

The height of the letter F is bisected to give the center line for its lower arm. Point **B** is found by measuring one-half of a full-stroke's width up from the halfway line. The dimension from this point to the top guideline finds the extent of the upper arm.

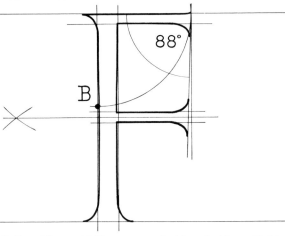

N.B.: The middle arm of the letter E is located higher than its counterpart on the letter F. However, in each case, their extent and the angle of their serifs is found by a line angled at 88 degrees.

How to Construct the Obliques: K, Y

After establishing the full-width upright of the letter K, project its arms from a point on the halfway line. The upper arm is drawn at an angle of 46 degrees to the horizontal, the lower arm at an angle of 44 degrees.

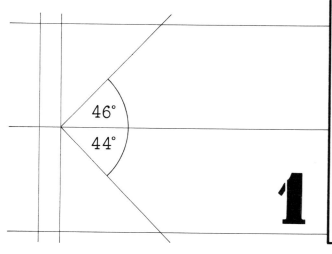

1

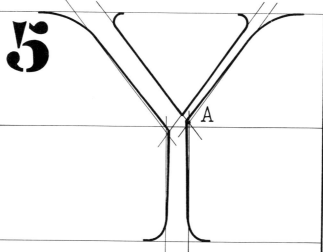

2

The upper arm is one-half the width of the full-stroke lower arm, the latter ending with a flourish similar to that in the letter R.

To construct the letter Y, first establish the outer edge of its left arm. This is described by a line drawn at 52 degrees from a point on the top guideline down to the halfway line.

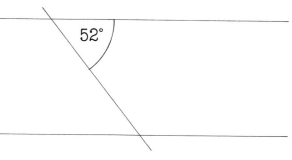

3

From the point of intersection with the halfway line, measure one full stroke's width to the right. From this point the outside edge of the right arm is projected at an angle of 54 degrees. Add lines to describe the inside edges of the left and right arms. The arms are full- and half-stroke width, respectively.

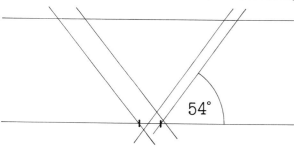

4

5

The upright can now be introduced. Draw a vertical line from A (the intersection of the right-hand sides of both arms) to establish its right-hand edge. Then draw in the left edge of the full-width stroke.

Slight entasis occurs on the upper stem of the upright stroke and the outer side of the lower arms.

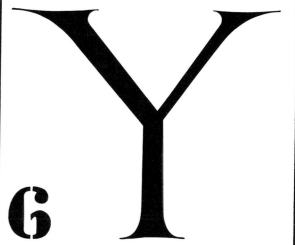

6

How to Construct the Obliques: N, X

The apex of the letter N occurs at a point on a line drawn one-quarter of a wide stroke's width above the upper guideline.

From this point, a diagonal is then drawn at an angle of 46 degrees. One full-stroke width below this, a second diagonal is drawn to connect with a line drawn one-half of a full stroke's width under the baseline. This point of intersection finds the outer edge of the right upright.

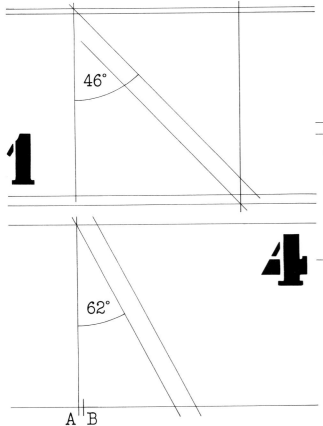

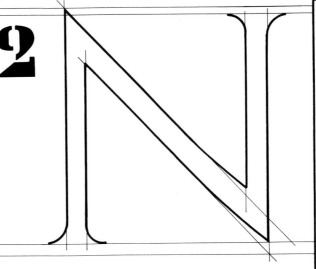

When the diagonal stroke is drawn, a subtle curve is introduced along its length to bring its lower point onto the baseline.

From point **B** on the baseline, project a left-to-right diagonal at an angle of 64 degrees. This describes the left edge of a stroke one-half the full-stroke width.

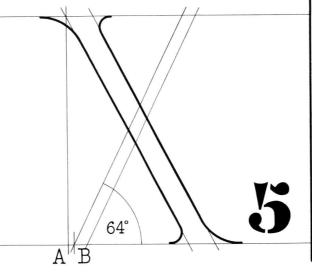

Both the upright strokes are seven-eighths of a wide stroke in thickness.

To construct the letter X, first mark off two points one-quarter of a wide stroke apart on the baseline. From point **A**, project a vertical line to the top guideline. From this point, project a right-to-left diagonal at 62 degrees. This describes the left edge of a full-width stroke.

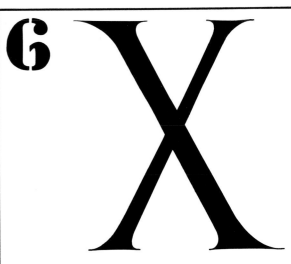

As with other oblique serifs in the Roman alphabet, the outer versions are slightly larger and extended.

182

How to Construct the Obliques: A, V

1

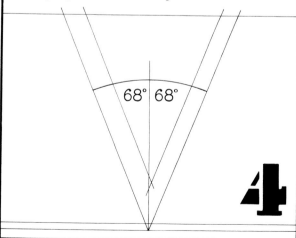

70° 68°

The apex of the letter A is found one-quarter of an upright thickness above the upper guideline. The left-hand stroke is then drawn from this point at 70 degrees and the right-hand stroke at 68 degrees.

The width of the left-hand stroke is three-quarters that of the full width of the right-hand stroke.

The crossbar is located on the halfway line of an "inside leg" measurement from the crotch of the A to the baseline, and is one-half a full-width stroke in thickness.

2

Depending on the method of construction used, there are several optional methods of forming the apex of the letter A.

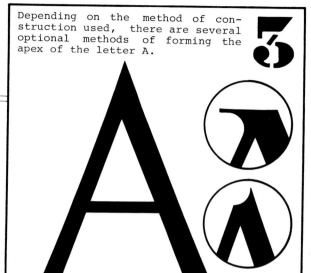

3

The letter V is a slightly wider version of an inverted A. Its point is found one-half of an upright stroke's thickness below the baseline. Each oblique stroke is then projected at 68 degrees.

4

68° 68°

5

The right-hand stroke is three-quarters that of the full-width left-hand stroke. Unlike the A, this letter form is then reduced to normal height by curving each stroke and bringing its point back onto the original baseline.

The subtle bowing effect toward the point of the V prevents this letter from appearing too pinched.

6

How to Construct the Obliques: W, Z

1 The construction of the letter W is, essentially, that of two overlapping V's. First, construct a letter V as described on page 183.

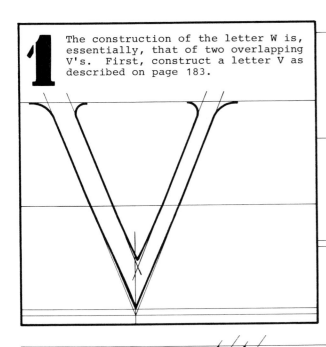

2 Then construct a second letter V so that the left edge of its left arm cuts the right edge of the right arm of the first V on the halfway line.

Notice how the points of the two V's that comprise this letter are bowed to bring them onto the original baseline. **3**

4 The letter Z's oblique is a full-stroke's width and is drawn at an angle of 54 degrees. From the points where each line connects with the upper guideline, measure back one-half a full-stroke's width. Both oblique lines are then curved along their length to meet these new points.

54°

The points where the left side of the oblique stroke meets the baseline and the (now curved) right side of the stroke meets the top line find the extent of the Z's horizontal bars. Both bars are one-half the thickness of a wide stroke.

6

5 80°

62°

Notice how the base of the oblique stroke sits slightly above the baseline and the lower bar rocks gracefully on the baseline. Also, note the subtle tilting of both serif faces, the lower being more acute and subtly elongated at its upper point.

How to Construct the Obliques: M

The left leg of the letter M is three-quarters the thickness of a full-width stroke. It is drawn at an angle of 84 degrees, its left edge climbing to a point one-quarter of the thickness of a wide stroke above the top guideline.

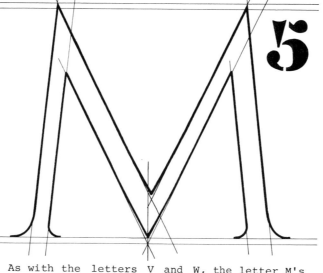

1

The M's second leg descends from the top of the left leg and is drawn at an angle of 64 degrees. This stroke is full width in thickness, its lower edge connecting with a point on a line that is one-quarter of a wide stroke below the baseline.

2

The third leg begins at the point below the baseline and climbs back at an angle of 64 degrees. Its width is three-quarters that of a wide stroke and its left edge connects with a point on the line above the top guideline to form the apex of the fourth leg.

3

4

The fourth leg completes the basic form. At a thickness of a wide stroke, this leg descends at an angle of 84 degrees.

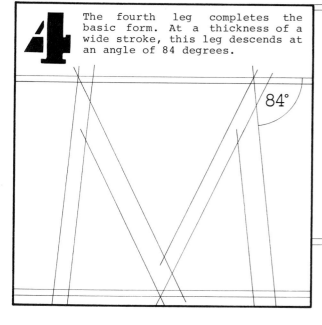

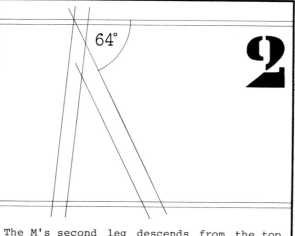

5

As with the letters V and W, the letter M's lower point is curved and brought back onto the original baseline to avoid an acute appearance.

6 Also, as with the letters V and W, a slight entasis occurs along the length of the two inner strokes.

How to Construct the Curves: O

The construction of the letter O begins on a center point on the halfway line around which a full letter-height circle is described.

Through its center, draw an inclined vertical with an angle of 82 degrees. A circle with a radius of one full stroke's width is then described around the center giving points A, B, C, and D.

1

Point A is the center for a circle describing the inside of the upper part of the letter. Its radius is found by measuring three-eighths of a full stroke's width from the upper guideline.

2

Using the same radius, transfer the compass point to point C to describe the inside of the lower part of the letter.

3

Point D acts as the center for an arc that reduces the right-hand side of the letter. Its radius is found by measuring back one-quarter of a full stroke's width from the intersection of the full circle on the halfway line.

4

Using the same radius, transfer the compass point to point B and describe the same arc on the left-hand side of the letter.

5

The thinner parts of the letter O are a little less than one-half a full stroke's width. These should enlarge gradually into the full thickness.

6

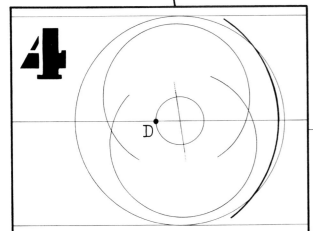
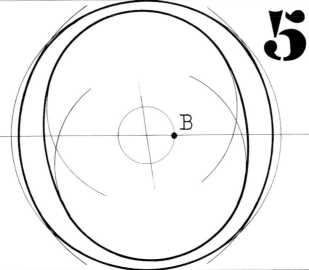
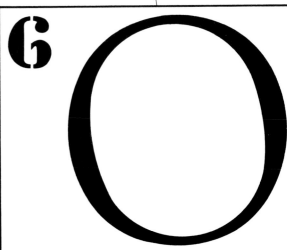
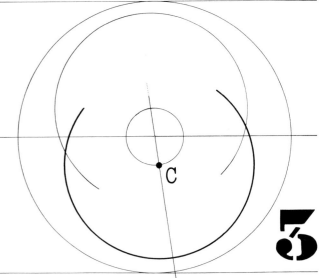

How to Construct the Curves: Q, D

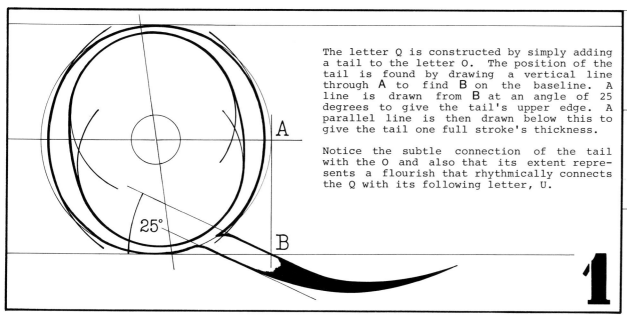

The letter Q is constructed by simply adding a tail to the letter O. The position of the tail is found by drawing a vertical line through A to find B on the baseline. A line is drawn from B at an angle of 25 degrees to give the tail's upper edge. A parallel line is then drawn below this to give the tail one full stroke's thickness.

Notice the subtle connection of the tail with the O and also that its extent represents a flourish that rhythmically connects the Q with its following letter, U.

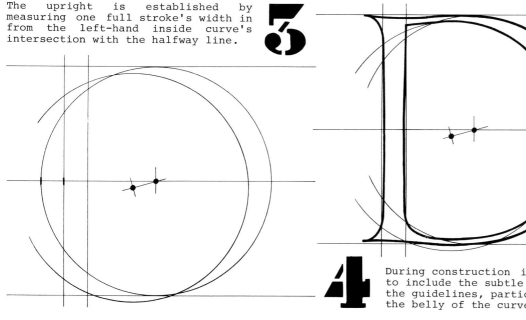

1

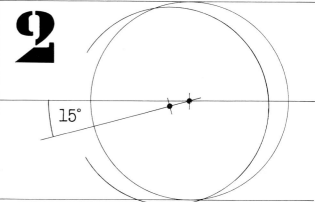

2

To construct the letter D, first establish the center for its outer curve with a point on the halfway line. From this draw a line angled at 15 degrees from the horizontal.

Along this angled line measure one full stroke's width to find the center point for the inner curve.

3

The upright is established by measuring one full stroke's width in from the left-hand inside curve's intersection with the halfway line.

4

During construction it is important to include the subtle deviation from the guidelines, particularly that in the belly of the curves.

5

Another important aspect of the letter D is the slightly raised lower serif, a trait common to the letters B, E, and L.

How to Construct the Curves: C, G

1

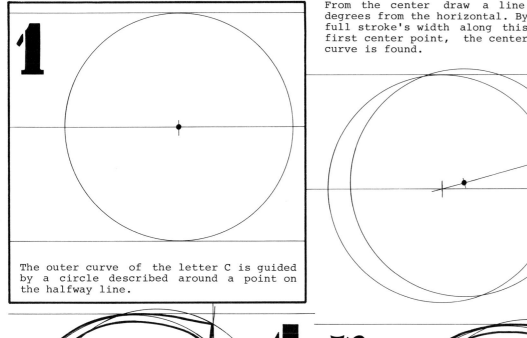

The outer curve of the letter C is guided by a circle described around a point on the halfway line.

From the center draw a line angled at 15 degrees from the horizontal. By measuring one full stroke's width along this line from the first center point, the center for the inner curve is found.

2

3

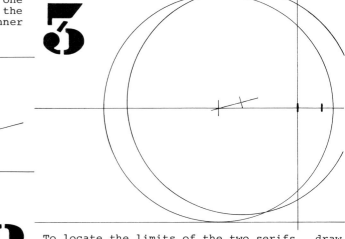

To locate the limits of the two serifs, draw a vertical guideline one and a half full-stroke widths in from the point at which the inner circle intersects the halfway line to the right.

Again, notice that the lower curve thickens and straightens just before it connects with the vertical tail.

N.B.: In both C and G, the main curve reaches its greatest width below the halfway line.

4

5

Make sure that the upper and lower curves straighten and thicken slightly as they merge into the serifs.

N.B.: The face of each serif is angled slightly from the vertical, and the upper arm is heavier than the lower one.

The construction of the letter G is identical with that of the C up until step 3. The difference is the G's vertical tail, which is one full stroke in width. Its outer edge coincides with the vertical guideline.

G

6

How to Construct the Curves and Loops: J, U

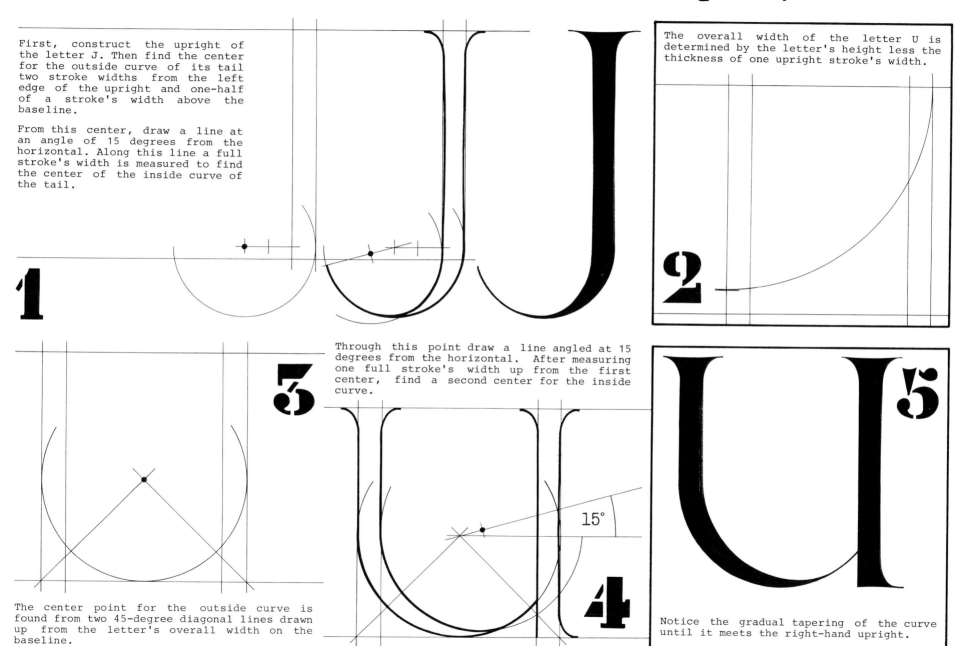

1 First, construct the upright of the letter J. Then find the center for the outside curve of its tail two stroke widths from the left edge of the upright and one-half of a stroke's width above the baseline.

From this center, draw a line at an angle of 15 degrees from the horizontal. Along this line a full stroke's width is measured to find the center of the inside curve of the tail.

2 The overall width of the letter U is determined by the letter's height less the thickness of one upright stroke's width.

3 The center point for the outside curve is found from two 45-degree diagonal lines drawn up from the letter's overall width on the baseline.

4 Through this point draw a line angled at 15 degrees from the horizontal. After measuring one full stroke's width up from the first center, find a second center for the inside curve.

15°

5 Notice the gradual tapering of the curve until it meets the right-hand upright.

How to Construct the Curves and Loops: S, P

Construction of the letter S begins with a vertical line angled at 86 degrees.

One-quarter of a wide stroke is then measured above the halfway line and the distance between this and the upper guideline is bisected to give the center of a circle. Do the same for the distance between the original halfway line and the baseline.

1

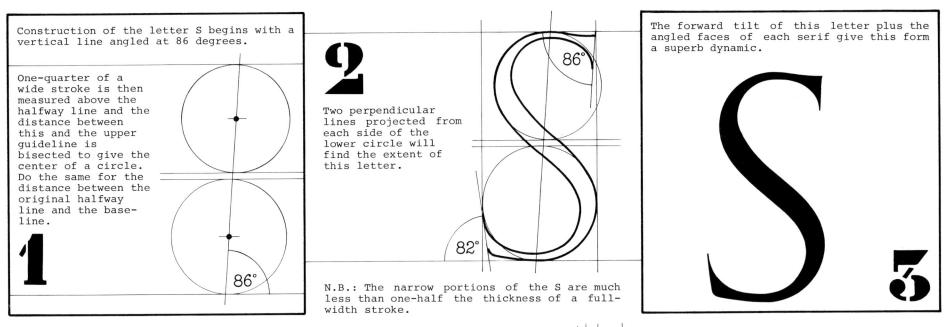

Two perpendicular lines projected from each side of the lower circle will find the extent of this letter.

N.B.: The narrow portions of the S are much less than one-half the thickness of a full-width stroke.

The forward tilt of this letter plus the angled faces of each serif give this form a superb dynamic.

Begin the letter P by establishing its upright stroke. Then draw a line one full stroke's width below and parallel to the baseline. Next find a halfway line between this lower baseline and the top guideline.

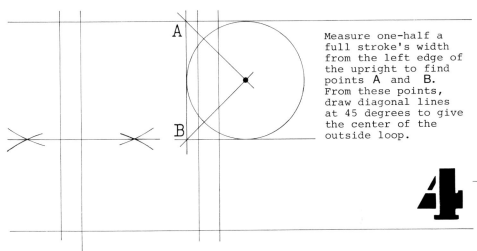

Measure one-half a full stroke's width from the left edge of the upright to find points **A** and **B**. From these points, draw diagonal lines at 45 degrees to give the center of the outside loop.

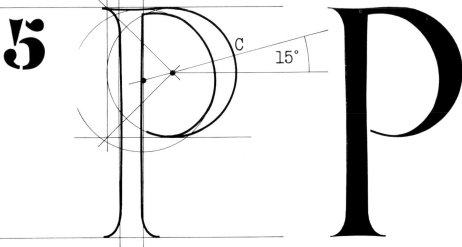

Then draw a line from this center, at 15 degrees to the horizontal. The point where this line cuts the right edge of the upright stroke becomes the center point for the inside loop. The radius for this circle is found by measuring from its center to within one full stroke's width from **C**.

How to Construct the Loops: B

To construct the letter B, first draw a line the distance of one full-width stroke above and parallel to the baseline. Then establish the upright stroke and bisect the distance between the upper baseline and the top guideline.

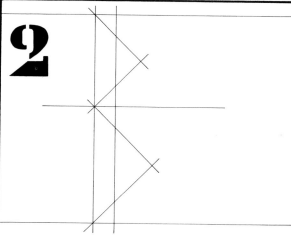

Next, draw diagonal lines at 45 degrees from the points where the left edge of the upright is cut by the top guideline, the "halfway" line, and the lower baseline.

The diagonals locate the center points, from which two circles acting as guidelines for both the outer loops are inscribed.

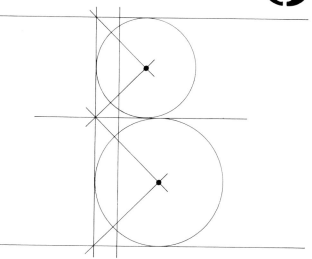

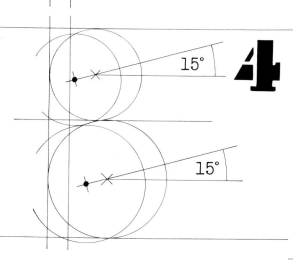

From each center point now draw a line at 15 degrees from the horizontal. Along these mark two further points one full stroke's width to the left of each original center. These give the centers for circles acting as guidelines for both the inner loops.

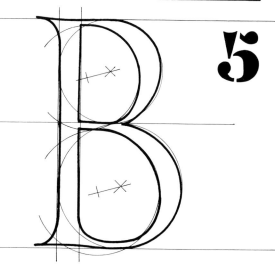

When forming this letter, notice that the horizontal connecting bars have individual qualities that extend the nature of the loops. The thickness of the connections is about a third that of the full stroke's width.

Notice the raised upright base and its gentle curve along the baseline. This feature is common to the letters D, E, and L.

How to Construct the Loops: R

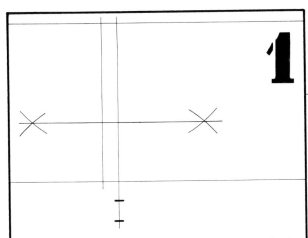

To construct the letter R, first establish its upright stroke. Then measure the distance of two full-stroke widths below the baseline. Bisect this increased vertical dimension to find the depth-of-loop line.

Next, measure one-half of a full stroke's width from the left edge of the upright and draw a perpendicular line to connect at **A** and **B**. From these points, draw two diagonal lines at 45 degrees to find the center of a circle describing the outer edge of the loop.

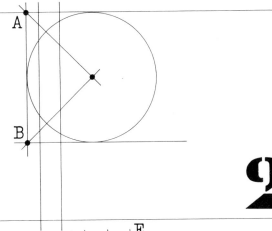

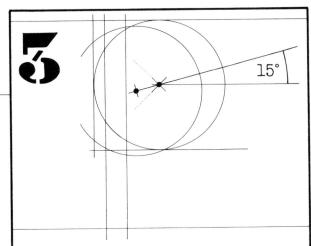

From this center now draw a line at 15 degrees to the horizontal. One full stroke's width along this finds the center for a circle of the same radius that describes the inner edge of the loop.

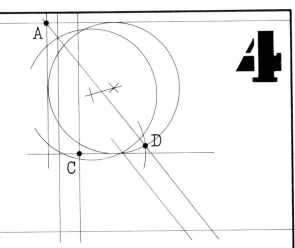

Using this same radius, place the compass point on **C** and mark its length at **D** on the outer edge of the loop. A line drawn from **A** to cut **D** gives the outer edge of the tail.

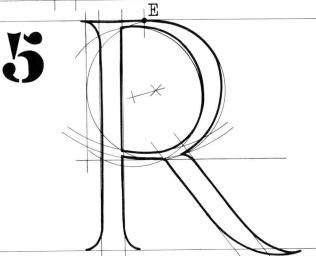

The loop is connected to the upright by marking point **E** one full stroke's width to the right of the inside upright edge on the top guideline. Place the compass point on **E** and connect the lower edge of the loop by touching the depth-of-loop line. Its inner connection is found one-third of a full stroke's width away.

N.B.: There is a subtle curve at the point of connection between tail and loop. The tail is a full stroke's width and its flourish ends below the baseline.

Lowercase Roman and Sans Serif Lettering

This lowercase, or minuscule, alphabet accompanies the Roman capitals described on pages 178–92. Essentially, lowercase characters retain the proportional principles that govern the construction of the capitals. However, the half serifs on the letters b, d, h, and so on are slightly angled from the horizontal. Also, the full-length vertical strokes are usually drawn to a height just above that of the capitals.

N.B.: As opposed to Roman capitals, which enjoy more generous spacing, the lowercase letters are easier to group, because they contain a less varied range of forms. Their mainly rounded shapes, and the spaces they define, appear rather like links in a chain: too compacted and they merge, too loose and the chain breaks.

abcdefghijklmnopqrst
uvwxyz 1234567890

2 abcdefghijklmnopqrst
uvwxyz 1234567890
1234567890

In this lowercase sans serif alphabet, the full-length vertical strokes remain at the same overall height as their capital counterparts. Also, numerals used in sans serif alphabets are usually the same height as capital letters. These examples, however, display both the regular and the more useful nonranging numerals. In both Roman and sans serif styles of nonranging numerals, a lowercase O is used for zero. Also, remember that the tails, or descenders, on lowercase letters (such as the j, p, and q) dictate a wider line spacing than usual in order to avoid collision with the ascenders.

Distorted and Perspective Lettering

Lettering can be enlarged or reduced by simply covering the selected letter or word with a regular grid. The letter or word is then redrawn into an enlarged or reduced grid with the same number of squares as the original grid.

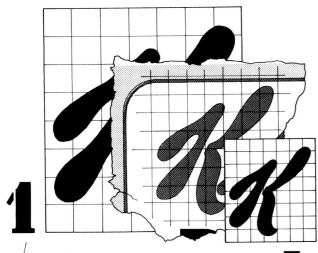

1

2 Also using grids, lettering can be made to distort. First, establish the letter or word, then cover it with a regular grid having its lines numbered for reference.

3 Then freehand a distorted grid, using the same number of lines as its regular version. The letter or word can now be outlined in response to the suggested distortion and, if necessary, traced for its transfer into the recipient design.

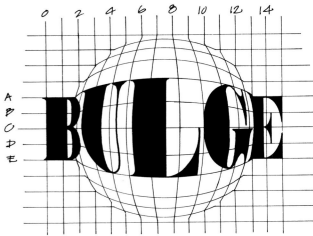

4

Words can also be transformed into perspective settings. A quick method is to project lines from a station point through a horizontal line to a baseline marked off with letter widths and spaces and angled to represent the degree of acuteness.

The horizontal line now becomes the baseline for the lettering in perspective. Horizontal guidelines that determine various heights should be marked on the right and extended to meet the vanishing point on the left.

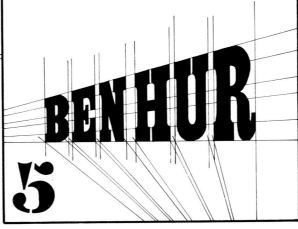

5

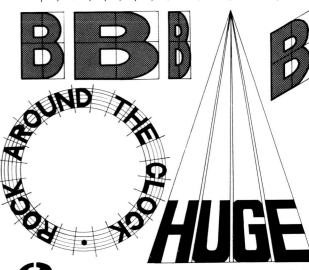

6 Letters and words can be expanded, condensed, foreshortened, curved, and angled into limitless spatial positions.

8 PRESENTATION TECHNIQUES

A "Psychology" of Presentation

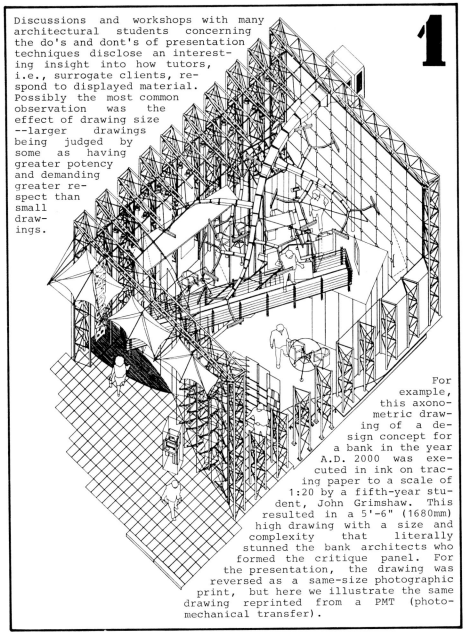

1

Discussions and workshops with many architectural students concerning the do's and dont's of presentation techniques disclose an interesting insight into how tutors, i.e., surrogate clients, respond to displayed material. Possibly the most common observation was the effect of drawing size --larger drawings being judged by some as having greater potency and demanding greater respect than small drawings.

For example, this axonometric drawing of a design concept for a bank in the year A.D. 2000 was executed in ink on tracing paper to a scale of 1:20 by a fifth-year student, John Grimshaw. This resulted in a 5'-6" (1680mm) high drawing with a size and complexity that literally stunned the bank architects who formed the critique panel. For the presentation, the drawing was reversed as a same-size photographic print, but here we illustrate the same drawing reprinted from a PMT (photomechanical transfer).

Paradoxically, the reduction of large, rendered drawings into smaller formats is also seen by some students as improving their prowess--especially when resized using the Cibacopy color process. Diminished size is seen to increase content richness and to diminish any imperfections in the original.

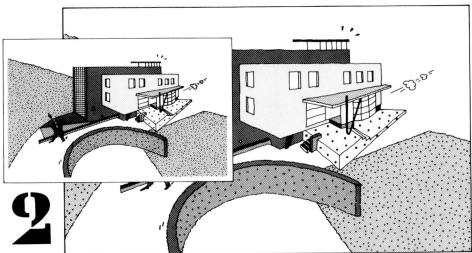

2

Also, drawings worked in ink were felt to portray a greater sense of permanence and credulity compared with drawings worked in graphite--especially when mounted under glass. This favoring of ink over graphite also refers, possibly, to the need to communicate over distance. For example, if a drawing is to be produced at a large scale for presentation to a large panel of viewers, the intensities of line have to be adjusted so that they match the distance over which the drawing is viewed. Failure to increase the boldness of ink line weights and graphite grades over extended viewing distances will, inevitably, cause a breakdown in communication. For instance, this table illustrates a maximum viewing distance for each of the ink line weights and graphite grades shown.

3

Graphite Grades	Ft	M
4H	2	0.6
2H	4	1.3
HB	7	2.0
2H	9	2.7
4H	11	3.4
Technical Pen Nibs	Ft	M
0.18	3	0.9
0.25	4	1.2
0.35	5	1.5
0.5	7	2.0
0.7	8	2.5

A "Psychology" of Presentation

4

Informed students saw boredom and distraction in the critique panel as the main enemies of presentation. However, to have one's design proposal reviewed first in a day of crit's was found by some to be a challenge. This was because the panel was fresh and would spend more time "grilling" the opening student. Meanwhile, to be reviewed first or, especially, second was more beneficial than being seen last, as by the end of a long session panelists had become jaded and less useful to the student.

Students saw their role in a critique as "marketing" their design ideas. Consequently, many thought it wise to introduce their scheme against a set of clearly verbalized or published objectives--as this would tend to head off any prejudice in the panelists. Furthermore, some felt it worthwhile to open their presentation display with conceptual drawings taken from the design process in order to provide insight into their precedents and design route.

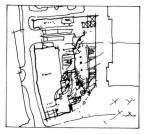
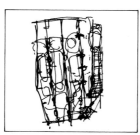

5

It was generally felt that irritating displays were avoided when plan drawings were presented with their north points facing in the same direction. Similarly, uniformity of sheet sizes, drawing scales . . .

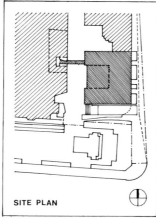

SITE PLAN

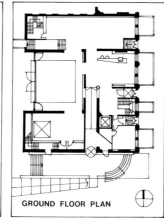

GROUND FLOOR PLAN

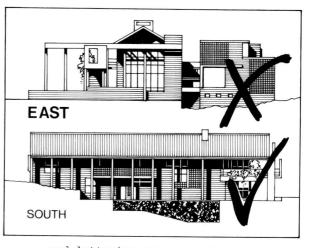

EAST

SOUTH

. . . and lettering was seen to aid communication. For example, some students discovered that their lettering on design drawings had dominated the drawings, or had been too elaborate in style and caused distraction.

6

7 A fascination for models was seen to distract critics from displayed drawings. When this situation was anticipated, students would only disclose their models as a climax to the presentation sequence.

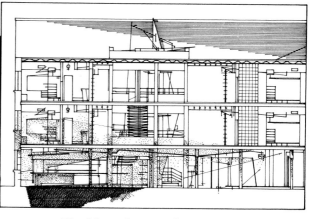

8 Finally, when used to underline decisions concerning building materials, quality of setting, and interior schemes, etc., color was seen to bring an added dimension to communication. Even when presentation deadlines are pressing, drawings could be selectively color rendered.

Traditional and Experimental Presentation Layouts

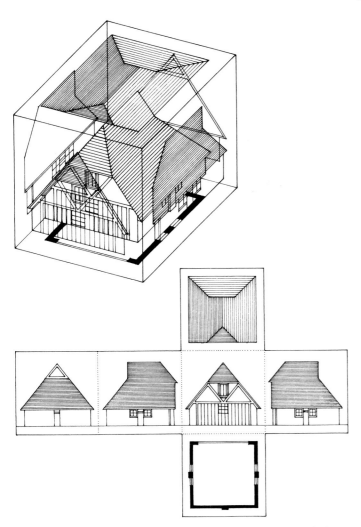

1 Traditional forms of layout have evolved from the development of first angle projection. This convention sees an architectural design as visualized within a "glass box," with the significant faces of the conceptual form as projected onto the inside of the glass in "first angle projection," or the outside of the glass in "third angle projection." When conceptually opened flat, the layout, depending on the convention used, places the plan either above or below its elevations.

2 However, many architects will devise their own layouts and even tailor a different layout for each individual project. In contrast to traditional layout, the influence of the restricted entry format of international design competitions and their widespread publication has caused designers to experiment with variations on traditional layout. As a result, more adventurous forms of layout have evolved. These are characterized by variation in the scale of orthographics and the squeezing together, overlapping, and layering of graphic information within the format. Such layouts are carefully planned and are reminiscent of how an artist might plan an abstract composition.

The Basic Presentation Sequence

1 In design presentation, the respective viewpoints of orthographics each play a coordinating role in a spatial narrative. For example, the progressively descending scales of the location plan, neighborhood plan, and the site plan, traditionally introduce and orientate the viewer who, from an overhead viewpoint, "arrives" on the site for a closer analysis of its nature via diagrams, sketches, sections, etc.

2 An important link in presentation between the results of a site analysis and the ensuing design is the diagramming of the design strategy.

N.B.: To avoid confusion, all plans along the sequence of presentation should be shown with the same orientation. Traditionally, these are coordinated with their north points in an upward position.

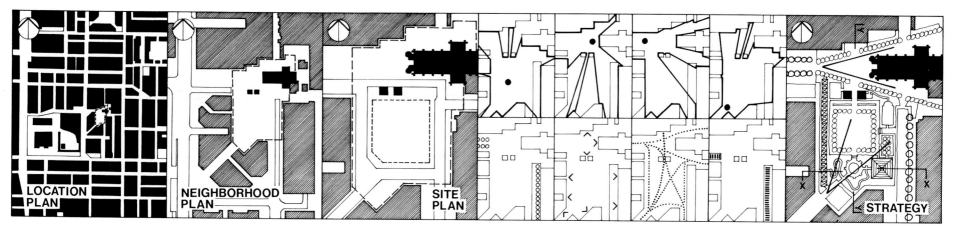

LOCATION PLAN

NEIGHBORHOOD PLAN

SITE PLAN

STRATEGY

The design proposal is then presented via the overhead view offered by the plan that, operating as a horizontal section, slices the form at key levels. These are coordinated in scale and, either horizontally or vertically, related directly to the head-on views of the external appearance and internal workings offered respectively by the elevation and the section. When more than one story is involved, floor plans should be vertically or horizontally stacked.

3 The site section moves the spectator's viewpoint horizontally away for a more distant and sliced impression of the impact of the form on the surrounding environment. The opportunity for contextual presentation is provided when a ground floor plan is shown directly on a site plan, and when elevations embrace events beyond the face of the form they portray.

4

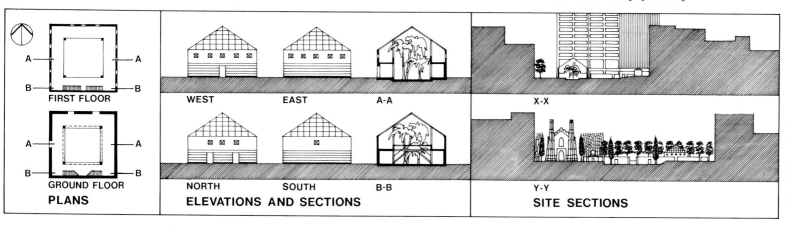

A — A
B — B
FIRST FLOOR

A — A
B — B
GROUND FLOOR
PLANS

WEST EAST A-A
NORTH SOUTH B-B
ELEVATIONS AND SECTIONS

X — X
Y — Y
SITE SECTIONS

Traditionally, wall presentations end with a summation of the design described by a "three-dimensional" drawing, such as an axonometric or a perspective, or a small-scale model.

A Gallery of Alternative Drawing Types

Beyond the basic range of orthographics there is a series of drawing types that provide alternative viewing points or, when combined as composite graphics using two or more systems, allow hybrid vehicles for the communication of more complex or more spatially enhanced information. One such graphic combination unfolds the plan and elevation in direct relationship. In flattening the two, it provides a true-to-scale and simultaneous view of both horizontal and vertical planes.

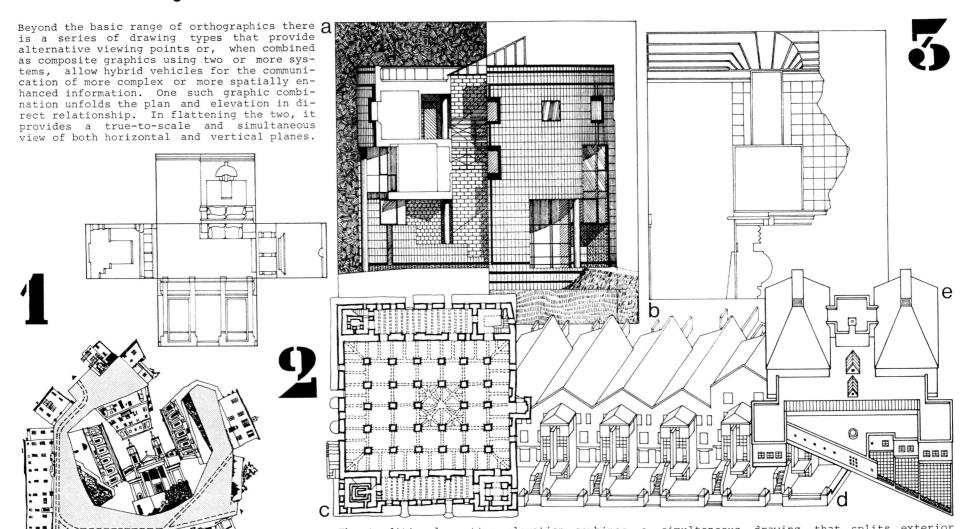

An unusual variation on this unfolding theme is found in the color restoration work of designer Giovanni Brino. In order to study the contextual relationship of facade colors in Turin's streets and piazzas, he flipped back elevations at 45 degrees to produce a montage of streetscapes.

The traditional section elevation combines a simultaneous drawing that splits exterior appearance with a view of interior elevations (a). Such graphics are generally associated with symmetrical forms. Interior wall elevations (b) are usually drawn by interior designers and visualized without their surrounding sectional cut for an exclusive concentration on internal events. More elaborate ceiling designs will call for a reflected ceiling plan (c). This version of the plan is true-to-scale and drawn as if viewed as the reflection in a continuously "mirrored" floor plane. One variation on the plan oblique (axonometric) is the elevation oblique (d), which simply substitutes a true plan for a true elevation, which is then projected back into the illusion of space at the same scale. Another variation involves the use of a true plan placed square-on, with the elevations projected vertically (e). The drawings are derived from the work of Rick Mather, Michael Graves, Jeremy Dixon, and John Tuomey.

A Gallery of Alternative Drawing Types

The worm's-eye-view plan projection--commonly known as an "up-view" axonometric--flips the true-to-scale plan for a paraline projection drawing that provides the designer with an impossible vantage point that is located below the ground plane. The resultant graphic view gives simultaneous glimpses of exterior and interior wall planes together with a focus on the ceiling plane. This drawing is based on the work of James Stirling and Michael Wilford.

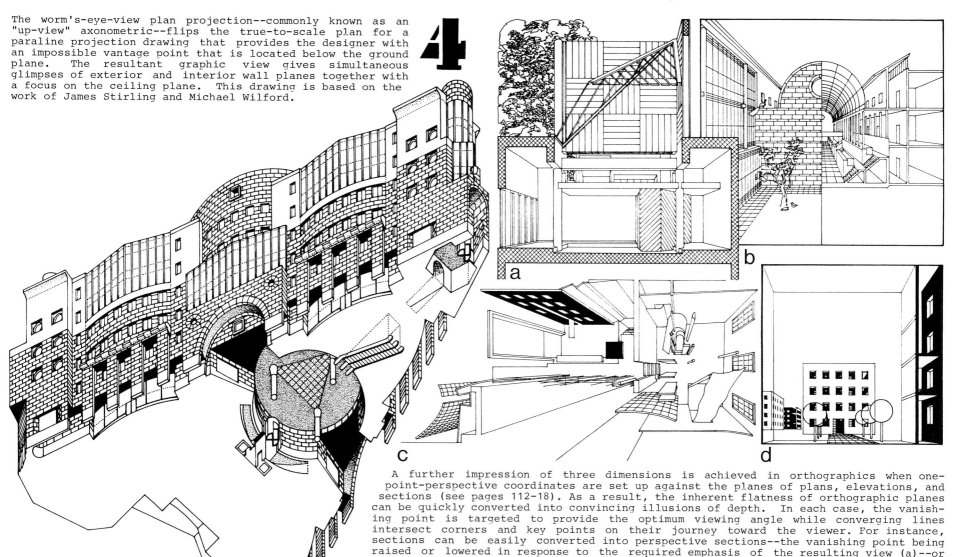

A further impression of three dimensions is achieved in orthographics when one-point-perspective coordinates are set up against the planes of plans, elevations, and sections (see pages 112-18). As a result, the inherent flatness of orthographic planes can be quickly converted into convincing illusions of depth. In each case, the vanishing point is targeted to provide the optimum viewing angle while converging lines intersect corners and key points on their journey toward the viewer. For instance, sections can be easily converted into perspective sections--the vanishing point being raised or lowered in response to the required emphasis of the resulting view (a)--or they can be split into elevation and section and projected both forward and backward (b). Similarly, simple plan projections can be used to look upward into worm's-eye views of interiors, or downward to produce aerial, or bird's-eye, views (c). As we have seen on page 114, the pseudo perspective places a true-to-scale elevation within a perspective setting. A realistic-looking impression is achieved when the vanishing point is placed at normal, scaled eye level and overlapping forms are inserted in the illusory foreground space (d). The illustrations are based on the work of Franco Purini and Laura Thermes, James Stirling and Michael Wilford, Zaha Hadid, and Matthias Ungers.

Exploding, Cutting, and Dissolving Orthographics

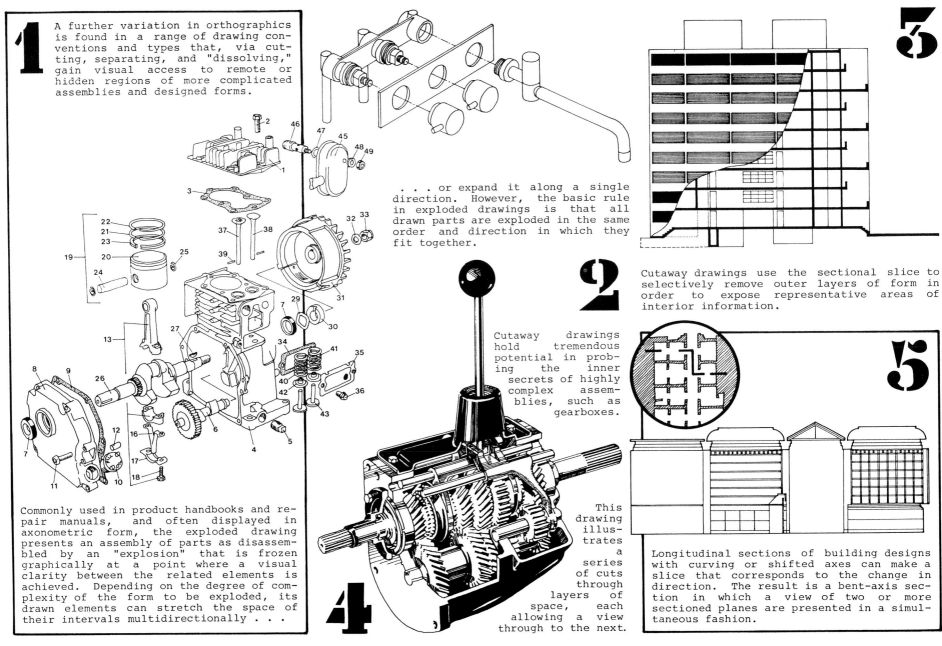

1 A further variation in orthographics is found in a range of drawing conventions and types that, via cutting, separating, and "dissolving," gain visual access to remote or hidden regions of more complicated assemblies and designed forms.

. . . or expand it along a single direction. However, the basic rule in exploded drawings is that all drawn parts are exploded in the same order and direction in which they fit together.

3

Cutaway drawings use the sectional slice to selectively remove outer layers of form in order to expose representative areas of interior information.

2

Cutaway drawings hold tremendous potential in probing the inner secrets of highly complex assemblies, such as gearboxes.

5

Commonly used in product handbooks and repair manuals, and often displayed in axonometric form, the exploded drawing presents an assembly of parts as disassembled by an "explosion" that is frozen graphically at a point where a visual clarity between the related elements is achieved. Depending on the degree of complexity of the form to be exploded, its drawn elements can stretch the space of their intervals multidirectionally . . .

4

This drawing illustrates a series of cuts through layers of space, each allowing a view through to the next.

Longitudinal sections of building designs with curving or shifted axes can make a slice that corresponds to the change in direction. The result is a bent-axis section in which a view of two or more sectioned planes are presented in a simultaneous fashion.

Exploding, Cutting, and Dissolving Orthographics

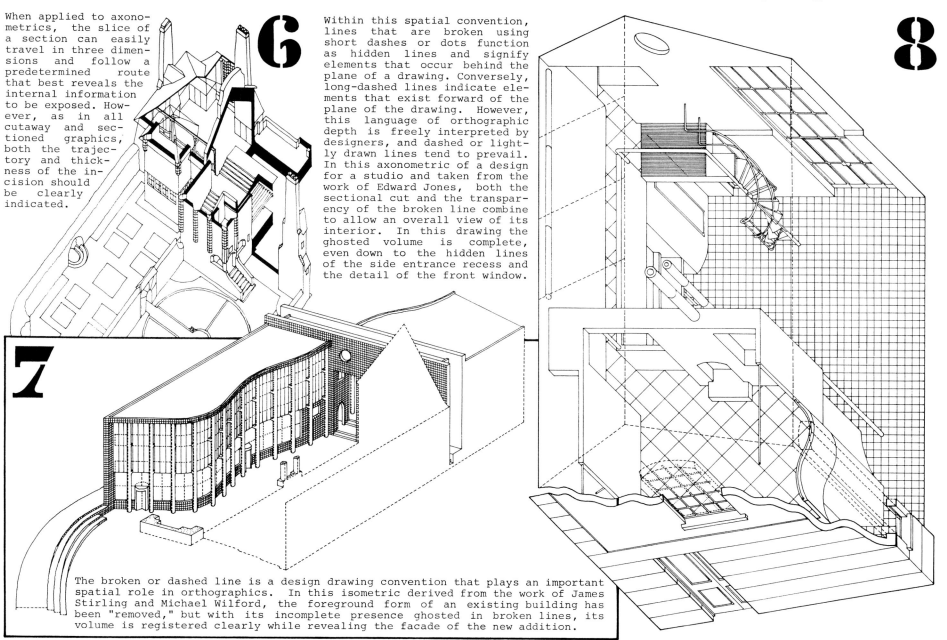

When applied to axonometrics, the slice of a section can easily travel in three dimensions and follow a predetermined route that best reveals the internal information to be exposed. However, as in all cutaway and sectioned graphics, both the trajectory and thickness of the incision should be clearly indicated.

Within this spatial convention, lines that are broken using short dashes or dots function as hidden lines and signify elements that occur behind the plane of a drawing. Conversely, long-dashed lines indicate elements that exist forward of the plane of the drawing. However, this language of orthographic depth is freely interpreted by designers, and dashed or lightly drawn lines tend to prevail. In this axonometric of a design for a studio and taken from the work of Edward Jones, both the sectional cut and the transparency of the broken line combine to allow an overall view of its interior. In this drawing the ghosted volume is complete, even down to the hidden lines of the side entrance recess and the detail of the front window.

The broken or dashed line is a design drawing convention that plays an important spatial role in orthographics. In this isometric derived from the work of James Stirling and Michael Wilford, the foreground form of an existing building has been "removed," but with its incomplete presence ghosted in broken lines, its volume is registered clearly while revealing the facade of the new addition.

Multiview Design Drawings

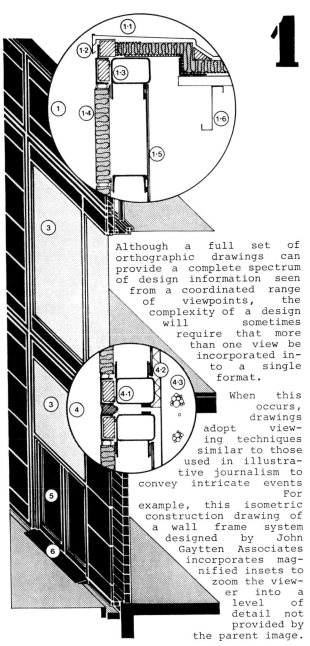

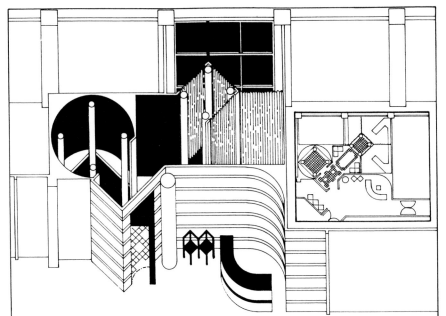

1

The use of insets to communicate aspects of related spatial information can be found in all forms of design drawing. Here, an axonometric incorporates its own plan as an integral part of its format in order to show the broader setting of its more selective projection. This design for a beauty salon was derived from the work of Patrick Dignan and Douglas Read.

Although a full set of orthographic drawings can provide a complete spectrum of design information seen from a coordinated range of viewpoints, the complexity of a design will sometimes require that more than one view be incorporated into a single format.

When this occurs, drawings adopt viewing techniques similar to those used in illustrative journalism to convey intricate events For example, this isometric construction drawing of a wall frame system designed by John Gaytten Associates incorporates magnified insets to zoom the viewer into a level of detail not provided by the parent image.

2

3

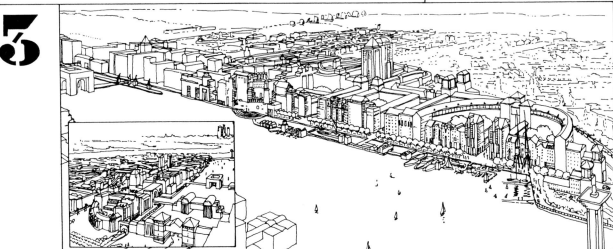

This perspective of a proposal for a River Thames dockside village by Form Design attempts to extend the directional confinement of its main aerial view by inserting an alternative glimpse within its frame of reference. This need for a second look taken from another vantage point represents the first step in the production of sequential perspectives that, when made at eye level, can take the viewer on a visual walk around the space of the designer's intentions.

How to Use Key Drawings in Presentation Layouts

1

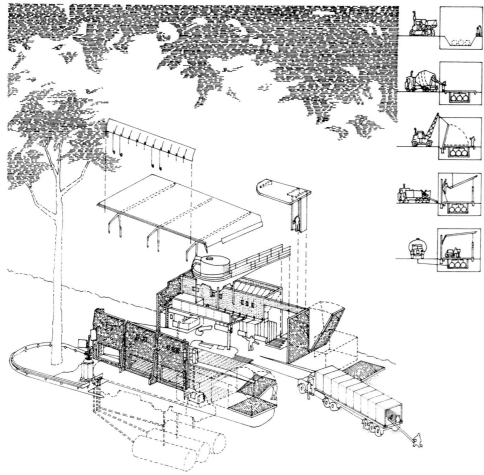

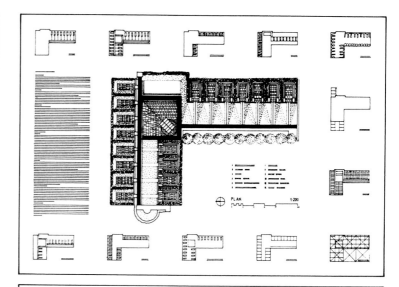

Layouts should be adapted to the uniqueness of each design project and be generated by the range of drawing types needed to adequately describe its complexity. Also, within a layout design, certain types of drawing may be modified in order to fulfill specific communication roles (see pages 200-201). However, the emergence of the key drawing as the central communication vehicle in the presentation usually involves the recycling of a graphic type that has already proven its worth in summarizing the concept earlier in the design sequence. Indeed, the extensively published key drawings of many well-known buildings are more widely known than their physical counterparts--one key drawing often capturing the essence of an architectural intent and, through media exposure, becoming a mental icon "visited" and "revisited" in the mind's eye. Having been identified as the best graphic model to describe the design, this drawing type can be employed on a large scale and function as the referential centerpiece of a layout against which smaller scale and subordinated information can be arranged.

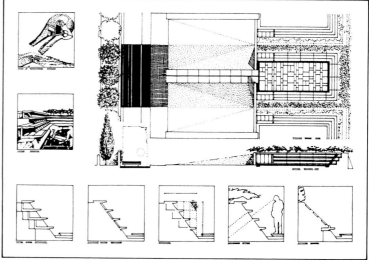

These individual sheet layouts are by John Pardey and Ronald Yee. They demonstrate the impact of a clear and visually accessible design statement arranged around a simple grid layout. Each sheet fronts with its own key drawing as centerpiece, and each uses the grid to frame the key drawing in different ways by supplementary and smaller scaled information.

205

An Introduction to Layout Design

The first step in layout design involves an understanding of the figure-ground illusion. For example, when an image is positioned at the dead-center of a mount, an optical effect causes the image to appear lower than its actual physical location on the surround--a visual phenomenon in which the "figure" appears to be sliding down its "ground."

1

2

This illusion can be corrected by positioning the image slightly higher than halfway on its support sheet. An ideal image-mount proportion is equal frame width top and sides, with a slightly deeper width at the bottom.

3

SITE PLAN
MUSEUM OF THE 19th CENTURY

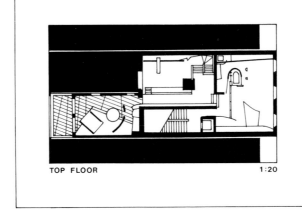

TOP FLOOR   1:20

On both portrait (vertical) and landscape (horizontal) formats, this compensatory image-frame relationship not only visually stabilizes the artwork, but allows for the introduction of lettering as an integral component of the layout. Indeed, in visual terms, title blocks and captions will function as important "bracing" and "connecting" elements in the layout design.

4

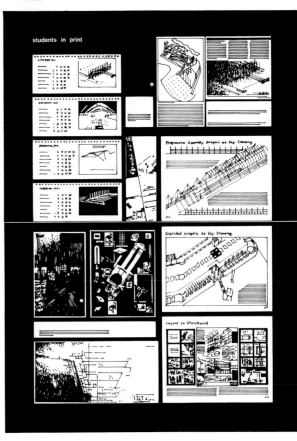

students in print

Therefore, the juxtapositioning of multiple- and dissimilar-sized images together with their annotation on one mount is a figure-ground design problem. As a general rule, layouts should avoid the boredom of symmetry and the visual "holes" caused by large areas of meaningless and empty space. Such problems are avoided when a vertical, horizontal, and/or diagonal order is introduced in which the spaces between and around the images are as considered as the relationships between the images themselves.

An Introduction to Layout Design

5 The first stage in layout design is to gather together all the graphic components that will be required to clearly communicate the design in question. Initial layout development can employ a series of trial-and-error thumbnail sketches that, arranged against the structure of a background grid, aim to sequence and orchestrate each graphic component into an overall composition.

7 . . . or will the layout be devised as one single composition occupying an overall format provided by several sheets? Such decisions will be governed by the spirit of the design concept and the roles played by the different drawing types enlisted within the design sequence (see page 205).

6 However, depending on the complexity of the design and its selected scale, or range of scales, an early decision determines the use of sheets in the overall format. For instance, will the layout comprise a set of individually composed sheets . . .

8 However, the function of the background grid should be approached both as a compositional stabilizer and liberator. In other words, its structure should be used to harness the various graphic components into a clear narrative, but it should also be used to create new and dynamic graphic relationships.

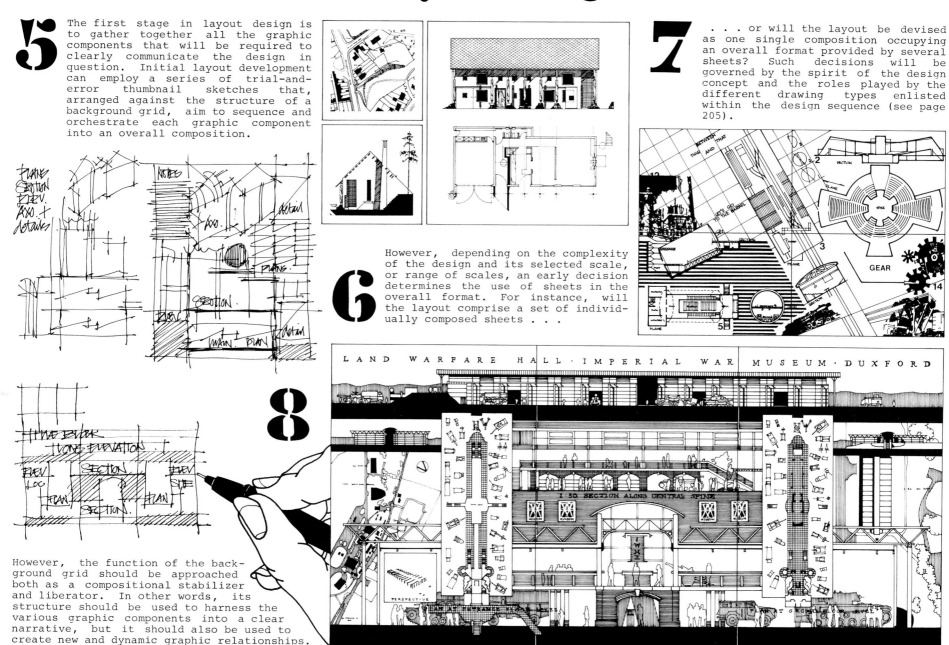

LAND WARFARE HALL · IMPERIAL WAR MUSEUM · DUXFORD

How to Window-Mount Artwork

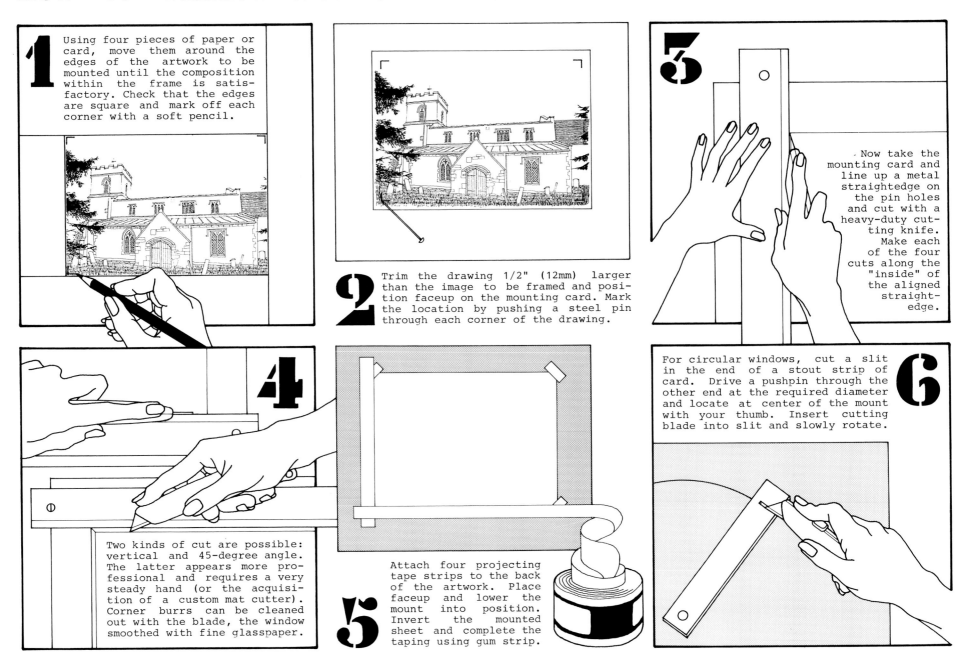

1 Using four pieces of paper or card, move them around the edges of the artwork to be mounted until the composition within the frame is satisfactory. Check that the edges are square and mark off each corner with a soft pencil.

2 Trim the drawing 1/2" (12mm) larger than the image to be framed and position faceup on the mounting card. Mark the location by pushing a steel pin through each corner of the drawing.

3 Now take the mounting card and line up a metal straightedge on the pin holes and cut with a heavy-duty cutting knife. Make each of the four cuts along the "inside" of the aligned straightedge.

4 Two kinds of cut are possible: vertical and 45-degree angle. The latter appears more professional and requires a very steady hand (or the acquisition of a custom mat cutter). Corner burrs can be cleaned out with the blade, the window smoothed with fine glasspaper.

5 Attach four projecting tape strips to the back of the artwork. Place faceup and lower the mount into position. Invert the mounted sheet and complete the taping using gum strip.

6 For circular windows, cut a slit in the end of a stout strip of card. Drive a pushpin through the other end at the required diameter and locate at center of the mount with your thumb. Insert cutting blade into slit and slowly rotate.

How to Heat-Mount Artwork

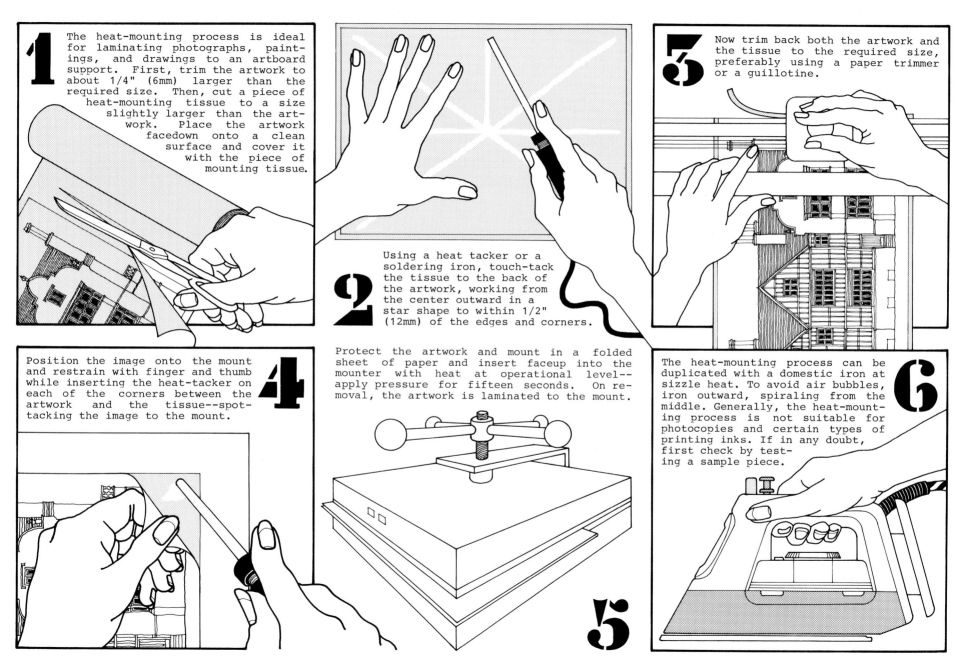

1 The heat-mounting process is ideal for laminating photographs, paintings, and drawings to an artboard support. First, trim the artwork to about 1/4" (6mm) larger than the required size. Then, cut a piece of heat-mounting tissue to a size slightly larger than the artwork. Place the artwork facedown onto a clean surface and cover it with the piece of mounting tissue.

2 Using a heat tacker or a soldering iron, touch-tack the tissue to the back of the artwork, working from the center outward in a star shape to within 1/2" (12mm) of the edges and corners.

3 Now trim back both the artwork and the tissue to the required size, preferably using a paper trimmer or a guillotine.

4 Position the image onto the mount and restrain with finger and thumb while inserting the heat-tacker on each of the corners between the artwork and the tissue--spot-tacking the image to the mount.

5 Protect the artwork and mount in a folded sheet of paper and insert faceup into the mounter with heat at operational level-- apply pressure for fifteen seconds. On removal, the artwork is laminated to the mount.

6 The heat-mounting process can be duplicated with a domestic iron at sizzle heat. To avoid air bubbles, iron outward, spiraling from the middle. Generally, the heat-mounting process is not suitable for photocopies and certain types of printing inks. If in any doubt, first check by testing a sample piece.

How to Use Overlays in Presentation

One of the many ways of employing overlays in design presentations is to use progressive cross-sections--composed of opaque dry-transfer color and ink on acetate--to unfold large interior spaces.

2 A second overlay might then introduce a section taken at a convenient point near the middle of the interior.

3 An overlay reconstruction of an interior design concludes with a third section taken at a point just inside the near elevation.

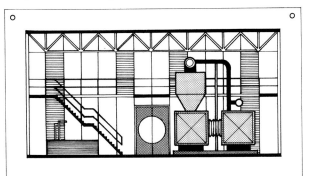

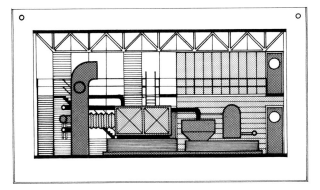

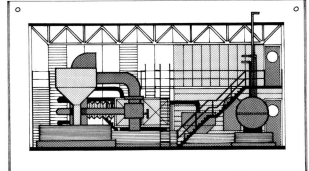

1 Being presented first, the farthest section might incorporate an interior view of the back wall elevation together with objects placed immediately in front of its plane.

N.B.: Selection of the point at which this and the subsequent section occur is made in response to the availability of views through unworked areas of clear acetate.

N.B.: The sequence can be extended by adding a fourth overlay which, in carrying the exterior front elevation, places the observer outside the building.

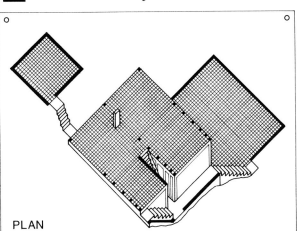

PLAN

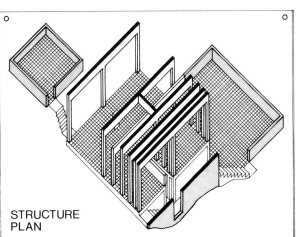

STRUCTURE PLAN

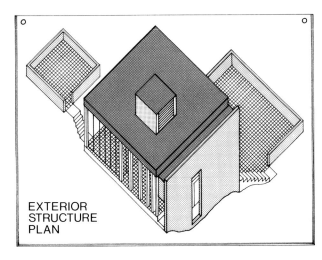

EXTERIOR STRUCTURE PLAN

4 Another overlay sequence, again using opaque dry-transfer color and ink on acetate, reconstructs a building design in the horizontal plane. In this sequence, the plan represents the first layer of presented information.

5 The second overlay superimposes structural elements, partition walls, and, if scale or viewability allows, furniture and figures.

6 This sequence is completed by a third layer of acetate that overlays the external envelope--the result representing a regular axonometric.

How to Use Overlays in Presentation

Complex design solutions can be communicated using the overlay method in wall displays and brochures. The progressive buildup of superimposed layers of information is mainly used to explain in-depth site appraisals and intricate planning proposals, but it can be utilized for many forms of design communication.

Overlays can be worked on tracing paper or on acetate sheets. However, the latter are more successful when more than two layers of information are involved.

1

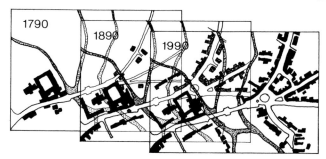

2

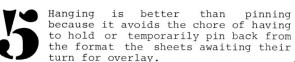

Labeling and titling can occur at the various stages in overlay presentation. However, as with all the other information contained on the sheets, make sure that labels or titles do not conflict on completion of the overlay sequence. One method is to employ a color-coded system, i.e., different colors of lettering at different levels--with the strongest colors being on the lower sheets.

3

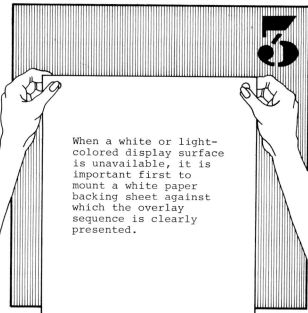

When a white or light-colored display surface is unavailable, it is important first to mount a white paper backing sheet against which the overlay sequence is clearly presented.

The set of overlay material can be pinned directly to the display surface. The pinning operation--as with the binding of brochures--acts as registration and should be carried out carefully.

4

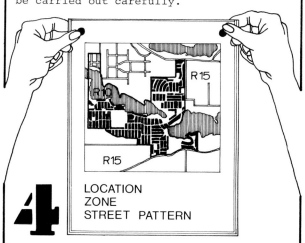

LOCATION
ZONE
STREET PATTERN

5

Hanging is better than pinning because it avoids the chore of having to hold or temporarily pin back from the format the sheets awaiting their turn for overlay.

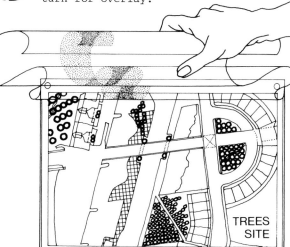

TREES
SITE

The hanging method simply necessitates punching two holes through the set of overlays, which are then reinforced with eyelets. The sheets are then hung in sequence on hooked pushpins or substantial chart tacks, leaving the designer free during presentation.

6

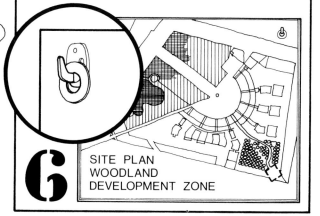

SITE PLAN
WOODLAND
DEVELOPMENT ZONE

How to Compile a Brochure

1

Within a highly competitive job market, the brochure, or report, has become a widely used vehicle in design communication--either to clients, or to advertise one's ability to potential employers, astute students compiling and mailing brochures of their work when making long-distance job applications. Brochures act as miniature exhibitions that, like slide presentations, reveal their contents sequentially but with the potential for a greater emphasis on written information. Being portable and conducive to reproduction, they can function to store or proliferate ideas. They can also complement or duplicate wall displays for circulation to a wider audience.

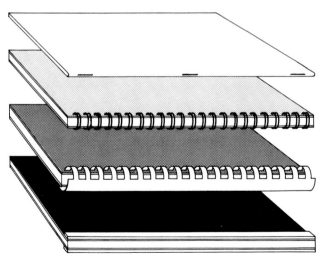

4

For more permanent binding, brochures can be stapled, spiral-bound in plastic or wire spines, or, for a really professional appearance, assembled via the vinyl rivet method.

Table of Contents

2

Many styles exist for brochure presentation, but each is likely to consider a uniform method of ordering its contents. A basic structure might include title page, preface, introduction, an organized system for paragraphs and sections, and, if applicable, a conclusion, bibliography, and index.

Photographs, drawings, and glossy diazo prints can be laminated on thin card for use as full-page illustrations. These might be overlaid with pages of clear acetate carrying inked, dry-transfer, or photocopied information. For a sneak preview effect, windows cut into a preceding page can isolate a selected area of an illustration or frame captions or titles.

5

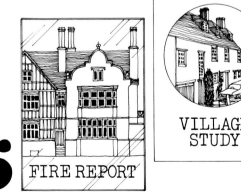

3

When brochures are intended to double for, or supplement, a wall display, their binding method should allow for rapid disassembly. Binding methods for this purpose include the spring-back folders and slide-on plastic spines.

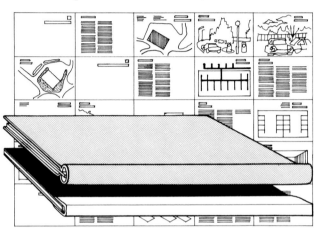

6

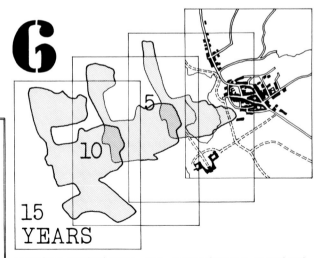

Overlay techniques can superimpose statistical data on pictorial images in tables, charts, and graphs; more complex material can be transmitted via a succession of transparent acetate pages worked in ink and dry-transfer color.

How to Compile a Brochure

The use of a grid should accommodate all the essential ingredients of a brochure's design. It should establish column widths, picture and caption areas, and margins.

A basic, easy-to-read layout for portrait format brochures using photographic illustrations is the single column of typewritten text with a width dictated by that of a regular and compatible print size.

This format allows the insertion of prints into text, a direct location with their reference prescribing page layouts.

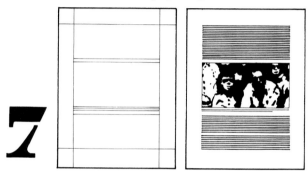

7

As a general rule, always allow a generous center-spread margin so that the inside edges of columns of text and illustrations do not disappear down the central gutter when the brochure is opened. However, stapled and spiral-bound brochures are easier to handle when their contents are filled with illustrations. The latter allow foldout material to be inserted . . .

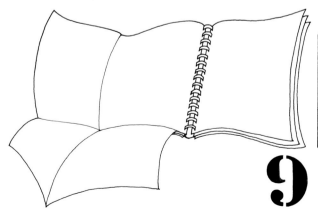

9

Another flexible arrangement for portrait formats is a double-column layout: a wider column incorporating text and key illustrations, a narrow one containing key illustration captions together with support illustrations located whenever possible adjacent to their text reference.

8

10

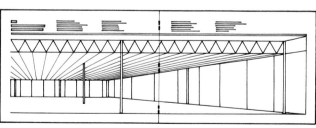

. . . while the former offer the potential of double-page-spread exploitation.

11

The wider landscape formats are easier to design and more digestible to peruse when organized into a series of columns. These can be designed against a grid to carry either:

a

Solid text

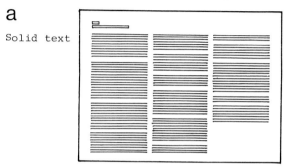

b

Related combinations of text and illustrations.

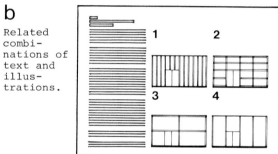

c

Full-page illustrations with annotation responding to the three columns.

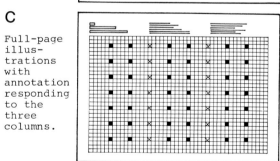

N.B.: It is important not to overcomplicate drawings for brochures; simple, confident linework creates a clean impression and is better equipped to survive reduction.

How to Use an Overhead Projector

1

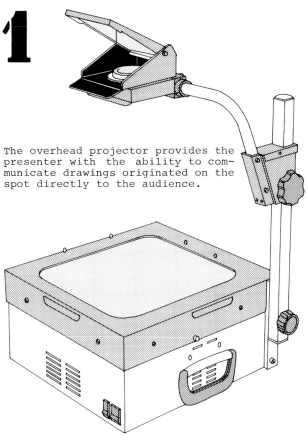

The overhead projector provides the presenter with the ability to communicate drawings originated on the spot directly to the audience.

Alternatively, acetate drawings and diagrams can be prepared prior to a presentation. Here are a few pointers for clarity of communication when preparing acetate transparencies: keep your transparencies as simple and uncluttered as possible; use only one theme on each transparency, and keep any text short and to the point. To enable easy reading from a range of distances, lettering size should be

no smaller than this.

Using the custom acetate pens or adhesive film, employ color to accentuate and differentiate the image but beware of confusing the viewer with too many colors.

2 Overhead projector images should be prepared within a safe area--approximately 1" (25mm) in from the edge of the transparency format. This ensures that the edges of graphics are not lost in projection. The safe area should be drawn on card which functions as a backing sheet during the preparation of the acetate.

3 Using the special OHP pens and/or adhesive film, material for transparencies can be traced directly from original material (see facing page). These can begin as line drawings on plain paper that have been resized and reproduced on acetate film using a photocopier capable of accepting acetate.

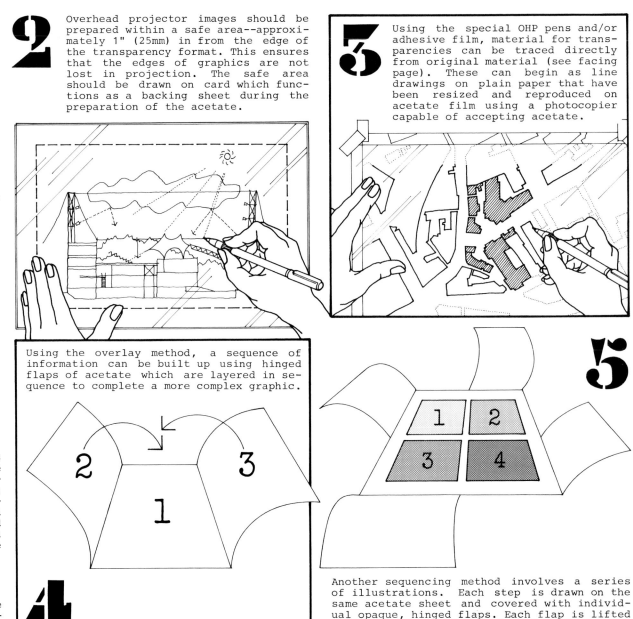

4 Using the overlay method, a sequence of information can be built up using hinged flaps of acetate which are layered in sequence to complete a more complex graphic.

5 Another sequencing method involves a series of illustrations. Each step is drawn on the same acetate sheet and covered with individual opaque, hinged flaps. Each flap is lifted in the appropriate sequence to reveal the stages of information.

How to Enliven Statistical Graphics

Statistical diagrams such as graphs, tables, bar charts, or histograms and matrices, etc., can be made more visually exciting and more readable through the addition of color and support imagery. A fast method is to integrate--via photomontage or direct tracing--relevant images from magazine photographs. This reportage technique can convert a potentially dull visual into an attractive and professional-looking graphic for wall displays, reports, and (when traced) especially for overhead projector transparencies.

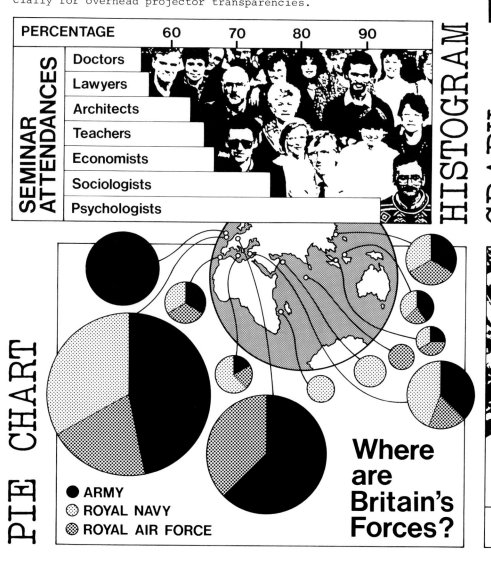

HISTOGRAM

SEMINAR ATTENDANCES

PERCENTAGE   60   70   80   90

Doctors
Lawyers
Architects
Teachers
Economists
Sociologists
Psychologists

PIE CHART

- ● ARMY
- ◉ ROYAL NAVY
- ◉ ROYAL AIR FORCE

Where are Britain's Forces?

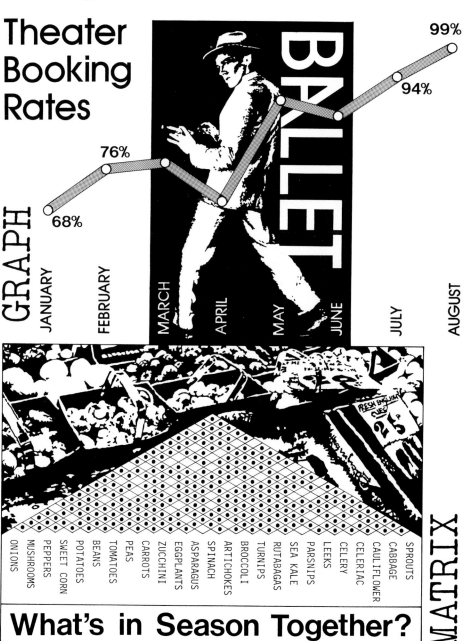

Theater Booking Rates

GRAPH

BALLET

99%
94%
76%
68%

JANUARY   FEBRUARY   MARCH   APRIL   MAY   JUNE   JULY   AUGUST

MATRIX

ONIONS
MUSHROOMS
PEPPERS
SWEET CORN
POTATOES
BEANS
TOMATOES
PEAS
CARROTS
ZUCCHINI
EGGPLANTS
ASPARAGUS
SPINACH
ARTICHOKES
BROCCOLI
TURNIPS
RUTABAGAS
SEA KALE
PARSNIPS
LEEKS
CELERY
CELERIAC
CAULIFLOWER
CABBAGE
SPROUTS

FRESH ENGLISH CUES 25 P

What's in Season Together?

How to Present with Projectors

The advantages of projector presentations are numerous. For example, in darkening a room for projection, the audience becomes captive, their center of attention being focused on the projected image. Information in a slide package is disclosed--uninterrupted by viewers--in a predetermined sequence, its order and timing of exposure being totally controlled by the designer. By comparison with wall displays, slide projections also allow the presenter to assume different positions in relation to the audience, such as in front, side, or rear--a freedom limited only by the length of the hand control cable or the power of a remote.

2 All forms of image can be combined as a means of disclosing various design concepts, such as images photographed from magazines or all kinds of artwork photographed in color or in monochrome, together with lettering, composite images, and even diagrams.

Live commentaries can take advantage of a pointer, an indicator projecting an illuminated arrow to draw attention to screened detail. Pointers are sometimes built into the projector, into the hand control, or supplied as separate devices.

N.B.: Most projectors allow slide shows to be projected by remote control. Spoken commentaries can also be tape-recorded to synchronize with an automated or manual display. Specific moods can also be induced by adding tape-recorded music or appropriate sound effects.

3

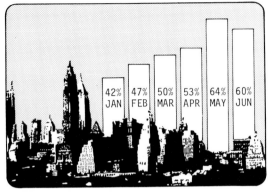

Statistical diagrams such as graphs, tables, bar charts, and so on can be made more visually exciting for projection as slides by adding color and support imagery. A fast method is to photograph a diagram integrated with relevant magazine photographs. This technique can convert a potentially dull visual into a professional-looking and digestible screened image (see page 215).

6

There is also the visual diversity of multi-screen projection. Two, three, four, and up to eight banks of projectors are sometimes enlisted to project visual fragments of information.

N.B.: It is important that multiscreen displays not contain overly complex information --particularly in written form. If text or detailed graphics are used, these should be screened for longer periods within a pre-planned sequence of presentation.

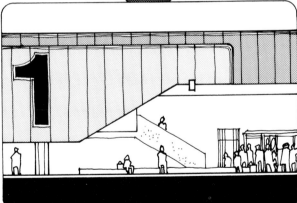

4 When producing orthographic drawings for conversion via photography into slides, the designer should be aware of the contrast needed for clarity in projection. Simple drawings using strong ink lines together with dry-transfer tone or color work well for such images (see page 34).

5

216

How to Rostrum-Shoot Artwork

1

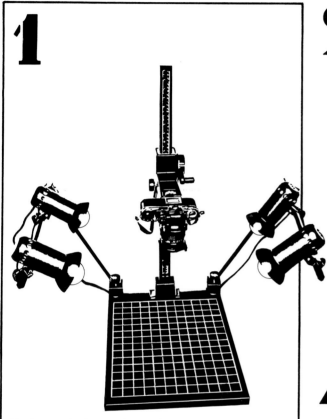

Rostrum photography using a copying stand is the alternative to the use of tripod with flash or floods. Even illumination is provided by four lamps positioned above the copying board, and for this reason, direct sunlight should be avoided when in use. If color-balanced lamps are not provided, attachable blue filters are recommended when photographing most colored artwork. A Macro lens should be fitted to an SLR camera loaded with a film of the slowest possible speed. Focusing is a meticulous operation involving moving the entire camera back and forth. For exposure, set a delayed action to eliminate camera shake. During focusing and exposure, care should be taken to avoid shadows cast by the user onto the artwork.

2

Make sure that the artwork format is compatible with the proportions of the ultimate transparency. Also, especially when producing perspectives for conversion into slides, make sure that artwork responds to a clear frame of reference. Otherwise, the appearance on the projected slide of unworked areas of paper around the frame will tend to countermand the illusion of perspective depth.

4

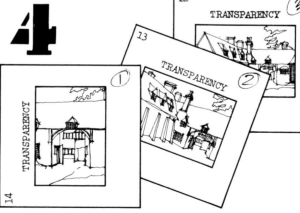

When presenting short slide sequences made from a single drawing, project those taken "inside" the format first so that the audience's realization of the singular nature of their source is delayed.

3

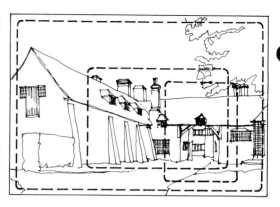

The macro lens allows several different slide images to be made from one perspective drawing. For example, a two- or three-stage sequence of slides can be derived using selected frames of reference, and working from "inside" the perspective to its outer frame. In such sequences, the close-ups (those taken inside the perspective) will obviously magnify the nature of the technique and paper texture.

5

The copying stand is also useful for photographing three-dimensional material. For instance, a simple but effective method for titles is to glue strips of paper end-on to pre-drawn lettering on a backing sheet. When illuminated obliquely--achieved by switching off two side lamps--the resultant light and shadow effect offers a dramatic source for slide-presented credits, etc.

217

Some Slide Presentation Techniques

1

A 35mm color slide presentation of a site analysis is a fast, professional method of orientating critique or client panels prior to their confrontation with design proposals.

a For example, a presentation package might include series of slides processed from shots photographed progressively along a pre-planned route around and about the site environment. In functioning as serial vision "stills," these could take the viewer on a "walk" through the space of the design setting and, if required, focus on factors having particular impact on the ultimate design proposal.

b Also, in order to avoid time spent explaining shot locations, a series of corresponding slides could be made from rostrum photographs of the site plan. Before each shot, a **V** symbol--cut from colored paper--can be positioned on the plan to denote location and direction of each of the on-site photo-graphs. After process-ing, each site plan location slide is then paired off with its on-site counterpart for a twin projection. During the presen-tation sequence, the **V** on each success-ively projected site plan "animates" to the position from which the view on the adjoining image was photographed.

30 TRANSPARENCY 6
PIER
FISHING MUSEUM + FISHERMANS HOME - SITE PLAN

VIEW ALONG DUKE STREET FROM SITE 6
Color

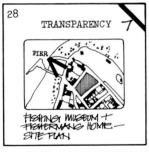

28 TRANSPARENCY 7
PIER
FISHING MUSEUM + FISHERMANS HOME - SITE PLAN

VIEW OF SITE EDGE FROM HARBOR 7
Color

29 TRANSPARENCY 8
PIER
FISHING MUSEUM + FISHERMANS HOME - SITE PLAN

CORNER OF SITE FROM BANK STREET 8
Color

2

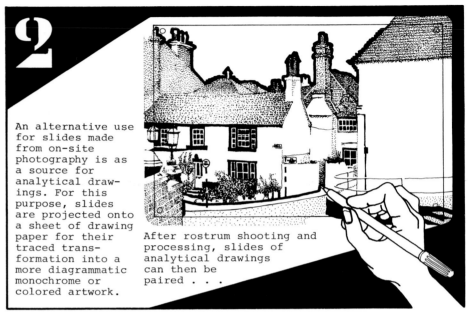

An alternative use for slides made from on-site photography is as a source for analytical draw-ings. For this purpose, slides are projected onto a sheet of drawing paper for their traced trans-formation into a more diagrammatic monochrome or colored artwork.

After rostrum shooting and processing, slides of analytical drawings can then be paired . . .

3 . . . with their on-site source images in a twin projector sequence which, apart from taking the viewer on a site tour, also displays two perceptions--one via the mechanical eye of the camera, another using the analytical eye of the designer.

MAIN PIAZZA - CHURCH OF ST. ANTHONY

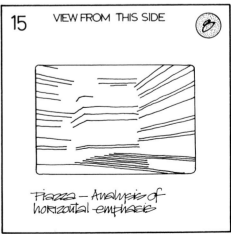

15 VIEW FROM THIS SIDE

PIAZZA - Analysis of horizontal emphasis

Some Slide Presentation Techniques

Slide presentations are also useful for introducing a building design within its setting. Site drawings, traced from on-site slides projected onto drawing paper, could then receive composite drawings of the proposed architecture viewed from different vantage points.

These could then be photographed on the rostrum, processed as slides, and then twin-projected alongside their source slides for a "before" and "after" impression to communicate the impact of the form on its environment.

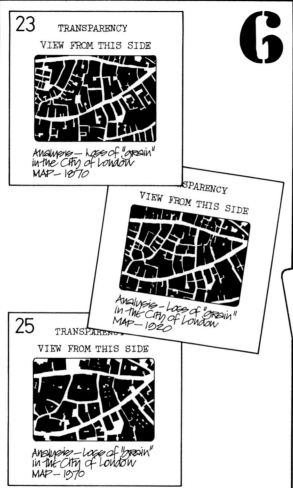

A progressive buildup of the elements in a complex design analysis, urban growth patterns, and phases in the construction of buildings and the like can be presented in an "animated" form. Stages in the assembly of monochrome or colored artwork destined for transformation into 35mm slides are simply rostrum photographed for a projected sequence in which each screened image brings a component of information not present in the last.

Apart from including some of the sequences already described, a more ambitious slide presentation could package the entire design process, from initial key ideograms to final presentation drawings. Also, modelscope photographs processed as slides could take viewers on a trip around the inside of models.

How to Make Slides for Projector Presentations

As slide presentations are often remote-control projections, some form of written narration is required. In "silent" presentations, the insertion of credits, captions, etc., into the slide package greatly enhances one's communication prowess.

A basic method of making do-it-yourself credits is to produce rostrum photographs that exploit the colors of dry-transfer lettering affixed to contrasting self-colored backgrounds, monochrome or colored site prints, or appropriate photographs culled from color magazines.

1

A further possibility is the production of composite slides, i.e., a double exposure combining either lettering or line drawings or both with a colored image. This process requires a slide copier and two 35mm color slides. The first slide should be a slide-mounted "litho" film negative taken of lettering, a drawing, or a combination of the two, the second a color transparency taken of a suitable background.

4

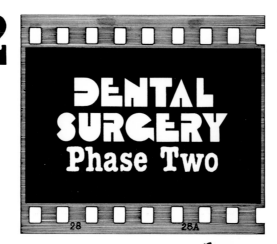

2

Another method is to rostrum photograph typewritten or black dry-transfer lettering on a white background using 35mm "litho" or line film. The resultant negative is then slide-mounted to project its reverse image, i.e., white on black.

Next, place the background color slide into the slide carrier on the slide copier, focus, and shoot, using color film. Then remove the original slide and, if not using a multiple-exposure camera, rewind the film back to its original position. Finally, insert the slide-mounted "litho" negative into the slide carrier, focus, and reshoot as a double exposure.

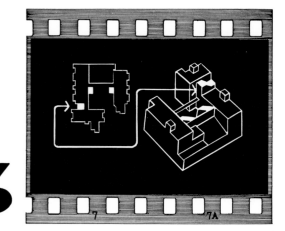

5

Using the same process, line or line and hatched drawings made in black-on-white paper can be rostrum photographed to project them as a reverse image. All kinds of linear artwork can be used as source material, even thumbnail sketches achieving the same potential conversion into images with billboard proportions.

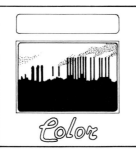

3

6

The processed result is a composite image of a color slide superimposed on a white image, the latter resulting from the opaque areas on the "litho" negative acting as a stencil, allowing only the light of the image to fall on the reexposed film.

How to Make Slides for Projector Presentations

When making slides it is important to predetermine the position of the drawing or lettering on the negative so that its subsequent superimposition coincides with the more opaque areas on the reexposed frame of the recipient color film. For instance, if parts of a title or drawing on the negative are double exposed so that they coincide with transparent areas on the color image, they will be lost.

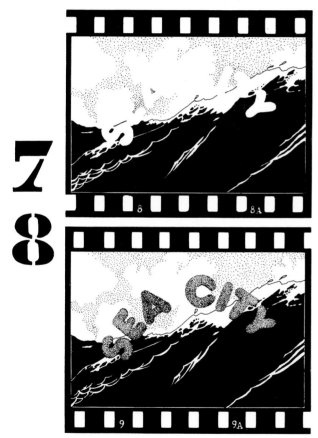

This problem can be overcome, however, during the second exposure by inserting a colored gel between camera and negative. The subsequent shot then causes the lettering or drawing on the negative--together with the color of the gel--to be exposed on the color film as an opaque image.

Another exciting dimension of composite slide making is the fusion of a model or a drawing of a building design with a color slide of its proposed setting. This process requires a setup in a blacked-out room comprising a projector, a back-projection screen (which could be made from a suspended, battened sheet of heavy-duty tracing paper, or a thin, white bedsheet), and camera with tripod.

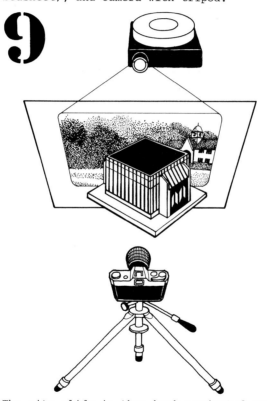

The site slide is then back-projected onto the screen, with the model supported or suspended in front of the screened image. N.B.: In order to allow a drawing to take part in a composite slide, it should be heat-mounted to a card and then cut to shape prior to insertion from the side or suspension from above, between camera and screen.

The next stage is critical. The model or drawing must be side illuminated so that stray light does not fall on the screen. This is done by a careful positioning of the model or drawing in front of the screen, together with the manipulation of the black-out curtain so that a chink of daylight falls across the faces.

Finally, check the composition through the viewfinder, shoot the composite image, and process.

N.B.: The use of a telescopic lens will compensate for any focal discrepancy caused by excessive distance between the face of the model or drawing and the screened background image.

How to Make a Multislide Presentation

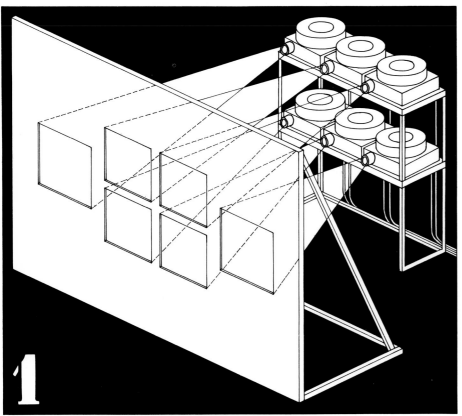

A highly sophisticated form of slide presentation involving banks of projectors, a tape recorder, and a custom-built display unit has been used by students. This is a fully-automated and back-projected presentation comprising especially-made slides and using the techniques described on pages 218-21 to communicate the story of a design sequence from site appraisal to building proposal. By enlisting the automatic time-lapse facility on a six-pack projector unit, it involves sequences of 35mm slides projected at various speed cycles. For instance, slower slide cycles occur in the extreme left- and right-hand screens. These act as reference images, such as location plans during the site appraisal, or floor plans during the communication of the final building design. Meanwhile, the central bank of four screens becomes more animated--showing either multiviews from the points recorded on the site plan, or interior perspectives or details corresponding to the viewing point recorded on the floor plans. The presentation is accompanied by a tape-recorded and synchronized "soundtrack." The display unit is constructed from timber-braced Masonite--its screen apertures being filled with heavy-duty tracing paper.

A simpler but equally impressive automatic slide-tape presentation can also be assembled using three projectors loaded exclusively with landscape format slides. When aligned to form a continuous image, the potential of this projector setup allows the achievement of a panoramic wide-screen formed from three projected slides that have been carefully photographed for the purpose.

Alternatively, the bank of three projected images can be used individually or in differently linked permutations. For example, one such site presentation featured an interview with a local character. His tape-recorded responses provided the "soundtrack" while a sequence of slides--taken during the interview and showing him in the act of response--occupied center-screen. Simultaneously, and to either side of the "speaking" person, a more slowly cycled sequence of slides illustrated the areas and objects to which his dialogue referred.

N.B.: A more professional cycling of projected slides is achieved with the "fade" facility--available on some projectors.

Credits

223

Index